Image into Identity

STUDIA IMAGOLOGICA
AMSTERDAM STUDIES ON CULTURAL IDENTITY

11

Serie editors
Hugo Dyserinck
Joep Leerssen

Imagology, the study of cross-national perceptions and images
as expressed in literary discourse, has for many decades been one
of the more challenging and promising branches of Comparative
Literature.
In recent years, the shape both of literary studies and of international
relations (in the political as well as the cultural sphere) has taken a
turn which makes imagology more topical and urgent than before.
Increasingly, the attitudes, stereotypes and prejudices which govern
literary activity and international relations are perceived in their full
importance; their nature as textual (frequently literary) constructs
is more clearly apprehended; and the necessity for a textual and
historical analysis of their typology, their discursive expression and
dissemination, is being recognized by historians and literary scholars.

The series STUDIA IMAGOLOGICA, which will accommodate scholarly
monographs in English, French or German, provides a forum for this
literary-historical specialism.

Image into Identity
Constructing and
Assigning Identity in
a Culture of Modernity

Edited by Michael Wintle

Amsterdam - New York, NY 2006

Cover illustration: ©René Magritte, Transfer (1966),
c/o Beeldrecht Amsterdam 2006

Cover Design: Erick de Jong

The paper on which this book is printed meets the requirements of "ISO
9706:1994, Information and documentation - Paper for documents -
Requirements for permanence".

ISBN-10: 90-420-2064-4
ISBN-13: 978-90-420-2064-1
©Editions Rodopi B.V., Amsterdam - New York, NY 2006
Printed in the Netherlands

CONTENTS

ACKNOWLEDGEMENTS

This book has evolved from an international research project run from the Faculty of Arts at the University of Hull (UK) from 1999 onwards, which was also entitled 'Image into Identity'. I am grateful to the Dean and Deputy Dean for Research in the Faculty at that time for their support for the project, including financial assistance. With the aid of generous grants from the British Academy and from the University of Hull's research support funds, a successful international conference was held at the University of Hull in September 2000, at which no fewer than 130 papers were delivered by scholars from all over the world. The intellectual exchange generated at that conference richly rewarded the efforts of the organizers, among whom Steve Burwood, Jacky Cogman, and Jamal Shahin deserve special mention. We are grateful to the conference participants for their energy in the discussions, which eventually led to the assembly of the present volume. Most of the chapters of this book were originally delivered as papers at the conference, and after lengthy and careful selection, they have been fully revised for inclusion in the collection, some five years after the conference was held. I am immensely grateful to the conferees, and especially to those commissioned to revise their contributions for inclusion here, for their enthusiasm, input and patience during the inevitable delays in the editing process. I am also grateful to Steve Burwood and to John Osborne (who co-authored the Introduction), for their help in selecting the papers from well over one hundred in order to arrive at the coherence of the seventeen presented here. In the final process of editing, I am indebted to Menno Spiering for preparing the manuscript for press, to the Institute for Culture and History at the University of Amsterdam for financial assistance, and to the editorial staff at Editions Rodopi for their patience and professional assistance.

Michael Wintle,
Amsterdam

LIST OF FIGURES AND TABLES

NOTES ON CONTRIBUTORS

BRIGITTE ADRIAENSEN recently finished her doctorate at the Catholic University of Leuven on the poetics of irony in the work of Juan Goytisolo. Her main interests are in the theory of irony, postcolonial theory, trauma theory and the relationship between ethics and literature. She has published on the work of Juan Goytisolo, José Saramago, and on postcolonial theory in Latin America.

MARNIX BEYEN teaches contemporary political history at the University of Antwerp. His main fields of research are the role of historical and literary representations in the shaping of national identities and the evolution of parliamentary culture in twentieth-century Belgium, France and the Netherlands. His most recent book is *Oorlog & verleden: nationale geschiedenis in België en Nederland* (2002).

ADRIAN CHAN is at the Australian National University. He has been working on the language of discourse in Sinology as Visiting Fellow in the Research School of Pacific and Asian Studies. He previously taught Politics at the University of New South Wales in Sydney. His *Chinese Marxism* was published by Continuum Books in 2003, and he is now finishing a volume on Orientalism in Sinology.

STEF CRAPS is a lecturer in English literature at the University of Ghent. He holds a licentiate's degree and a PhD from the Catholic University of Leuven and an MA from the University of Hull. He is the author of *Trauma and Ethics in the Novels of Graham Swift: No Short-Cuts to Salvation* (Sussex Academic Press, 2005).

ANN DAVIES is a Lecturer in Spanish in the School of Modern Languages at the University of Newcastle. She researches primarily on Spanish cinema but also has an interest in the generic narratives of Carmen, Don Juan and the vampire. Her monograph, *The Metamorphoses of Don Juan's Women: Early Parity to Late Modern Pathology*, was published by Edwin Mellen in 2004.

MARY ANNE FRANKS is currently completing a JD at Harvard Law School, and is also a Teaching Fellow in philosophy at Harvard University. She received her DPhil in 2003 from Oxford University, and her dissertation offered a critical feminist engagement with the work of Slavoj Zizek. She has previously taught ethics and religion, and recently worked in the Investigations Division of the International Criminal Court in The Hague. Her research interests involve engaging simultaneously with continental philosophy, psychoanalytic theory, and the law to address violence and conflict.

PAUL GILBERT is Professor of Philosophy at the University of Hull, and is currently working on the ethics of cultural identity. His recent publications include *Peoples, Cultures and Nations in Political Philosophy* (Edinburgh UP, 2000), and *New Terror, New Wars* (Edinburgh UP, 2003).

JOY JAMES teaches at the University of British Columbia in the Centre for Research in Women's Studies and Gender Relations, and at the Emily Carr Institute of Art, Design and Media, in the Critical, Cultural, and Historical Studies programme. Her research interests focus on an examination of current applications of contemporary imaging technologies in cross-disciplinary projects set at the intersections of art, science and technology.

JOEP LEERSSEN studied at Aachen University and University College Dublin, took his doctorate at the University of Utrecht in 1986, and was appointed Professor of Modern European Literature at the University of Amsterdam in 1991. He works on cross-cultural perceptions, representations and stereotypes, especially in Irish literary and cultural history; on the development of cultural nationalism; and on the history and methodology of the humanities.

NURIA LÓPEZ-FERNÁNDEZ graduated in English Language and Literature from the University of Oviedo (Spain) in 1997 and took her PhD at the same university in 2001. Her postgraduate research has been focussed on South Asian literature written in English, within the theoretical framework of gender and postcolonial studies. She holds an MA in Commonwealth and Postcolonial Literatures from the University of Leeds, and has worked as a Lector in Spanish in the University of Sheffield. Currently she is a Lector in Spanish in the School of Education at the University of Wales, Newport.

HENRIETTE LOUWERSE is a lecturer in Dutch in the Department of Germanic Studies at the University of Sheffield. Her research interests focus on migrant writing in the Netherlands, especially Hafid Bouazza. She is also interested in women's writing in any language. Her publications include 'Sweet is the Whisper of Yon Whispering Pine: Migration and the Pastoral in Hafid Bouazza's *Paravion*', *Dutch Crossing* 28 (2004).

GAY MCAULEY taught theatre and film in the Department of French Studies at the University of Sydney from 1973 to 1998, and she founded the interdisciplinary Department of Performance Studies in Sydney in 1988. Her major research and teaching interests include the following: performance analysis, documentation of performance, participant observation of the rehearsal process, problems of translation for the stage, and the study of the spectator in live performance. Her book,

Space in Performance: Making Meaning in the Theatre, published by the University of Michigan Press, was awarded the 2000 Rob Jordan Prize by the Australasian Drama Studies Association.

JACQUELINE MAINGARD lectures in film and television in the Department of Drama: Theatre, Film, Television at the University of Bristol. Her research interests are in representations of identity in the cinema, specifically African/South African cinema. She has recently completed a book on *South African National Cinema* for the Routledge National Cinema series. Her short film, *Uku Hamba 'Ze – To Walk Naked* (South Africa, 1995), has been internationally screened and is distributed by Third World Newsreel.

ANGELINE MORRISON is a writer and lecturer at University College Falmouth in Art History and Visual Culture. Her research interests lie in monochrome painting, blank space, indeterminacy, 'race', hair and identity. She has delivered papers on mixed 'race' identity at the Tate Britain's 'Whiteness Study Day' in February 2000, and on Afro hair at Tate Britain's 'Black History Month' study day. She is currently compiling a database of UK-based visual artists who consider themselves to be of mixed 'race' identity.

JOHN OSBORNE is Director of American Studies at the University of Hull. For ten years he edited the magazine *Bete Noire*, and has published approximately a hundred essays on modern poetry and the visual arts in books and scholarly journals in the UK, the US and Poland. His current projects are a critical monograph on the poetry of Philip Larkin, and a volume of essays selected from the papers given at the international Larkin conference which he organized at the University of Hull in July 2002.

PHIL POWRIE is Professor of French Cultural Studies at the University of Newcastle upon Tyne. He has published *French Cinema in the 1980s: Nostalgia and the Crisis of Masculinity* (Oxford UP, 1997), and *Jean-Jacques Beineix* (Manchester UP, 2001). He is the editor of the anthology *Contemporary French Cinema: Continuity and Difference* (Oxford UP, 1999), co-editor of the anthology *The Trouble with Men: Masculinities in European and Hollywood Cinema* (Wallflower, 2004), and co-author with Keith Reader of *French Cinema: An Introduction* (Arnold, 2002). He is the general co-editor of the journal *Studies in French Cinema*.

TOM VERSCHAFFEL studied history at the Catholic University of Leuven and at the European University Institute (Florence). Since 1988 he has been a researcher for the National Fund for Scientific Research (Belgium/Flanders) in the History De-

12 STUDIA IMAGOLOGICA

partment at Leuven. Since 2004 he has held an associate professorship at the Coutrai campus of the University of Leuven. His main research concerns the intellectual and intellectual history of the eighteenth and nineteenth centuries, and more specifically the history of historical writing and of popular representations of history and cultural nationalism. His most recent book is (with Raf de Bont) *Het verderf van Parijs* (UP Leuven, 2004).

MICHAEL WINTLE is Professor of European History at the University of Amsterdam, where he directs the degree programmes in European Studies. Prior to 2002, he held a chair of European History at the University of Hull, UK, where he had taught since 1980. His current research interests are in European identity and especially the visual representation of Europe, cultural aspects of European integration, European industrialization, and the modern social and economic history of the Low Countries.

INTRODUCTORY

CHAPTER 1

THE CONSTRUCTION AND ALLOCATION OF IDENTITY THROUGH IMAGES AND IMAGERY: AN INTRODUCTION

John Osborne and Michael Wintle

Image, identity and postmodernity

The critical study of the relationship between cultural stereotype and cultural identity has been, until recently, conducted mainly in the field of International Relations, and more particularly in that specialism of Comparative Literature known as 'imagology'. Elaborated notably in Hugo Dyserinck's 'Aachen Programme' (see Dyserinck 1982 and 1988), imagology dealt largely with the historical contextualization and debunking of national and ethnic stereotyping in literature, with an emphasis on the nineteenth and early twentieth centuries. The present collection of essays aims to extrapolate from this literary-historical basis by analysing the ways in which the dominant social discourses and imageries construct identity, or assign subject positions, in relation to categories such as race, nation, region, gender and language. Applying such deconstructive concepts as difference, Othering, Orientalism, hybridity, liminality and translatability to these discourses and their attendant imageries, the authors of this collection destabilize the category distinctions on which they are predicated, and thereby excavate the power relations implicated in the prevailing iconographies.

This volume does not intend to explain, step by step, the received understanding of a particular established field. It is more investigative and adventurous a collection than that would allow; the coverage is geographically global, multidisciplinary, and theoretically eclectic, but its arrangement in four sections on race, nation, gender and text is designed to make it intelligible and accessible. The unifying, overarching theme is the construction and allocation of identity, especially through images and imagery.

In keeping with the 'de-mythologizing' approach, which Dyserinck championed as centrally important to the critical study of national imagery, all the chapters query, and most systematically oppose, essentializing discourses that proffer the illusion of a holistic selfhood. In these essays identity is always socially mediated and, therefore, relativistic, provisional and performative. That is to say, identity is wholly or partially the precipitate of social discourses that the critical process is trying to render conscious and, to that extent, to liberate us from. The authors are not proposing that we can dispense with the concept of the self, but rather that we should stop employing images to invest it with a permanency and authenticity it cannot sustain.

In the case of national identity, for instance, the authors are mindful that nationalism is a comparatively recent ideology and that nation states efface their novelty by an appeal to ancient and invariant tradition. Where such a legitimating tradition does not exist, it is often retrospectively invented through the visual trappings of state and tribe. The 'national costume' of Scotland (including the kilt) was largely concocted in the eighteenth century, that of Wales in the nineteenth. The earliest national anthem seems to have been the British in 1740, while most European national flags derive from the French revolutionary tricolour of the 1790s. Sometimes the nationalistic appeal to the sanction of perpetuity entailed outright forgery: in the 1760s James Macpherson put Highland Scotland on the cultural map by inventing a 'Celtic Homer' named Ossian, whose Gaelic strophes Macpherson actually pillaged from Irish ballads. Vaclav Hanka did something similar for the Czechs with his fake medieval manuscript the *Kralodvorsky Rukopis*; Baron Hersart de la Villemarque (Kervarker) composed the supposedly ancient Breton poetry in *Barzaz Briez*; while Edward Williams, under the adopted name of Iolo Morganwg, published bogus druidic lore which he attributed to a sixteenth-century Welsh bard. In parallel, nation-state imagery can and has been adapted for deployment at nation-regional level. Taking the example of Belgium, two of our authors (Verschaffel and Beyen) demonstrate that the same historical and literary representations with which the young nation state attempted to legitimize its independent existence in the nineteenth century were later used by Flemish intellectuals to create a new, Flemish identity, and finally even to undermine the Belgian nation itself.

One of the sources of the authors' desire to de-naturalize identity and instantiate unfixity in our very conception of the self is a shared belief in deracination as a defining feature of modernity. In this collection, the international is more typifying than the national, itineracy more characteristic than autochthony, routes more expressive than roots. An example is the way the Belgian scholar Brigitte Adriaensen examines the depiction of Arab culture in works which the Spanish author Juan Goytisolo wrote in Morocco and France; or the British scholar Phil Powrie's analysis of French and American film versions of the Spanish *femme fatale*, Carmen. This sort of focus on the exilic, cosmopolitan and ethnically diverse calls into question the binary opposites on which the dominant discourses rely: hence, the study of immigrant minorities, far from bolstering the imagined homogeneity of the host society, tends to cast everyone in the role of *emigré*, even if the majority are internal rather than external exiles. Indeed, immigrants are often victimized for the extent to which they remind the indigenous population of its own insecure sense of belonging.

Much the same applies to gender. Even those chapters primarily concerned with the use of images to construct national identity remark the way in which typical representations of the patriotic male meld military prowess with heterosexual prowess, while the essays on such 'queer' novels as Virginia Woolf's *Orlando*, Pierre Loti's *Madame Chrysanthemum* and Juan Goytisolo's *Count Julian* agree that the unhousing of narrative from the false givens of nation and race is simultaneously an unmooring of sexual certitudes. In these and other ways, the chapters in this book accept the modern shift from a universe to what Henry Adams called 'the multiverse', from Thomas More's 'utopia' to Foucault's 'heterotopia' (Adams 1918). At one level of meaning, then, the entire volume testifies to a peculiarly modern aspiration: in the words of the gay American poet Frank O'Hara, that human beings acquire the grace to live as variously as possible.

At the same time, however, many chapters are at pains to establish the political limits of polymorphous image exchange. In a world that distributes power unequally, cultural transmission is not free, but may represent colonial appropriation, gender oppression, Orientalist distortion of the Other, or a refusal to acknowledge difference. Mary Anne Franks' stark declaration that 'a recent study of Internet pornography revealed that 98.9% of all consumers are male' undermines claims not only that the pornographication of our culture is emancipatory, but also that the world wide web is contributing to a postmodern state of endless diversity without hierarchy. Angeline Morrison's account of 'the cultural appropriation of the natural 'Afro' hairstyle' considers whether there might be sound political reasons for limiting contemporary theory's inclination to de-naturalize the human body. And Adrian Chan's provocative chapter 'On Being Chinese' avoids constructing a 'true' Chinese identity while forcibly demonstrating the falsity of prevailing Western constructions. In short, this book explores both the use of images to construct identity and the distribution of power undergirding the dominant imageries (or, more crudely but vividly, who defines whom).

Even here, however, the reader is continually made aware of imagery's disrespect for the protocols of power. Time and again, these chapters affirm the compulsion of language to posit Otherness; the inadvertent rebelliousness that leaks from purposive discourse; and the fictive, protean, anti-determinist tendency of images to undermine the very writs of convention they were intended to uphold. Hence, Marnix Beyen demonstrates how the farcical Belgian figure of Thyl Ulenspiegel was in 1867 transformed into a Francophile icon of liberal progressivism, only to become an emblem of illiberal Flemish nationalism that during the Second World War was sometimes recruited to Nazi collaborationism. Joy James' analysis of Pierre Loti's *Madame Chrysanthemum* brings out the homo-erotic subtext that perpetually threatens to unsinew the patriarchal and imperial values entailed in its Orientalization of woman. Gay McAuley's analysis of rehearsals for an Australian production of Molière vividly demonstrates the malleability of even the most canonical of theatrical texts. All these essays concur that the more emphatically images seek to concretize identity, the more they admit its amorphousness; or, to put it the other way round, that the elusiveness of the self exposes the inherent instability of the imagery that would (but cannot) fix it. In short, this collection is unified by a sense of the fugitive nature of both image and identity.

The structure of the book

Joep Leerssen is one of today's most renowned exponents of the discipline of imagology, and he sets the tone in an introductory essay which has as its primary aim the exposure of cultural essentialism in the guise of claims about identity. The notion of 'identity' (as in 'identity politics') has come to loom large in political and ideological discourse, and articulates a crucial link between private individuality and collective presence. On the basis of textual and visual examples from the last four centuries, Leerssen's article (taking its cue from *Begriffsgeschichte* or conceptual history) explores the roots and changing meanings and connotations of the concept of 'identity'. While the primary import of 'identity' nowadays seems to stress the notion of existential specificity and cultural/moral salience, it also implies a no less crucial claim to historical continuity and 'permanence through time'. Thus the term 'identity' has developed to occupy, eventually, an ideological-semantic space formerly held by the notions of 'character', 'tradition' and even 'cultural distinctness'. In all these respects, it can be historically demonstrated that 'identity' is a reification and indeed internalization of social attitudes, perceptions and stereotypes. The article concludes that 'identity' in its current usage has come to mask a recent, dangerous drift towards neo-essentialism.

The rest of the book is divided into four sections, which cover different thematic areas in which images of one kind or another are used to construct patterns of identity: race, nation, gender and text. These divisions are organizational useful, but sometimes analytically deceptive: many of the essays cover more than one area, and there are many overlaps and internal connections, as one would expect. In the first section, on *Immigration and Race*, Brigitte Adriaensen's essay deals with the representation of Arab culture in post-Franco Spain, through the prism of the work of Juan Goytisolo. Born in Barcelona in 1931, Goytisolo is a contemporary Spanish writer actually living alternately in Marrakech and in Paris. He devoted many of his essays and literary works to the reassessment of the Arab heritage in Spanish and European culture. In his capacity as an expert on Spanish literature from the sixteenth century onwards, he offers us a revision of the national Spanish canon from a (post)colonial point of view. His continuing emphasis on the importance of the 800-year presence of Arab culture in the Iberian peninsula has generated work marked by the profound influence of Américo Castro and Edward Said. However, despite Goytisolo's attempts to represent Oriental culture from a non-Western, non-Orientalist perspective, many critics blame him for idealizing Arab culture, for representing it through 'Third World images', or for strengthening the antithesis between the Occident and the Orient. This chapter sets out to demonstrate that the postcolonial/multicultural dimension in his work cannot be analysed without taking into account its traumatic disposition. Looking at the Goytisolo's work as a whole, the majority of its protagonists suffer from intense traumas and identity crises. The reasons for this traumatic experience are often linked to the oppression in Franco's regime, concerning both cultural (Arab) and sexual (homosexual) difference. Exile, racism and war experience in the European context form another important topic. The resulting analysis of the expression of trauma and of its relation with the representation of Arab culture permits a better understanding of Goytisolo's work, and of the sheer complexity of the identity issues involved, and their representation.

Henriette Louwerse's essay on what she terms Hafid Bouazza's 'Ghostly Demarcations of Arab Identity' approaches the complexity of identity formation from a similarly international perspective. Bouazza is a Dutch writer of Moroccan origin, who made his debut in the Netherlands in 1996 with the collection of short stories, *De voeten van Abdullah*, and caused a considerable literary stir. Unlike most so-called migrant writers, Bouazza was hailed as a serious author and the first migrant to produce 'real' literature, rather than an amalgam of journalism and therapeutic self-expression. The stories draw on common presumptions that exist in the Western perception of North Africa, ranging from the small currency of cultural cliché to the ruthless typecasting of racism. Playfully exploiting cultural expectations, the stories further appear to echo the one-dimensional views that are predominant in the West, demarcating the Arab world as both exotic and cruel, romantic and perverted, horrifying and fascinating. A first reading might yield the impression of a writer who has freed himself of the restrictions imposed by his society of origin. However, a closer examination reveals that Bouazza is acutely aware of the pitfalls which any exotic/native opposition harbours, and that he uses the potential offered by this binary opposition to the full. What seems to set out as a satire of the exotic and the Other quickly develops into a mockery of the native, the reader, 'us'. The mockery ultimately targets precisely 'our' ingrained tendency to think of the relatively homogeneous cultural community of the West 'we' imagine ourselves to be as the 'proper' readership of this work. Louwerse illustrates Bouazza's cunning double-dealing through a detailed discussion of two stories from the collection, 'Spookstad' and 'Abdullah's Feet'.

Jacqueline Maingard's chapter focuses on the way in which South African identities are constructed in its cinema. She illustrates how national identity is variously framed in different films, against the backdrop of colonialism and apartheid. One set of images is drawn from films that reflect a desire for Afrikaner identity to be paraded as the national identity, and the exemplary film here *is De Voortrekkers* (1916). Branded on its release as 'South Africa's national film', it presents an alliance between the British and Afrikaners while constructing black people as either barbarous or servile. A second set of images is drawn from a series of work by white film-makers about black identities after the National Party took power in 1948. In *Jim Comes to Jo'burg* (1949), for example, the city plays a central role in the representation of black and white identities: it is both a place where black servant is pitted against white 'boss', and where a new black identity is possible, primarily through the black jazz of the period. Images of poverty and deprivation alongside the feisty community spirit are frequently the milieu within which characters and their identities are positioned. A third set of images is taken from more recent films made by both black and white anti-apartheid film-makers. Images from these films extend and politically re-align elements of images seen in earlier films. *Mapantsula* (1988), for example, is set in the urban spaces of Johannesburg and Soweto. The images toy with individual stereotypes in the divided urban milieu of apartheid South Africa, where the stakes are high for shifting identities. Each set of images constructs, positions, and imagines identity in complex and sometimes problematic ways, casting light on the interrelationship of these constructions of identity with questions of national identity and national cinema.

Finally in this section grouped around racial identity, Angeline Morrison takes on the complexity of identity and its imagery through what eventually became a mere fashion accessory, the 'Afro' hairstyle. In the late 1960s, there were campus revolts in black universities in the US, and whilst the primary motivation was political, it was combined with an evangelical zeal for educating black students out of their obedient following of white fashion and beauty dictates. Morrison's chapter explores the various consequences – both historical and personal – of choosing to wear Afro hair 'naturally' (i.e. to forgo chemical straighteners, wigs, hairpieces, etc.). For from its beginnings as an African-American statement of pride in history, identity and beauty, the 'Afro' became a 'must-have' accessory for fashionable young white people. Once it went out of fashion, the style then became a way to ridicule the natural ethnic characteristics of members of the African diaspora. However, 'Afro' hair's appropriation into white fashion was a way of undermining the style's semiotic significance, and there was a relationship between natural 'Afro' hair styles and the imagined homeland. The signifying power of hair is, for African diasporans, far more problematic than for Europeans; fashion can do more than simply make statements about image, for it can sometimes actually create identity.

The second main section of the book is on national and regional identity, perhaps the most prolific identity theme in the literature, certainly in the discipline of history. To set the scene, Paul Gilbert's essay on 'Republics, Tribes and National Identities' observes that if, as Benedict Anderson has taught us, nations are imagined communities, then the style in which they are imagined determines the character of the corresponding national identities. Contestations of national identities may reflect profound philosophical differences as to the nature of political communities. Gilbert takes the 'unresolved question' of Northern Ireland as an instructive case. He suggests that Augustine's critique of Cicero is the source of the cultural nationalist conception of community which recent writers (like Thom and Viroli) have recorded as replacing an earlier republican one. However, he goes on to argue, the republican conception may itself take a nationalist form, delimiting membership of the nation differently and thereby potentially generating conflicts between competing nationalisms. This is not to say that republican nationalism is not a culturally constituted phenomenon. Rather it conceives of and employs culture differently from so-called cultural nationalism. This distinction is illustrated by the contrast between Anglo-Irish constructions of Irish identity, for example by Burke or Yeats, and confessional constructions of national identity in the north of Ireland.

Two studies follow of the relatively new state of Belgium, one national in scope, and one concentrating on the regions in this oft-divided country. First, as Tom Verschaffel shows, when Belgium obtained its independence as the result of a romantic revolution in 1830, the young nation state immediately felt the urge to legitimate its own existence by the creation and consolidation both of a national identity and of a national history. These were strongly interwoven. It was in the mythological forefathers of ancient times, the *Belgae* who had fought against Julius Caesar, that the national identity was recognized in its purest form. Moreover, a love of freedom was considered not only as the main characteristic of the Belgians, but as the guiding principle of their history. Through the (re)presentation of the national past, the national identity was constituted. The urge to create the Belgian nation as one, and as different from other nations, led not only towards the writing of many 'national histories', but also to the multiplication and popularization of the national past through a large-scale historical culture, including genres like historical drama, historical novels, historical pageant and historical painting. These were meant to incite the public – the compatriots – to believe in and to be devoted to the specificity of the country. The visual arts had a mission to exemplify the national identity, and this again led to historicism. The 'national style' was to be discovered in the artistic tradition; artists had to adhere to this tradition and take the 'great' Belgian painters from the past (especially Rubens) as their masters. But they also had to contribute in an even more direct and explicit way to the constitution of the national identity. The historical iconography that was elaborated through the visual representation of the various episodes and heroes of the national past was nothing other than the direct visualization of that identity. The 'visible' past was the image of nationality.

Marnix Beyen then illustrates in Chapter 9 the role of literary and visual imagery in the complex and ever-shifting field of national and political identities in Belgium by following the vicissitudes of the folk hero called Thyl Ulenspiegel in the nineteenth and the first half of the twentieth century. Originally a farcical figure popularized in chap-books, in 1867 Ulenspiegel was transformed by the Francophone, Romantic author Charles De Coster, in his *Légende d'Ulenspiegel,* into an icon of what he considered to be traditional Belgian values: liberty, independence, tolerance and social sensitivity. Thus, Ulenspiegel became a hero of patriotism and of progressive liberalism. But the message of De Coster appeared to be so polyphonous that his Ulenspiegel, throughout the century that followed the appearance of the *Légende*, became the icon of very different, sometimes even oppositional discourses of identification. Strangely enough, the image was most powerfully dispersed by those circles that at first sight were most removed from everything De Coster had stood for: the anti-Belgian, anti-liberal, usually Catholic Flemish Nationalists. During the Second World War, the image of Thyl Ulenspiegel was even frequently used in collaborationist Nazi propaganda. During this process, the image underwent considerable transformations: whereas the Belgian-patriotic version remained fairly close to the folkloric and good-hearted figure of the chap-books, in Flemish Nationalist imagery and discourse he was increasingly transformed into a severe-looking, powerful warrior. This evolution of the Ulenspiegel image was not dictated solely by the conscious manipulation of political actors, but also by some intrinsic qualities of the image – as it was forged by De Coster – and of the meanings that this image engendered. In other words, the evolving Ulenspiegel image was both product and producer of identities. This aspect may be illuminated by the fact that Ulenspiegel, as an unintended by-product of his nationalization, also became a model of masculinity, and therefore of gender identity. Thus, by studying the image of Ulenspiegel in its visual and non-visual aspects, Beyen is able to illuminate not only the power of images in identity building, but also the constant intertwining of national and gender identities.

Finally in this section on national identities, Adrian Chan undertakes a critical examination of what it means to 'be Chinese'. Chan suggests Orientalism had impacted on 'being Chinese', the Chinese identity, before the publication of Said's *Orientalism* (1978), which saw the Orient as an 'integral part of European material civilization', using a 'supporting vocabulary' in its discourse. While defining what it is to be Chinese is an expanding niche in Sinology, Chan argues that the Chinese identity remains ambiguous. Chinese culture was introduced to the West by Christian missionaries who, since the time of Matteo Ricci in the sixteenth century, have distorted China's cultural texts and invalidated her cosmogony as strategic necessities in their higher calling of saving souls. The early missionaries and translators of Chinese cultural texts gave Chinese culture a Creator-God and Heaven. This view often persists in modern Sinology, which sees a natural affinity between classical Chinese culture and Christianity, and which uses a Christian framework in these comparative enterprises. Chan suggests that Said was perhaps too generous in exempting post-1960 East Asianists from Orientalism, for Orientalist Sinology remains popular. The image of the Chinese which the West has constructed is not, contests Chan, an accurate rendering of Chinese identity.

The third section concerns itself with gender in the representation of identity through imagery. Stef Craps offers a critical reading of Virginia Woolf's novel *Orlando* (1928), focusing on its representation of gender and sexuality. This reading takes its lead from queer theory, particularly from Judith Butler's theory of the performativity of gender. From that perspective, all forms of gender identity and all sexual practices are social and cultural; patriarchy and heterosexism privilege some identities and practices over others, defining them as normal or natural. Queer theory is intent on the disruption of all taken-for-granted assumptions about what constitutes legitimate gendered subjectivity. It expects its cause to be furthered by the proliferation of transgender phenomena, which it sees as actively subversive of naturalized models of gender and sexuality. Craps uses queer theory to shed new light on the many instances of transgender behaviour in *Orlando*. He argues that Woolf's text, which figures a sex-changing, cross-dressing and bisexual protagonist, upsets the logic on which our gender reality is based, making us doubt virtually everything we thought we knew about gender and sexuality.

In Chapter 12, Mary Anne Franks takes a wider and contemporary approach to the imaging of gender, and explores the intersection of two eternal cultural obsessions: money and sex. The so-called 'sex industry' takes in billions of dollars every year, and its manifestations are inescapable – from news-stands and video stores to the Internet; its influence and production has reached baffling proportions. But the term 'sex industry' is a misnomer – and it is a misnomer that has immunized pornographic rhetoric from full-scale political/ideological critique. The term presents pornography as a level playing field, as a space for both sexes to make choices freely and explore desire. Pornography markets itself ideologically as explicit images of sexual interchange, unrestricted to any gender identity. Internet pornography in particular promises 'something for everyone', and this rhetoric is adopted by many feminists who laud the pornographic space as a place where women too can access and indulge their own sexual desires. But it is important to distinguish this rhetoric as ideological: this is only one level, or side, of the discourse of pornography. For its practice indicates something altogether different. Most consumers of Internet pornography are male. The advertisements for pornographic web sites are almost exclusively directed at men – even the so-called lesbian and 'male nude' sites are fashioned largely for the male audience. The subjects of pornography are overwhelmingly women, the younger the better (note the enormous popularity of 'teen' and 'little girl' pornography) and the depictions are almost invariably violent. This chapter exposes this and other internal contradictions within the rhetoric of pornography, to 'traverse the fantasy', in a Lacanian-Zizekian sense, not with the purpose of determining its 'truth' of woman (as the object of pornography) but to reveal some truths of man (as maker/consumer of pornography). As Roland Barthes asserted, to gauge the political weight of an object one must not look at things from the point of view of the signification, but from that of the signifier, of the thing which has been robbed. The chapter investigates the metaphor of colonization used by many feminists to describe the patriarchal oppression/repression of the female body, and the implications this has for identity and sexuality. The psychoanalytic/ideological/literary sediment in pornographic rhetoric is examined, and the case is made that pornography, in its ideological interpellation of both women and men into its discourse of phallic-defined sexuality, creates not only a male identity which naturalizes violence and degradation of the female, but also a female identity of false consent – disciplining women to internalize a sexuality that must always stipulate their 'ontological' status as lacking the 'necessary' presence of violence in sexual relations.

In Chapter 13, Nuria López examines the role of imagery in both gender and national identity, studying the relationship between women's image and national identity in the Indian nationalist movement. The fight of oppressed nations against colonialism requires the dismantling of the imperialist image of the colonized, and the formation of a new and alternative national identity which allows the oppressed to assert themselves against the oppressor. In the Indian context, British colonization first began to be attacked by the creation of an Indian national identity which could distinguish Indian social and religious customs, culture and traditions from the British ones. The traditional position of Indian women in Indian society and in the Hindu and Muslim religions became an important symbol of Indian culture, and therefore, a significant element of the national identity with which Indians wanted to fight the British oppression. If the Social Reform Movement led by some Bengali intellectuals at the beginning of the nineteenth century had promoted the Westernization of Indian women, national identity at the end of that century required a completely different image of Indian women. The perfect Indian woman was she who maintained the 'traditional feminine virtues', such as chastity, patience, devotion and personal sacrifice. Education was also considered an important feature of the new Indian woman, although it first needed to be demonstrated that it did not jeopardize her traditional position in society and her outward appearance. In this sense, the education of women became a controversial and even contradictory issue in the creation of an Indian national identity. The feminization of the nationalist movement was intensified when Gandhi became the leader of the nationalist spirit in India. The Mahatma turned the activity of spinning, traditionally carried out by women, into a symbol of the passive resistance to colonialist rule. If this symbolism idealized Indian women's traditional manual work and served to make them a more visible part of the nationalist movement, it also reinforced the traditional image of women as passive full-time workers in the household. Once again, the image of Indian women suffered contradictory effects for the sake of the creation of a national identity which needed to be genuinely Indian. These changes in the ideal image of Indian women during the evolution of the nationalist movement show the close relationship between image and identity during this period of Indian history. The image of Indian women and the national identity of Indians became interrelated elements in the nationalist project, the former changing to suit the necessities of the latter, and the latter using the former as one of its most powerful anti-colonialist weapons.

In the final section of the book, entitled *Text and Identity*, four authors take films, a novel and play to explore the subtleties of identity construction through text-based media. The first two essays concern themselves with various film versions of the Carmen story. The figure of Carmen has been a particular focus of interest for film-makers since the beginning of cinema's history. The need for cinema to resurrect and recreate her, time and again, suggests not only the enduring power of the Carmen figure but its ability to be repackaged and re-presented for different audiences at different times. Ann Davies' chapter, on 'Resurrecting Carmen', examines different ways in which the cinema has perceived Carmen in terms both of gender and of ethnicity. It considers the Carmen story in terms of the tension between the bourgeois and the Bohemian, a tension that is the site of negotiation but with the former holding the balance of power in the form of a dominant spectatorial gaze. Davies argues that the notion of Carmen as Other in terms of gender is intricately related to the notion of her Bohemian Otherness. The chapter concludes that Carmen illustrates the complexity of the Other as spectacle and the precarious negotiation involved in audience construction of identity. The result is a perpetual need both to destroy and to resurrect images of the Other in a *fort-da* movement between loss and retention of identity: hence Carmen's constant resurrection in the cinema.

The second essay on Carmen, by Phil Powrie, in Chapter 15, compares and contrasts two versions of the story: *Carmen* (1942), by the French director Christian-Jaque starring Vivianne Romance, and *The Loves of Carmen* (1948) by the US director Charles Vidor, with Rita Hayworth. Theoretical paradigms in film studies related to *film noir*, gender studies, and the more recent one of costume studies are employed, and the hypothesis is advanced that anxieties caused by World War II were focused on and worked out through leading *femmes fatales* of the period in a move typical of *film noir*, punishing women for their access to the world of work, and in the case of the American film, access to a culture of consumerism. What makes these films more interesting than the standard *noir* analysis, however, is the displacement of anxiety onto the Hispanic Other, and the somatization of anxiety in melodramatic excess located in costume and music. This problematizes identity differently, for here French and American national cultures underlie the overtly constructed Hispanic culture. Powrie concludes that the fissures in problematized national identities allow the emergence of the dark heart of the films: a vulnerable masculinity constructed differently according to different cultural frameworks. The key to the films is the soldier who fails (most obviously in the case of the French film), rather than the *femme fatale* who is punished for her independence. Star images can help us to understand how national identity is negotiated. These two films, which both featured the major female star of the period, show us how audience identification is encouraged, so that the stars can be used to negotiate social change in their respective societies, especially relating to the role of women, who 'embody the nation'. However, a story chosen because it is easily recognizable also poses problems precisely because of the ease of recognition. The new identity represented by Carmen is a threat because it too is anchored in female identity, and not sufficiently nationally representative. The films therefore work to marginalize the national specificity of the character through exoticization and hystericization. In so doing, they have their cake – 'women are the future of the nation' – and they eat it – 'but what women want is excessive and dangerous, so we will show how they are eccentric and kill them off'. Women may well (briefly) embody the nation, but the price to pay is a dead body or a consuming body. Either way, men, weak and infantilized though they may be, still win.

In Chapter 16, Joy James presents a theoretical model of the way in which, in nineteenth-century France, various forms of visual and textual representation installed unauthorized constituencies and marginal subjectivities in the larger body politic. Pierre Loti's *Madame Chrysanthemum* (1887), a fictionalized travel narrative built around the author's time in Japan, is one of the earliest articulations of what has come to be known as the 'Madame Butterfly' story. The Butterfly narrative, at its inception and as it has evolved over the past century (most prominently in relation to Puccini's *Madama Butterfly*), displays colonialist and imperialist responses to gender, race, and class in the construction and representation of the self and Other. The Butterfly theme presents a tenacious though infinitely unstable link from the time of its emergence as a dynamic representation of European Orientalism to its contemporary manifestation in the David Cronenberg/Henry Hwang 1993 film *M. Butterfly*. Loti's representation of Chrysanthème is a complex one, and carries multivalent meanings: he constructs and re-presents a popular, dominant stereotype of the 'Oriental' woman, but his writing also subverts the assertion of a stable normative masculinity. The nineteenth-century European project was concerned with asserting and maintaining Western supremacy through, in part, the definition and construction of a rigorously heterosexualized male bourgeois identity. However, the presence of a homoerotic or homosocial theme in Loti's work complicates his involvement in this project. James examines and contextualizes the material conditions that lay behind and were indexed by the way that the Orient, 'woman' and normative male sexuality were constituted in relation to one another, both in Loti's writings, and in the rather brilliant representation of these complex relationships over a century later in Cronenberg's *M. Butterfly*.

Finally, in Chapter 17, Gay McAuley draws on a contemporary performance project in which a group of Australian actors, starting from what they designated a 'neutral' translation of Molière's *Dom Juan*, modified the text in order to produce an Australian vernacular version, without adapting the fiction to locate it in an Australian setting. A comparative analysis is presented of five different versions of a fragment from this play: the original French, two published British translations, and the Australian 'neutral' and vernacular versions. The minor textual differences are examined, and comment is offered on the significant impact these have in performance, on the ways in which this rehearsal process can construct characters and narrative moment, and on the value of rehearsal studies for cultural theorists interested in identity formation. Even when working with classic plays, actors frequently modify the text during the course of the rehearsal process, either consciously through cuts and changes, or unconsciously through slips of the tongue and failures of memory. The text is thus reworked to fit the meanings being constructed by that group of actors through their performance. While this process occurs to a greater or lesser extent in any text-based rehearsal, it is greatly accentuated when the work involved is a translation from another language. Translation seems to destabilize the authority of the text, performance problems are likely to be seen first and foremost as translation problems, and the tendency is to amend the text rather than search harder for a performance solution. This means that the rehearsal room is a wonderful place to observe the interface between cultures, and the role of language in the construction and representation of identity.

Collectively, then, these essays confirm for us the instability of constructed identities, despite their power, and the ability of images to mould them. We have assembled here wide-ranging illustrations of the interaction between already-constructed identities and new or mutating imagery. For not only are identities shown to be transient, but we also witness the instability of the images themselves, and the unpredictability and lack of certainty involved when images are linked to identity. Images can be indeed used in the construction of identity, thus vindicating the title of 'Image into Identity', but this collection demonstrates that they are more reliable as a tool for the analysis of identity politics than as part of the arsenal of would-be identity-constructors, whatever the medium.

References

Adams, Henry. 1918. *The Education of Henry Adams; an Autobiography.* Boston: Houghton Mifflin.
Dyserinck, Hugo. 1982. 'Komparatistische Imagologie jenseits von "Werk-immanenz" und "Werktranszendenz"' in *Synthesis* 9: 27-40.
Dyserinck, Hugo. 1988. 'Komparatistische Imagologie. Zur politischen Trag-weite einer europäischen Wissenschaft von der Literatur' in Dyserinck, H. & K.U. Syndram (eds) *Europa und das nationale Selbstverständnis. Imagologische probleme in Literatur, Kunst und Kultur des 19. und 20. Jahrhunderts.* Bonn: Bouvier: 13-38.
Said, Edward W. 1995. *Orientalism.* New York: Pantheon.

CHAPTER 2

THE DOWNWARD PULL OF CULTURAL ESSENTIALISM

Joep Leerssen

Just that downward pull of human nature,
Coming to try it on;
The downward pull of human nature,
Just trying to take you by the storm.
    John Martyn, 'The Downward Pull of Human Nature'

Essentialism and culture

In considering human affairs and the traffic between individuals and societies, we often tend to take for granted that such affairs and traffic are determined by the inner constitution of the partners involved. Patterns of behavioural interaction will be explained in terms of the inner, essential nature of the actors involved, much as the nature of a chemical reaction is determined by the elements involved.

This explanation of human interaction from the inner make-up of the participating actors I term essentialism. A notorious, but telling example is that of the Italian savant Cesare Lombroso, who explained criminal behaviour in terms of the mental and even physical characteristics of 'the' criminal, *L'uomo delinquente* (as his 1876 book was entitled). Nowadays, such biological explanations of behaviour are less crude, but still popular. Especially since Richard Dawkins, in his influential book *The Selfish Gene* (1976), re-formulated Darwinian evolutionary schemata in terms of survival strategies, not of organisms, but of the DNA material of which those organisms are the phenotypical expression, much animal behaviour has been explained in terms of strategies towards siring or protecting as many offspring samples as possible; and this explanatory model has also been extended to the field of human culture. Human behaviour, in the analysis of 'sociobiologists', 'evolutionary biologists', 'evolutionary psychologists' *et hoc genus omne*, is heavily mortgaged by millennia-old, engrained, instinctive patterns which in some primal past proved to be effective strategies to survive and procreate. The explana-

tory pattern is, in fact, older than Dawkins and reaches all the way back
to Freud's *Totem and Taboo* (1913).

For all its popularity, evolutionary psychology is surrounded by criticism and indeed scandal. The criticism focuses on the unfalsifiable nature
of the explanations offered. Not only is there no way to test or check the
conditions of life in the 'primal horde' of some unspecified Very Long
Time Ago, so airily invoked as furnishing the behavioural blueprint of
human characteristics; it also appears as if any behavioural or social trend
in present-day society (usually Western, American/European society,
discounting possible different patterns in other parts of the world) can
be retroactively fitted with a narrative prequel, relating how the trend in
question may possibly have helped males to sire offspring numerously,
and females to rear their offspring successfully. The one-explanation-fits-
all nature of such deterministic explanatory narratives seems at times
closer to Kipling's 'Just So'-stories (which, in Lévi-Straussian terms,
means that such explanations are properly speaking mythical) than to
scientific procedure with its need for testable hypotheses and experimen-
tal proofs. It is no surprise, then, to see evolutionary psychology exhibit
an unfortunate tendency to gravitate, Lombroso-style, towards rationalizations of human inequality (between the sexes or between the races) as
being somehow pre-ordained.[1] This is a version of what I call essentialism.

In defining essentialism as I do here, I am aware that I depart slightly
from the more stringent definition of the term as offered originally by

[1] There is a large body of controversy on sociobiology and evolutionary psychology. Scholars agree that the ascription of a volition or a teleology to genes and DNA
packets ('selfish', 'strategy', 'successful') is a stylistic conceit, a narrative strategy, on
the part of Dawkins and his followers; but no-one has yet proven that the case can be
stated at all without in some manner anthropomorphizing biochemistry or the mecha-
nism of survival statistics, i.e. that the conceit is not just in the manner of presenting
the case but even in the conceiving of it, in which case the entire theory would be just
that: a conceit. There are various cases of sociobiological or evolutionary-biological
models being used to rationalize perceived sexual or racial differences as somehow
the natural outcome of natural selection, thereby also reifying such perceived differences as being objectively factual - an assumption which shows a remarkable insouci-
ance concerning the risk of having one's observations tainted by racist or sexist bias.
Examples in point are Herrnstein & Murray 1994, Rushton 1995, and Browne 2002.
An apologia for evolutionary psychology and sociobiology is Barkow et al. 1992; for a
strenuous critique, see Malik 2000, as well as Rose & Steven Rose, eds 2000. Also,
Derksen 2004: 3-5, points out the irony that social (evolutionary) psychologists still
maintain the taxon of 'race' as a meaningful human aggregate, whereas it has been
wholly abandoned by anthropologists.

Karl Popper.[2] On the whole, however, the word has entered general usage and accordingly has obtained a greater semantic bandwidth. It is usually seen nowadays more or less in the sense used in these pages: locating and explaining the meaning of things in and from their inner, internal essence (rather than in their function and interaction with the rest of the world). Sexual essentialism, for instance, will hypothesize that differences between men and women are irreducible because they result from their specifically masculine or feminine, inner nature; racial essentialism will argue similarly with regard to ethnic groups. Such essentialism usually stands in contradiction to constructivism (which holds that observable behavioural or moral differences between the sexes, or between races, are the result of social conventions and socialization patterns rather than of natural proclivities). Here, the opposition between essentialism and constructivism usually collapses into the debate of nature vs. nurture or nature vs. culture.

Now, if we see culture as a counterpart to nature (i.e. as the sum of human behaviour which is not biologically circumscribed by our physical functioning in the natural world), then the notion of cultural essentialism would seem, at first sight, a contradiction in terms. Sexual and racial essentialism will call, not *cultural*, but *natural* (physical, biological) factors into play: physical differences between men and women, or between Central Africans and North Europeans, in order to rationalize perceived or actual differences in behaviour, values or mentality. The notion of cultural essentialism therefore needs some further scrutiny.

To be sure, cultural differences (*perceived* cultural differences!) between societies have long and widely been explained from physical causes. We have already taken stock of its crudest, somatic-biological or evolutionary mode. Another prevalent way of doing so is, for instance, climatological: differences (perceived differences) between Spaniards and Swedes have been explained from the determining circumstances of climate and temperature. Temperature has, as it were, been used to explain temperament. Such climatological-physical explanations have been prevalent from the early modern period onwards (Zacharasiewicz 1977). We encounter it, not only in banal colloquial stereotypes, but also in literary history handbooks like Hippolyte Taine's *Histoire de la littérature anglaise* of 1864. We may even suspect Max Weber's thesis on Protestantism and the work

---

[2] Initially in *The Open Society and its Enemies* (Popper 1945). Later, in *The Poverty of Historicism* (Popper 1957), he came to equate essentialism with anti-nominalism.

ethic of carrying some climatological overtones. Why else should we
always conceive of Protestantism as being peculiarly suited to 'cool',
'cerebral', and individually moralistic Northern Europe, despite the contrary evidence of cases like Polish and Irish Catholicism, and Protestant
Geneva?

Another physical-determinist way of explaining cultural difference is
geographical. In the eighteenth century, Haller conceived of the Alps as
a landscape designed to inculcate a sublime sense of awe and 'natural
piety' in its inhabitants. Similarly, there has for centuries been a widespread cliché to the effect that Dutch culture has been formed by the
proximity of the sea and the constant struggle against inundations; and in
his *La Méditerranée* (1949), Fernand Braudel argued that mountainous
coasts in the Mediteranean yielded cultural patterns common to Corsica
and Epirus.

Such rationalizations of the link between landscape and morals invoke untestable commonplaces. Their rhetorical speciousness may account for their widespread popularity but should not be mistaken for
scientific validity. They have been studied as tropes and commonplaces,
alongside other prejudices, commonplaces and stereotypes, by imagolo-
gists.[3]

But cultural essentialism is more than just a physical-determinist view
of culture; it involves all attempts to explain cultural variations from the
inherent, essential profile of the actors involved. To see cultural variation
rephrased as a difference between culture A and culture B; to see the
very notion of culture reduced to that of 'a culture', where 'a culture'
becomes almost a synonym for 'a society' or 'a country'; to apply an
elemental taxonomy of unit-cultures (each with its own specific profile
and *essence*), which between them differ enough to make comparisons and
contrasts possible: such pigeonholing of diversity patterns into homogeneous unit-essences is what here is termed cultural essentialism.

That reliance on homogeneous unit-essences is atomistic: it believes
that compounds, if subdivided finely enough, will prove to consist of
unitary elements which are homogeneous and consistent in themselves
('atoms'). So too cultural difference can be reduced (or so it is believed)
to a pattern of differences between constituent fundamental elements

---

[3] For an attempt to situate Braudel's Mediterranean thesis from an imagological
point of view, see Leerssen 1995. For imagology, see Dyserinck 1982, and Dyserinck
1988.

which each individually will be specific, homogeneous and undifferentiated. Hence one can formulate what I consider a specific, even defining characteristic of cultural essentialism: Cultural essentialism locates cultural difference *between cultures* rather than *within culture*. This definition also indicates its logical flaws.

Culture is diverse and allows for variation and differentiation. One might even go as far as defining culture as 'all those human patterns of behaviour which might also be done differently'. The human eye can only see light in the spectrum between infrared and ultraviolet; the act of swallowing with which we ingest food is an in-born reflex. Such pre-givens belong to the realm of 'nature', and as such allow for little choice. By the same token, they are (again, almost by definition), culturally a-specific: they are common to all humans and accordingly unsuitable as distinguishing criteria for cultural comparisons. But the question whether we consider it courteous or not to keep our lips closed while we chew food, or the fact that we can improve or alter our vision with optical instruments – such possible variations belong to the realm of culture. Culture is primarily *a way of doing things differently*, a pattern of behavioural differentiations. Those differentiations will run *within*, as well as *between*, the various sub-groups and aggregates into which one may subdivide humanity.

Human aggregates are never as homogeneous as our schemata and tropes would make them out to be. Human societies are no anthills. It follows from the very definition of culture that any society or aggregate of people will have its inner cultural differentiation – between regions, between genders, between communities, between age-groups, between social classes. Indeed, these sub-groups will within their own ranks have further subdivisions and differentiations. Even families, siblings, will differ among themselves, and the intensity with which these differences are experienced is no less for the smallness of the group-size: family conflicts and village feuds are every bit as intense, if not more so, as quarrels among political parties. Yes, even the individual is internally inconsistent and diverse. I may feel different about certain things on a Monday morning from the way I do on a Saturday evening; my opinions may change as I grow older or according to my moods, the company I am in, or even the state of my digestion; and about a good number of things I have mixed feelings. The etymological foundation under the word 'individual' (something that cannot be divided, exactly as in the

Greek 'atomos') is misleading.[4] There is no atomistic level in human
affairs, no consistent homogeneity of culture. Yet cultural essentialism
would have it so, and will marginalize in-group diversity for the sake of
argumentative clarity in inter-group comparison.

There is, in fact, no reason to privilege the cultural *differences between*
societies over their shared similarities. When comparing Spaniards with
Swedes, we may foreground all sorts of differences (use of garlic as an
ingredient in the cuisine; bullfighting as opposed to the reading of trilo-
gies on long winter evenings) and these oppositions, often anecdotal,
tend to obscure the more fundamental shared similarities: neither society
practices Shintoism or riding to hounds; neither condones cannibalism
or polygamy; both are constitutional monarchies; both allow divorce;
both owe their legal system to the Napoleonic *code civil;* and their university systems both derive from the West-European prototype of Bologna
as revised by Humboldt. Privileging differences over similarities is what
anthropologists call *exoticist:* exoticism will conflate the distinct and the
distinctive, will reductively believe that the true nature of a given society
lies in precisely those aspects in which that society differs most saliently
from the rest of the world. Exoticism reduces culture to picturesque
idiosyncracies. Comparisons between groups like Spaniards and Swedes
will implicitly reduce both to an ideal-typical extrapolation of 'your typical Spaniard' and 'your typical Swede'; examples that do not fit this sim-
plification will thereby become marginal, or at best 'exceptions that
prove the rule'.

In sum, cultural essentialism presupposes, fallaciously so, that *differ-*
ences between cultures are more meaningful than similarities between cultures, and also
more meaningful than differences within a given culture.

Image into identity

> Là où nous ne voyons rien,
> nous croyons qu'il y avait l'homme éternel
>   Paul Veyne, *Comment on écrit l'histoire*

Off-hand, one would hold an 'image' to be a representational derivative
of its 'original'. If I carry a picture of my children in my wallet, or in my

---

[4] One is tempted to speculate: is the tendency to lump 'others' together into
undifferentiated collectives with a simple character perhaps motivated by discomfort
at one's own inner fragmented inconsistency?

memory have a mental image of a city recently visited, such pictorial or mental images are considered derivations of a reality. 'Image' and 'reality' are, accordingly, counterpart terms; and unless one wishes to formulate Oscar-Wilde-style paradoxes to the effect that Life imitates Art, we usually hold empirical reality to be anterior to the image we form of it. Similarly, the relationship between identity and image. The former has greater ontological weight than the latter. Tartuffe's 'real' identity is that of a scheming hypocrite for all that he projects an image of pious and sentimental probity; historians are confronted with the distinction between Churchill as a public figure and the 'real' man behind the image.

The very phraseology 'image into identity' would appear slightly counter-intuitive, then, a mild oxymoron. We can understand how identities spawn images, but hardly the other way around. Yet, historically speaking, that is precisely how things have tended to work. Egregious examples like witch-hunts, cargo cults or Rastafarianism clarify the point but should not render it anecdotal. Images concerning people, human types or nations have arisen almost out of nothing, from literary commonplaces and intertextual formulae, and have solidified into belief systems and patterns of identification which in turn have given rise to the now-current set of tropes we call 'national identities' – tropes with which many of us, most of the time, actively identify and which thus have become real things in the real world.[5] In the course of the nineteenth century, an almost universal belief developed in Europe that each nation has its own specific identity, that this identity is historically permanent and sets off each nation from the rest of humanity, and that thus each nationality is individualized and characterized by its own 'national character' or 'volksgeist' (Leerssen 1999). This belief system has been at work throughout the nineteenth and twentieth centuries, has motivated many movements for national emancipation and nationalist separatism, and in many cases has led to the establishment of nation-states from Ireland to Estonia and Bulgaria. Ernest Gellner has summarized this process as the invention of nations by nationalism – close enough in its

---

[5] The 'realness' or ontology of things like 'national character' is problematic. In a Platonic division between concrete objects (the Eiffel Tower, my left elbow, this book) and notional abstractions (the square root of 3, the colour green, beauty), something like 'national character' or national self-identification occupies a problematic in-between position. Karl Popper has gone as far as proposing a separate, third ontological category for such things, 'world-3' (Popper 1979: 151-61). For an imagological application of this ontology, cf. Dyserinck 1982: 37-8.

phraseology to the idea that 'images' (in this case, national self-images)
can solidify into 'identity'. In many cases, it has been established that the
origins of these national-identitarian belief systems is, properly speaking,
mythical, or based on a literary or pseudo-historical imagination rather
than on empirical fact. The Basque instance provides a case in point.
While no-one would deny the separate existence and 'identity' of such a
thing as the Basque language, the set of symbols and cultural markers
which became the focus of an emancipatory and separatist Basque movement in the nineteenth century was partly a pseudohistorical fiction by
the French journalist Frederic Chaho, and partly the deliberate contrivance of the activist Sabino de Arana (Juaristi 2000).

Such trajectories are inherently 'pulled' by cultural essentialism, by a
belief that the nation in question exists, exists separately, and can be
objectively individuated by its inner propria and character. Indeed, the
very word 'character' itself, in its conceptual development over the centuries, illustrates this essentialist pull.

Character: from image into essence

The word 'character' begins its checquered career in Greek, and derives
from the verb *grattein*, meaning 'to scratch' or 'to draw' (as with a writing
stylus on a wax tablet). Anything 'scratched' is thus 'character' – witness
also one still-current meaning of the word, as in 'a book printed in Japanese characters'.

Thence the term was used to refer to sketches concerning social
types. Aristotle's pupil Theophrastos collected a series of such sketches
of social types as *èthikoi charakteres*, and the genre of the 'character sketch'
was kept alive in later manifestations such as La Bruyère's *Caractères* or
Elias Canetti's *Der Ohrenzeuge*. Dickens's *Sketches by Boz, Illustrative of
Every-day Life and Every-day People*, shows how the genre can morph into
that of the novel: it was Dickens's debut work, and led to the *Pickwick
Papers* and thence into more extensive narrative; yet Dickens's later novels still contained character sketches of such famous human or social
'types' as Mr Micawber, Mr Gradgrind and Uriah Heep (Smeed 1985).
The word *character* thus originally belongs to the realm of representation:
an emblem or sketch.[6]

---

[6] The same holds for similar words like *type* and *style*. *Style* is derived from the stylus
with which such sketches were made, the pen, hence penmanship or distinctive
'hand'; *type* is from the Latin *typus*, itself derived from Greek *tuptos*, meaning 'imprint',

Theophrastan 'characters' are sketches of human individuals who are remarkable for their 'typical' behaviour. The notion of typicality is double: on the one hand their behaviour is unusual, remarkable, stands out from the default; on the other it is representative of a type at large: the vainglorious soldier, the cocky young man-about-town, the absent-minded professor. In each case, it is the behaviour, the social pose, which counts: that too is the meaning of *èthikos* in Theophrastos's original title: sketches of an 'ethos', an ingrained behavioural pattern. What is noteworthy about this is that the word has to do with *outward social appearance*, how one comes over in one's environment. This meaning of 'character' is maintained in the English notion of character assassination: character may mean nothing more nor less than *reputation*, and even today it is possible to say that a certain individual was 'a man of good character', meaning that his standing among those who knew him was high.

It was only in the later seventeenth century that the word *character* seems to have taken an inward, essentialist turn and came to refer, not to how someone came over in his environment, but how he really was, deep down within himself (Van Delft 1993). In this most recent sense, most prevalent nowadays, character means one's inner psychological predisposition, the temperamental or moral profile of a given individual or group. To say that someone has an abrasive or amiable, an aggressive or a cooperative 'character' means to describe his own, inner personality. Character is this sense is less a description of behaviour than a motivational explanation.[7] People behave aggressively because such is their character; others laugh and joke a lot because they are of an easy-going character: the operative word in these two examples is 'because'. In other words, the notion of character has changed its meaning to refer, not to someone's impression upon society, but to his essence. This, too manifests

'stamp', 'imprinted impression'; its currency in the modern European languages appears to have spread together with book printing: it is rare before the mid-fifteenth century. Here as in other instances of conceptual development I have made grateful use of the evidence collected in the Oxford English Dictionary.

[7] The notion of motivation is complex and, like that of character, veers between the fields of a human psychology and literary poetics. In literary poetics and narrative it means that a character's actions are generated by his type of personality, and therefore make narrative sense. (Non-motivated acts or turns of event will be experienced as puzzling, random and implausible.) Indeed, the minimal narrative unit predicating an act on an actor is for that reason called called a 'motif'; cf. Dolezel 1972. In real-world behaviour, motivation likewise refers to the fact that a choice of action is deliberate and subjectively meaningful or plausible.

that 'pull of essentialism' which we see at work so often in these historical developments: that terms and concepts which at first refer to human
acts or interactions, later on come to refer to a generative essence.
National character[8] at first refers to a set of 'manners and customs'; and
while Montesquieu, in *L'esprit des lois*, already tried to underpin national
differences by climatological and physical determinism, Hume, in his
essay 'Of National Characters' vigorously refuted such essentialism in
favour of a more social-constructivist view. He pointed out that Jesuits
and army officers resemble each other across Europe, and that such
similarities obviously arise from a behavioural convergence resulting
from frequent mutual intercourse. Even so, the eighteenth century
tended to use 'character' as a means to create anthropological distinctions between 'nations' which in the process are categorized into meaningful taxonomical units. The process reached an end point in the
Encyclopédie of Diderot and D'Alembert, which concluded its entry on
nation by stating that

> chaque nation a sons caractère particulier; c'est une espèce de proverbe que
> de dire, léger comme un françois, jaloux comme un italien, grave comme un
> espagnol, méchant comme un anglois, fier comme un écossois, ivrogne
> comme un allemand, paresseux comme un irlandois, fourbe comme un grec.

Accordingly, an additional paragraph on *caractère des nations* is subjoined,
indicating that the difference between nations is primarily charactero-
logical, that these add up to a national taxonomy, and that the characters
in question are not a matter of reputation, stereotype or appearance ('image') but internal and essential properties of the nation in question ('identity'). The sub-entry gives a definition of 'national character' which runs
parallel to its definition of psychological character in general as a:

> certaine disposition habituelle de l'âme, qui est plus commune chez une
> nation que chez une autre, quoique cette disposition ne se rencontre pas dans
> tous les membres qui composent la nation: ainsi le caractère des français est
> la légèreté, la gaieté, la sociabilité, l'amour de leurs rois & de la monarchie
> même, etc.

Readers will be familiar with the intensification of national and cultural
essentialism that developed in the century following Diderot/D'Alembert's *Encyclopédie*. The notions of national culture, national character and
national identity became inextricably intertwined in the course of the

---

[8] For what follows, see more generally Leerssen 2000.

nineteenth century, leading to the development of Gobineau-style racism, 'Völkerpsychologie' (national psychology) in the style of Lazarus and Steinthal, and 'Wesenskunde' ('essentiology') in the style of Eduard Wechssler. We can trace the burgeoning of national-cultural essentialism in all human sciences. Linguists like Humboldt and Grimm disseminated the notion that each language carries within its structures a cognitive template which determines its speakers to one, rather than another, mode of coming to terms with the world – an early version of what is now better known as the Sapir-Whorff theory. Anthropology was no longer the 'proper study of mankind' as it had been practised by Enlightenment philosophers from Locke to Kant, but rather a comparative study of the fundamental differences between human societies or races; within this ethnographically oriented anthropology, the old-fashioned monogenist view that all humankind can be traced back to a common set of ancestors was gradually abandoned in favour of a polygenetic approach favouring the notion of radical differences, even biological-genetic differences, between the human races (Stepan 1982, Stocking1987). Again, philology (the historical study of language and literature), following Grimm, was similarly oriented towards the elucidation of the collective mentality of a given nation, and traced all literary culture back to a root system of tribal origins and myths (Leerssen 2004). Comparative linguistics schematized and systematized languages in terms of their salient differences and aligned them into a system which is racially ethnic in its taxonomic make-up, classifying languages into tribal-biological families with names like Germanic, Slavic and Celtic. Even the criticism of French and German culture polarized these twain into some anthropological irreconcilability between 'Romance' and 'Germanic', between *esprit* and *Geist*, *civilisation* and *Kultur*. Historians like Heinrich von Treitschke, Camille Julian and even Henri Pirenne explained the vicissitudes of their respective nations from the almost fatal necessity of their ethnic or geopolitical situation.

All this will be familiar to the reader. To see the nineteenth century as the heyday of essentialist and determinist thought is nothing new; similarly, we know that the pendulum swung back in the course of the twentieth century, and that in the latter part of the previous century we have seen an enormous lurch towards constructivism. Following Ernest Renan's *Qu'est-ce qu'une nation* of 1881, culture and history have come to be seen in terms of choices and contingencies, not of essence and determinacy. Entire disciplines have backtracked from their essentialist antecedents, and have instead developed a critique of essentialism into specialisms: anthropologists and philologists are now deeply concerned with the study, not of ethnic or cultural essences, but of ethnocentrism and cultural stereotype. In all related fields, structuralism and post-structuralism have rung out the 'metaphysics of identity' (Derrida's phrase), and have instead focused on patterns of significant differentia-tion (structuralism) or *différance* (post-structuralism). Deconstruction (pointing up the constructed nature of things which mask themselves as categorical pre-givens or as natural, rather than cultural, phenomena) has become predominant. After Foucault, things like tears, madness, sexual-ity, motherhood, death, the natural landscape, or codfish, have become matters for culture-historical, rather than biological or anthropological, investigation.[9]

And so, likewise, the concept of 'national character' has turned from an anthropological category into a culture-historical topic. Essentialism seems dead, a bygone paradigm like Ptolemaic geocentrism, the humoral theory in medicine, or the chemical belief in phlogiston.

Identity and constructivism

Does the mid-twentieth century signal the nadir, and thence the demise, of the downward pull of cultural essentialism? There are some indica-tions to that effect. One of these is a remarkable shift in the usage of the term identity. Like character, the notion of identity had, somewhere in the last three centuries, felt the essentialist pull. Originally the word referred to a *relation* between two identical objects or phenomena – as in phrases like 'this exhibit is a cudgel identical to the one with which the victim was murdered' or 'the Morning Star is identical with the Evening Star'. Thereafter, the term came to mean, as the Oxford English Dictio-nary puts it, 'The sameness of a person or thing at all times or in all circumstances; the condition or fact that a person or thing is itself and not something else; individuality, personality'. In other words, the con-cept has shifted from a relationship to an essence, and as such followed much the same semantic trajectory as 'character'. In the nineteenth and twentieth centuries, the identity of individuals and nations was seen in terms of 'the condition or fact of remaining the same throughout the

___

[9] On Foucault's importance for the renegotiation of the borders between anthro-pology and history-writing, see Veyne 1978; almost a theoretical prediction of the 'cultural turn' in the historical sciences.

various phases of existence; continuity of the personality', and thus added to the notion of 'national character' or 'volksgeist' a connotation of fixity, a hint of permanence through time. The semantic shift of the term in the last thirty years or so dramatically illustrates the rise of constructivism in social, cultural and political thought. Book titles on ethnic or national issues began to use the term 'identity' in collocations such as 'the search for identity', or 'the quest for identity', indicating that identity was not a categorical given, but rather the outcome of a historical growth process. Indeed, so far has this constructivist recalibration of the term progressed, that we nowadays take the constructed sense as the primary one, and implicitly use the word 'identity' to refer not to a pre-given essence, but to a pattern of self-identifications and a self-image. Identity, in other words, has been shifted from the objective to the subjective domain. As a result, earlier anthropological definitions of ethnicity in somatic terms (by kinship and blood lines) have been revised in favour of a more constructivist view. Ethnicity has become a shared self-image:

Ethnicity is also matter of subjective belief in common ancestry. Members of ethnic groups often have a subjective belief in their common descent. It does not matter whether or not an objective blood relationship really exists. Ethnic membership differs from the kinship group precisely by being a presumed identity (Liebkind 1999).

A recent scholarly conference held at the University of Ghent may serve as an example. It was entitled *Developing Cultural Identity in the Balkans: Convergence vs. Divergence*. The programme notes cautiously opened by hypothesizing that 'If something like a Balkan cultural identity does exist, it must have resulted from a long and intensive process' of 'contamination and hybridization'; 'national cultural identities' are presented as the result of 'a development', indeed from an 'ideological construction', involving not 'identities' *tout court,* but '(perceived) identities'. Perception and self-image are operative terms; similarly, and among the twenty-odd presentations, the eleven which use 'identity' in their titles all use it to denote something as subjective and historically variable as 'public opinion' or 'a common self-image'.[10]

---

[10] Victor Friedman: 'Turkism, Balkan Identity, and Balkan Linguistic Ideologies'; Razvan Dumitru, 'Vlaški Language and Vlasi Identity in the Vidin Region (Bulgaria)'; Ger Duijzings, 'Cultural Identities in the Borderlands of the Balkans'; Julia G. Krivoruchko, 'A Case of Divergent Convergence: the Cultural Identity of Romaniote

As these examples illustrate, the idea of identity has come to be used in a studiously anti-essentialist mode; its meaning has shifted to something like 'collective self-awareness' – a self-awareness which is acquired, malleable, and as such a historical variable rather than an anthropological constant; an ideological *construit* rather than a categorical *donnée*. In fact it seems to have met, and merged, with what is now its near-synonym: *culture*. Identity and culture have become almost interchangeable terms.

And back to Culture: post-constructivism, neo-essentialism
So to repeat the question posed at the beginning of the previous section: is essentialism dead? Not quite. Curiously, the demise of 'the metaphysics of identity' and the rise of constructivism in the humanities coincides with the rise of identity politics. Identity, for all that it is now used in a less stringently essentialist sense than before, also matters more urgently. Hyphenated identities abound. Consciousness-raising has affected all human aggregates who were marginalized by adult white Western males. The *Négritude* movement and the discussions around it; the cultural debates surrounding processes of decolonization and, in North America, the emancipation of African-Americans; the second feminist wave; the self-assertion of homosexuals and other sexual minorities: everywhere the emancipation of marginalized minorities was undertaken with the rallying-cry of 'identity'.

Thus, while scholars in the humanities have been deconstructing 'identities', these have become more prominently important factors in the field of societal relations and, concomitantly, in the field of the social sciences. As a result, the humanities now seem to be out of step with public opinion at large, and also with a certain section of the social sciences, which is still, or again, feeling the downward pull of cultural essentialism. As I write this, a Dutch television programme is scheduled for broadcast, trying to explain the fact that the German national soccer

Jewry'; Boyko Penchev, 'Tsarigrad/Istanbul and the Spatial Construction of Bulgarian National Identity in the 60s and 70s of the XIXth Century'; Nada Alaica, 'A Mixing of Cultural Identities: the Croatian Borderlands in the 19th Century'; Magdalena Elchinova, 'Alien by Default: the Identity of the Turks of Bulgaria at Home and in Immigration'; Zoran Terzic, 'Art from Somewhere Else: the Fuzzy Logic of Yugoslav Cultural Identities in the Light of War, Art and Literature'; Galia Lazarova Dimitrova, 'La redéfinition de l'identité nationale bulgare: le rôle des images médiatiques'; Andreas Hemming, 'Albania and the EU: how State Ambitions have Become Part of National Identity'. The conference was organized by the Centre for South-East European Studies at the University of Ghent, and held 12-13 December 2003.

team won the 1974 World Cup Final because of some underlying 'mentality' factor.[11] In popular culture, generalizations about the typical cultures and identities of various countries enjoy undiminished popularity, witness 'fun' books like *The Undutchables* or *The Xenophobe's Guide to*... These are, to be sure, post-modern and ironic about themselves, presenting their jokey references to ethic stereotypes as something not-quite-serious, a bit of a laugh, playfully 'mentioning' national clichés rather than actually 'using' and endorsing them.[12] At the same time, such publications belong to a range of discourse also informing us that 'men are from Mars and women from Venus', trying to pigeonhole the compound of inter-human variation into the matrix of ideal-typical human sub-classes (men, women, Dutch).

This essentialism also affects academic writing, or at least helps to create a climate in which such academic writing can gain wide popularity. An example in point is provided by the archaeological theories of Marija Gimbutas, according to whom a primeval, peaceful, matriarchal civilization in Europe was overrun by Indo-European masculine-dominated warrior tribes. The theory appealed to a wide, non-professional readership and fed into a New-Age-style, Bachofen-inspired feminism that was sympathetic, for other than purely scientific reasons, to Gimbutas's 'archaeomythology' (which claimed it could read, from artefacts and their embellishments, a 'holy scripture' of the Great Goddess').[13] A similar cross-over from social-activist identity politics into academic discourse was the theory by Leonard Jeffries (then a professor of Black Studies at City College, New York), in whose anthropological view of history whites (whose racial forebears developed in colder climes) featured as 'ice people', as opposed to blacks ('sun people'). In this scheme, 'ice people' were greedy and domineering by nature, whereas 'sun people' were giving, cooperative and intelligent. While these theories created something of a scandal in 1990s America, Jeffries continues to be held in high esteem by a devoted following, again (as in the Gimbutas case) for the social-activist, consciousness-raising potential of his theories rather than for their scientific accuracy (Hacker 1995).

---

[11] 'Een Duits geheim', broadcast 11 June 2004, Nederland 2 TV.

[12] On the distinction between the 'use' and the 'mention' of terms, and its importance for the idea of irony, see Sperber & Wilson 1981.

[13] For a vigorous denunciation of Gimbutas's ideological, rather than scientific, theories, see 'Im Bann der grossen Göttin: Marija Gimbutas' metaphysisches Matriarchat', chapter 6 in Brigitte Röder et al. 1996.

Identity politics and even the postmodern predominance of cultural relativism – which in itself is invaluable and necessary as an antidote against earlier ethnocentrism – thus seems, paradoxically, to feel the downward pull of cultural essentialism. Roger Sandall's book *The culture cult* (2002) has denounced a hypertrophy of cultural relativism which makes moral judgements impossible across cultural borders. Sandall denounces, in particular, the underlying assumptions that 'each culture is a semi-sacred creation', that 'all cultures are equally valid and must never be compared', and that 'the assimilation of cultures [...] is supremely wicked'.[14] Our retreat from ethnocentrism has left an essentialist reflex intact: in the reification of 'the culture' as an ultimate, non-negotiable fixity and moral horizon. Culture in such a view is not a praxis, but its underlying, determining condition, much as race used to be. It is still used, in short, to provide motivational explanation for acts, behaviour, choices; like 'character'.

Indeed, the term culture seems to be widely used to both describe patterns of behaviour and to offer a motivational account for them. The title of Geert Hofstede's book *Culture's consequences* indicates as much (Hofstede 1980, Hofstede 1994). 'Culture' here is something which semantically overlaps with notions like national character or identity, as the pre-given ethnic category determining along which lines patterns of behaviour will form. Hofstede outlines a number of attitudinal or behavioural patterns like 'power distance', 'uncertainty avoidance' and 'masculinity vs. femininity' and subsequently correlates these cultural patterns with the ethnicity of his test groups. I have elsewhere pointed out how Hofstede's correlations of ethnicity and cultural behaviour, for all that they claim to be empirically founded, owe more in fact to stereotyped preassumptions than to factual observation.[15] More to the point in the pres-

---

[14] Sandall 1992. See also Raymond Tallis's review in *Times Literary Supplement* (16 August 2002).

[15] Leerssen 1998. I argued there that Hofstede's model provides at best recognizable post-hoc rationalizations of values and behaviour, and does so by falling back on whatever available national stereotypes happen to fit the case. Since national stereotypes usually have it both ways (the Dutch as individualists *and* moralists, the French as gallants *and* cerebral formalists, the Swedes as sexually frank *and* brooding existentialists, the English as phlegmatic gentlemen *and* bullish football hooligans etc.), the availability of a fitting stereotype has no explanatory or analytical value. A proper empirical method should be predictive and falsifiable; e.g. by using national-characterological profiles outlining how a given nationality will *not* behave. So far such a falsifiable approach has not been fielded by Hofstede or his followers.

ent context, Hofstede's distribution of 'culture' is generally arranged by nationality or ethnicity: each nation apparently has its own culture. This perfect, seamless match between the categories of nationality/ethnicity and the distribution of cultural patterns (which, properly considered, should be highly puzzling and call for further clarification) is nowhere problematized.[16] Despite such flaws, Hofstede's model of cross-cultural comparison has made him one of the most widely quoted Dutch social scientists worldwide, and his model has become widely popular among the executive cadre of multinational industries in need of 'cross-cultural management' techniques.

There is, of course, a circular reasoning at work if we invoke 'culture' as an explanation or motivation for something (practices, attitudes, values) which we should properly call... culture. It is like saying that such-and-such a young man is unmarried 'because' he is a bachelor. Gerd Baumann put it aptly in giving us a cogent warning against such circularity in our idea of culture:

> Culture is not a real thing, but an abstract and purely analytical notion. In itself *it* does not *cause* behaviour, but denotes an abstraction from it, and is thus neither normative nor predictive but a heuristic means towards explaining how people understand and act upon the world (Baumann 1997).

Conclusion

The postmodern decades were the period of the 'air-quotes', that little gesture where two hands, gently clawing the air at shoulder level with index and middle finger, formed virtual quotation marks. Such air-quotes signalled a certain ironic distance *vis-à-vis* the words one deployed; indicating that these words were someone else's, not one's own, and that they should be used with reservations. Concepts like culture and identity were, for a while, given a constructivist encapsulation and carried, as it were, their own air-quotes with them. One discussed, not culture but 'culture', not identity but 'identity'. As postmodernism recedes into what has already been called 'post-irony', the habit of air-quotes is becoming corny and old-fashioned. Likewise, concepts of identity and culture are

---

[16] An admirable anthropological study of cultural patterns in Europe, Todd 1990, demonstrates much finer regional differentiations cutting across political, national and even linguistic barriers. Even an old-fashioned work like Van Gennep 1921 is much more reticent than Hofstede with regard to the problematic correlation between cultural variation and nationality.

gravitating slowly back from a constructivist to a neo-essentialist register, from denoting subjective belief systems to denoting objective conditions. After all, postmodernism with its epistemological relativism has itself taught us that, if everyone believes something, you might as well call it real ...[17]

Cultural essentialism (like sexual and racial essentialism) is still with us, and in the socio-political climate of the last ten years or so seems even to be making a comeback; not in the crass form of a century or so ago, but in complex new guises. Concepts like 'identity', 'character' and 'culture' have shifted semantically between themselves and between essentialism and constructivism, have variously denoted social interaction or inner motivating essence, have sometimes referred to an inner, fundamental predisposition, and at other times only to the subjective belief in such a predisposition.

The subdivisions of mankind into familiar ethnic groups, each with their own recognizable, predictable behavioural and moral attributes, seems to be a comforting and popular response to globalization and the increasingly intense proximity and intensity with which cultural traditions interact and intermingle. Eschewed by most cultural historians and cultural anthropologists nowadays, the nostrums of cultural essentialism enjoy either a continuing or a revived popularity in certain other branches of the social and human sciences; and to criticize them will often elicit the reproach of moralistic or scientistic rigidity, or political correctness.

If the purpose of this chapter is to warn against the ongoing, downward pull of cultural essentialism, this is not for moralistic or political reasons, but because, methodologically and logically, cultural essentialism is arguably *wrong*. It is not a different way of approaching things, alongside and amidst other, equally valid approaches; it is a flawed, misguided way of simplifying the complexities of cultural variation into the anecdotal predictability of stereotype. Surely the scholar's task is to understand and explain the complexity of the world, not to simplify it away. It

---

[17] This ontological ambiguity has created some debate in nationalism studies, in particular around the theories of Anthony Smith, who argues for an autonomous role for the factors of ethnicity and culture in nation-formation (against the socio-economic constructivism of scholars like Gellner; cf. Smith 1991). The extent to which those factors, ethnicity and culture, are themselves symbols (modern constructs) or primordial pre-givens has not been clarified and been contradictorily applied or interpreted by various scholars. The special issue of *Nations and Nationalism*, 10/1-2 (2004), on 'History and National Destiny: Ethnosymbolism and its Critics' addresses this issue.

is bad logic and makes for bad scholarship to explain human culture from human nature.

References

Barkow, J., L. Cosmides & J. Tooby. 1992. *The Adapted Mind: Evolutionary Psychology and the Generation of Culture.* New York: Oxford University Press.
Browne, Kingsley R. 2002. *Biology at Work: Rethinking Sexual Equality.* New Brunswick: Rutgers University Press.
Dawkins, Richard. 1976. *The Selfish Gene.* Oxford: Oxford University Press.
Delft, Louis van. 1993. *Littérature et anthropologie. Caractère et nature humaine à l'âge classique.* Paris: Presses Universitaires de France.
Derksen, Maarten. 2004. 'Ras, rede en racisme: de universitaire worsteling met politiek omstreden theorieën' in *Academische Boekengids,* 45 (July 2004): 3-5
Dolezel, Lubomir. 1972. 'From Motifemes to Motifs' in *Poetics* 4: 55-90.
Dyserinck, Hugo. 1982. 'Komparatistische Imagologie jenseits von "Werkimmanenz" und "Werktranszendenz"' in *Synthesis* 9: 27-40
Dyserinck, Hugo. 1988. 'Komparatistische Imagologie. Zur politischen Tragweite einer europäischen Wissenschaft von der Literatur' in Dyserinck, H. & K.U. Syndram (eds) *Europa und das nationale Selbstverständnis. Imagologische probleme in Literatur, Kunst und Kultur des 19. und 20. Jahrhunderts.* Bonn: Bouvier: 13-38.
Gennep, Arnold van. 1921. *Traité comparatif des nationalités.* Paris: Payot.
Hacker, Andrew. 1995. *Two Nations: Black and White, Separate, Hostile, Unequal.* New York: Ballantine.
Herrnstein, Richard J. & Charles A. Murray. 1994. *The Bell Curve: Intelligence and Class Structure in American Life.* New York: Free Press.
Hofstede, Geert. 1980. *Culture's Consequences: International Differences in Work-Related Values.* Beverly Hills: Sage.
Hofstede, Geert. 1994. 'Images of Europe' in *The Netherlands' Journal of Social Sciences* 30/1: 63-82.
Juaristi, Jon. 2000. *El linaje de Aitor.* Madrid: Taurus.
Leerssen, J.T. 1989. 'Over nationale identiteit' in *Theoretische Geschiedenis* 15(1988): 417-30, with postscript in vol. 16(1989): 361-5.
Leerssen, J.T. 1995. 'Een omzwerving rond Monte-Cristo. Mediterrane beeldvorming van Byron tot Bogart en Braudel' in Erp Taalman Kip, A.M. van & I.F. de Jong (eds) *Schurken en schelmen: cultuurhistorische verkenningen rond de Middellandse Zee.* Amsterdam: Amsterdam University Press: 9-24.
Leerssen, J.T. 1999. *Nationaal denken in Europa: een cultuurhistorische schets.* Amsterdam: Amsterdam University Press.
Leerssen, J.T. 2000. 'The Rhetoric of National Character: a Programmatic Survey' in *Poetics Today* 21/2: 267-92.

Leerssen, J.T. 2004. 'Literary Historicism: Romanticism, Philologists, and the Presence of the Past' in *Modern Language Quarterly* 65/2: 221-243.

Liebkind, Carmela. 1999. 'Social Psychology' in Fishman, J.A. (ed.) *Handbook of Language and Ethnic Identity*. New York: Oxford University Press.

Malik, Kenan. 2000. *Man, Beast and Zombie: what Science can and cannot Tell us about Human Nature*. London: Weidenfeld & Nicolson.

Popper, Karl. 1945. *The Open Society and its Enemies*. London: Routledge & Kegan Paul.

Popper, Karl. 1957. *The Poverty of Historicism*. London: Routledge & Kegan Paul.

Popper, Karl. 1979. *Objective knowledge: an Evolutionary Approach*, rev. ed. Oxford: Clarendon Press.

Röder, Brigitte, Juliane Hummel & Brigitta Kunz. 1996. *Göttinnendämmerung. Das Matriarchat aus archäologischer Sicht*. München: Droemer Knaur: 273-98.

Rose, Hilary and Steven Rose (eds). 2000. *Alas, Poor Darwin: Arguments against Evolutionary Psychology*. London: Jonathan Cape.

Rushton, J. Philippe. 1995. *Race, Evolution, and Behavior: a Life History Perspective*. New Brunswick: Transaction.

Sandall, Roger. 1992. *The Culture Cult: Designer Tribalism and Other Essays*. Oxford: Oxford University Press.

Smeed, John W. 1985. *The Theophrastan 'Character': the History of a Literary Genre*. Oxford: Clarendon Press.

Smith, Anthony D. 1991. *National Identity*. Harmondsworth: Penguin.

Sperber, Dan & Deirdre Wilson. 1981. 'Irony and the Use-Mention Distinction' in Cole, P. (ed.) *Radical Pragmatics*. New York: Academic Press: 295-318.

Stepan, Nancy. 1982. *The Idea of Race in Science: Great Britain, 1800-1860*. London: Macmillan.

Stocking, George W. 1987. *Victorian Anthropology*. New York: Free Press.

Todd, Emmanuel. 1990. *L'invention de l'Europe*. Paris: Seuil.

Veyne, Paul. 1978. *Comment on écrit l'histoire, suivi de Foucault révolutionne l'histoire*. Paris: Seuil.

Zacharasiewicz, Waldemar. 1977. *Die Klimatheorie in der englischen Literatur und Literaturkritik von der Mitte des 16. bis zum frühen 18. Jahrhundert*. Vienna: Braumüller.

IMMIGRATION AND RACE

CHAPTER 3

COMING TO TERMS WITH FRANCO'S LEGACY: TRAUMA AND CULTURAL DIFFERENCE IN THE WORK OF JUAN GOYTISOLO[1]

Brigitte Adriaensen

In her paper on 'Spectacle, trauma and violence in contemporary Spain', Cristina Moreiras Menor describes a rather desolate panorama of the Spanish cultural post-franquist scene as 'grounded in affliction' and inscribed in the logics of 'a wounded culture, a culture in shock' (2000: 135). Starting from an initial series of questions concerning the way the memory of the traumatic period of Franco's dictatorship and its abrupt end have been represented in cultural manifestations from the 1980s onwards, the author distinguishes three key concepts which allow her to classify the different ways in which this collective nightmare has been handled: spectacle, trauma and violence. The first concept is linked with the main features of what Guy Debord called the society of the spectacle (1983), namely dehistoricization, the simulacrum and superficiality of appearance. Historically, Moreiras Menor associates this attitude with the 'movida', the urban youth culture movement that arose in the 1980s in Spanish cities like Madrid, Barcelona, Vigo and Bilbao, which she considers 'the epiphany of the new culture of spectacle, opening up new and important spaces for the construction and representation of identities' (136). The second attitude is much more historically determined, and departs from the historical and collective trauma of Franquismo and Civil War in order to offer a broader interpretation of the present. The third attitude, in contrast, is formed by what Moreiras Menor calls a 'horrified gaze', and implies a 'foreignness of historical experience', translated into an extreme fascination with violence and a continuous 'acting-out designed to conceal the absence of meaning and eliminate any possibility of demonstrating affect' (ibid.: 138). These three concepts are linked to different narrative perspectives: in the case of spectacle, as 'distant spec-

---

[1] This article is a revised version of my earlier piece, Adriaensen 2001.

tators from without', in the case of trauma (for which Juan Goytisolo's autobiography *Coto Vedado* (1985) is mentioned as one of the main examples), 'as traumatized witnesses from within', and in the case of violence, 'as abject subjects at the centre of the crudest and most terrifying folds of that violence' (Moreiras Menor 2000: 138). The following analysis will demonstrate first that the narrative perspectives of 'trauma' and 'violence' are not always to be so neatly distinguished from each other, and second that in Goytisolo's case the intention to recover the historical memory concerning the Franquist period implies a more general revision of Spain's history, and especially of its problematic dealing with sexual and cultural otherness.

Before starting the analysis of Goytisolo's literary approach, it is first useful briefly to situate the author. Juan Goytisolo, who was born in Barcelona in 1931, is a rather controversial figure in Spain: his tireless and severe denunciation of the Spanish academic and intellectual environment is one of the main reasons for the rather reduced interest his work has received in Spanish research. The fact that he is not ready to accept stable categories or labels is certainly another factor that does not help to make him very popular: born in Barcelona, he always writes in Spanish and never supported Catalan separatism. A Communist militant for many years, he never actually joined the party as an official member. Married to Monique Lange, he openly acknowledged his bisexuality.

One of his major claims concerns the influence of Arab culture in the formation of Spanish identity. His reassessment of Arab cultural heritage and his condemnation of its continuous negation or obliteration since the sixteenth century (the Reconquista) is in many ways a continuation of the work delivered by Américo Castro in the 1950s. In *España en su historia. Cristianos, moros y judíos* (1948), or for example *La realidad histórica de España* (1954), Américo Castro had already stressed the need to recognize Jewish and Arab influences on Spanish culture, insisting on the fact that

> Our lack of knowledge will not be remedied by sustaining the fallacy that Spain has always been connected to Europe, and has followed in its life a course parallel to that of other Occidental peoples. [...] It is necessary to explain why today we still are a cultural colony of foreign countries; this is not the result of any 'enchanters', nor of some fatal destiny, but rather of the

course of life we have outlined for ourselves, all Spanish and Portuguese-speaking people in the world (Castro 1987: 9).[2]

Goytisolo considers himself a follower of Castro, his 'maestro', and decided to continue his research, mainly because in his opinion Castro's insights had not yet found acceptance. In a recent interview with Alfonso Armada he stated:

[AA:] And Américo Castro is a kind of uncomfortable mirror in which people don't like to recognize themselves because of the image it could project of ourselves?
[JG:] -Yes, it's an uncomfortable image, but we have to live with it. When people say that all this [he is referring to the taboo concerning the influence of Arab culture in Spain, and the persistence of a rigorous norm installed by National-Catholicism] has been overcome, it is evident that this is not the case (Armada 2000: 21).[3]

It is important to stress that Goytisolo succeeded in further developing Castro's theory thanks to his thorough study of Edward Said's theories about Orientalism. In one of his collections of essays, *Crónicas Sarracinas*, Goytisolo offers us a very interesting revision of the Spanish literary canon and historiography from a postcolonial point of view, and in many of his novels, mostly those written between 1970 and 1985, Arab culture is very prominent. Although the representation of the Orient in his work has already been analysed in great detail, there is one important point that seems consistently to have been overlooked: the identification with Arab culture and the foregrounding of homosexuality cannot be seen in isolation from the Franco regime and the immense trauma it entailed for Goytisolo.

In this context it may be useful to remark that Goytisolo's mother was killed in 1937 as a result of a bomb dropped on Barcelona by the

[2] All the translations in this chapter are mine. The original text is: 'Este nuestro no saber no se remedia sosteniendo la falacia que España siempre estuvo enlazada con Europa, y siguió en su vida un curso paralelo al de otros pueblos de Occidente. [...] Hay que sacar a la luz del día por qué todavía hoy seguimos siendo una colonia cultural del extranjero; esto no es obra de los 'encantadores', ni de un fatal destino, sino del curso vital que nos hemos trazado cuantos hoy hablamos español y portugués en el mundo.'
[3] '¿Y Américo Castro es una especie de espejo incómodo en el que no gusta reconocerse por la imagen que pueda proyectar de nosotros mismos? [AA] -Sí, es una imagen incómoda, pero tenemos que convivir con ella. Cuando la gente dice que todo esto está superado es evidente que no. [JG]' Armada, A. 'La mirada del que se sitúa a las afueras es más interesante que la del que está en el centro', entrevista con Juan Goytisolo'.

nationalist army. Goytisolo's resistance to the dictatorial regime and his affinity with Communism, together with other, rather personal reasons, accounted for his decision to go into exile in 1956. From then on, he would spend most of his time in Paris, travelling to Cuba occasionally (in support of the Castro regime). After some time he decided to go and live in Marrakech for almost half the year. Armada's remark that, 'since he left Spain in the middle of the 1950s, Juan Goytisolo has never again spent more than one month in the country where he was born' (2000: 21),[4] makes it clear that Goytisolo did not maintain any particular affective bonds with his native country.

In this chapter I will put forward the hypothesis that the interest in Arab culture in Goytisolo's work is indissolubly linked to the traumatic experience of the Civil War and the oppression by the Falange (the fascist movement founded by Primo de Rivera in 1933) and Franco. Indeed, the two novels which I propose to compare offer ample evidence of the traumatic impact of the dictatorship. So when Goytisolo comments, with regard to Américo Castro, that

> contrary to what this canonical criticism says, namely that he was only interested in reassessing Arab and Jewish elements in the history of Spain, what I think is that Castro's inquiry proceeds from the Spanish Civil War and from the reasons why it came about, and that this is why he found himself forced to reflect on the history of Spain (Armada 2000: 22).[5]

I would suggest that this statement applies equally well to the author himself.

The question which will guide the analysis is how Goytisolo's vision of the Franco regime has changed, how he has dealt with this traumatic experience, and how it has affected his representation of Arab culture in the course of his literary evolution. From *Reivindicación del Conde Don Julián*, his first really personal novel,[6] which was censored by Franco's regime and published in Mexico in 1970, to *Las semanas del jardín*, a sup-

---

[4] 'Desde que a mediados de los cincuenta se fuera de España, Juan Goytisolo no ha pasado nunca más de un mes seguido en la tierra que le vio nacer' (2000: 21).

[5] 'Yo creo que, contrariamente a lo que dice esta crítica canónica de que lo único que le interesaba era rescatar elementos árabes y judíos de la historia de España, lo que creo es que la reflexión de Castro parte de la Guerra Civil española y por qué se produjo, y esto le obligó a reflexionar sobre la historia de España'.

[6] 'Asumo todo lo que he hecho a partir de *Reivindicación del conde don Julián*. Hasta *Señas de identidad* era un miembro más de mi generación' (2000: 22). ('I take responsibility for all I have done since *Count Julian*. Until *Señas de identidad* I was just another member of my generation').

posedly anonymous work by 'A circle of readers' (Un círculo de lectores), published in 1997, how can we describe the transformations which the author underwent? More specifically, how is this personal and literary evolution reflected in two novels dealing with the same theme, the Civil War and the Franco regime, but written twenty-seven years apart?

Count Julian: *a renewed history of revenge*

One usually starts analysing a novel by summarizing the story it tells. In the case of *Count Julian*, however, this procedure proves rather problematic, as the novel presents itself as a radically innovative text which undermines traditional concepts of time, space, character and linear plot development. What we can say, though, is that the protagonist is a Spanish man living in Tangier who imagines that he becomes an Arab, and prepares a new invasion of his Spanish mother country through a rewriting of the legend of Count Julian. The protagonist, who is also the narrator of the novel, sets up a kind of dialogue with the other part of his split identity in the second person singular. At the end of the story the narrator intimates that his name is Alvaro, which is also the name of the protagonist of *Señas de Identidad*, the first novel of the trilogy completed by *Count Julian* and *Juan sin Tierra*. Just as in *Señas de Identidad*, the character of Alvaro seems to be largely autobiographical.

As the title of the novel indicates, the main topic is the claim or the revenge of Count Julian, an unmistakable echo of the legend with the same protagonist dating from the eighth century. According to this legend, Count Julian was outraged because King Rodrigo, the last king of the Visigoths, had raped his daughter Florinda. In revenge for this, he betrayed Rodrigo·by opening the doors of Spain to the Moors and allowing the invasion of the Iberian Peninsula by Tariq and his troops. This legend has a very long history. Before being given a completely new meaning by Goytisolo, it had already been commented on in a long series of romances and by many historians, for example, Menéndez Pidal, Ortega y Gasset and Américo Castro.

What interests Goytisolo about this legend is the link that it suggests between Islamic culture, violence and sexuality. In one of his essays, included in *Crónicas Sarracinas*,[7] Goytisolo points out that this legend is still very much present in the Spanish subconscious: according to his view, in contrast to the French representation of Arab culture, which is

---

[7] Cf. 'De *Don Julián* a *Makbara*: una posible lectura orientalista'.

characterized by exoticism, sexual liberalism and the escape from conservative bourgeois narrow-mindedness, in Spanish culture the Arab is readily associated with violence, rape, danger and (also) sexuality. The novel *Count Julian* sets out precisely to reverse this image: the Moors' invasion and the betrayal of Count Julian are presented as a triumph; the conquest of Spanish territory and the destruction of all its traditional values are portrayed as heroic deeds.

We are justified, therefore, in saying that Goytisolo realises a rewriting of an originally 'Orientalist' legend, and thus offers us a literary version of Américo Castro's historiographical theories. As such, *Count Julian* may be regarded as a severe condemnation of and act of resistance to all exponents of essentialist, traditionalist views of Spanish culture. The sense of anger manifest in the novel would then be directed against, for example, the protagonists of the Reconquista, the Catholic Kings Isabel and Fernando, who started the oppression of the Moors which led to their expulsion in the sixteenth century. However, *Count Julian* is basically a critique of Franco's dictatorial regime, and of the traditional, patriotic, Catholic values it advocated. This critique extends from the thematic level to the whole structure and conception of the novel, as is evidenced by the absence of traditional characters with an elaborated psychology, the ex-temporal situation (the whole story takes place in one day; twenty-four hours), the progressive disappearance of exterior reality in the narration of the story, the 'rape' of basic syntactic rules by the omission or different usage of many punctuation marks (e.g. the use of a colon instead of a full stop to mark the end of a sentence) and the absence of chapters or paragraphs.

But the breakdown of these traditional literary props is not the only reason why this novel is so shocking and so hard to digest: the traumatic disposition of Goytisolo's work is equally responsible for that. Reading his autobiographical books, *Coto Vedado* and *En los reinos de Taifa,* one becomes aware of the fact that the impact of the Civil War on the author can hardly be overestimated. In fact, the general evolution of Goytisolo's literary project may be understood as an illustration of the author's attempt to come to terms with this traumatic experience.

Goytisolo's literary project and the working-through of trauma

In order to develop this hypothesis further, we should first define some typical features of traumatic experience. One of its main characteristics is its belated character: a person who suffers from a trauma, does not actually live the event the moment it occurs, but rather relives it afterwards in a compulsive way. These symptoms, classified in different ways by experts,[8] are generally subsumed under the heading of Post-Traumatic Stress Disorder (PTSD).

According to Dominick LaCapra (1998: 40), the impact of trauma can be confronted in different ways. The 'acting-out' strategy consists in an endless, compulsive repetition of the event through nightmares, hallucinations and suchlike. One keeps going back to the event, finding it impossible to understand or to approach critically. A second characteristic way of coping with traumatic experience is designated as 'denial' or 'repression' by LaCapra. Its symptoms are considered to be complete numbness, or the avoidance of the event by means of silence or taboo. Against both of these responses, LaCapra defends the 'working-through' strategy, that is, a more constructive approach to the past, through a critical revision of it which would make it debatable again. However, in LaCapra's work none of these strategies is defined very clearly.

Reading the work of Shoshana Felman, Dori Laub, and Cathy Caruth, the relevance of all these theories for literary criticism becomes more apparent: in their opinion, narration, through testimony or diaries, and especially in the form of literary fiction, turns out to be a very effective tool in the overcoming of trauma. The advantage of literature over other discourses consists precisely in the different approach it proposes towards referentiality. If a traumatic event cannot be lived in an immediate way – since we do not experience it the moment it occurs but only as a result of our survival – a true and objective version of the facts is impossible to obtain. Literature, however, opens up an alternative way of understanding history because it does not aim at a causal, factual, referential understanding of the event.[9] In her commentary on Camus' novel *The Plague,* Felman asserts,

[8] Critics disagree on the meaning of the term 'trauma': some of them consider trauma as the event itself, and its belated experience as an effect of this trauma, while others define trauma as the symptoms that emerge after the event, as a result of the fact that the event itself was not actually experienced.

[9] Cf. Caruth 1996: 11: 'it is here, in the equally widespread and bewildering encounter with trauma [...] that we can begin to recognize the possibility of a history that is no longer straightforwardly referential [...]. Through the notion of trauma, I will argue, we can understand that a rethinking of reference is aimed not at eliminating history but at resituating it in our understanding, that is, at precisely permitting history to arise where immediate understanding may not' (Caruth 1996: 11).

This is why Camus' own testimony, as opposed to the journalist's, cannot be simply referential but, to be truly historical, must be *literary*. [...] Literature bears testimony not just to duplicate or to record events, but to make history available to the imaginative act whose historical unavailability has prompted, and made possible, a holocaust (Felman 1992: 108).

If we try now to link the theories of LaCapra and Felman to the work of Goytisolo, we can propose two hypotheses. First, if we accept Felman's claims regarding the potential impact of literature on the course of history, Goytisolo can be regarded as an example of a committed writer. He believes very strongly in the duty of the writer/intellectual to denounce and bear witness to abuses both past and present, and refuses to give way to the scepticism we find in many of his colleagues. While it is true that in his earlier work he devoted more attention to Spanish history, and particularly to Franco's dictatorship, his later novels do not avoid this topic but combine it with other, more recent polemics. In this way, Goytisolo both confirms the necessity of remembering the past (cf. *Las semanas del jardín*) and the need to bear witness to recent atrocities in Chechnya (*Guerra con Chechenia al fondo*) and Sarajevo (*Cuaderno de Sarajevo, El sitio de los Sitios*), and to the injustices of Europe's immigration policy (*La saga de los Marx*) or the treatment of homosexuality and transvestism (*Carajicomedia*). In *Coto Vedado* Goytisolo explains the need he feels to write against oblivion and to deal with trauma:

> As the mother, frustrated after an involuntary abortion and in order to overcome the trauma, impatiently searches for the appropriate form and occasion to become pregnant again, you suddenly feel in the dormitory of the place where you recover after an accident the violent pulsation of writing after long months of quiet sterility, the urgency and necessity of writing, to express yourself, not to allow that everything you love, your past, your experience, emotions, that which you are and have been to disappear with you, the resolution to fight with determination against oblivion (Goytisolo 1985: 33-34).[10]

Second, we can find an interesting illustration of the different strategies of the working-through process described by LaCapra in the evolution we observe in Goytisolo's work. Most critics agree that we can distin-

---

[10] 'Como la madre frustrada que después de un aborto involuntario busca con impaciencia, a fin de superar el trauma, la forma y ocasión apropiadas a lograr un nuevo embarazo, sentir aflorar bruscamente, en el dormitorio de la habitación en donde os reponéis del percance, la violenta pulsión de la escritura tras largos meses de esterilidad sosegada, urgencia y necesidad de escribir, expresarte, no permitir que cuanto amas, tu pasado, experiencia, emociones, lo que eres y has sido desparezcan contigo, resolución de luchar con uñas y dientes contra el olvido'.

guish between three periods, even though their limits are not always exactly the same. In the first period, between 1954 and 1970, Goytisolo presents himself as just another member of his generation, writing in accordance with the principles of social realism.[11] The second period stretches from the publication of *Señas de identidad* in 1967 to that of *Makbara* – the last novel dealing mainly with Arab culture and written in this destructive style – in 1980. The third, finally, lasts from *Paisajes después de la batalla* (1982)[12] to the present, and is designated by Randolph Pope as the 'Postmodern Goytisolo' (Pope 1995: 127-164).

Goytisolo's early novels: the period of denial
It is interesting to observe that these novels do not deal with the Civil War or the Franco regime in a very direct way. One obvious reason for this is censorship in Spain, but another reason is Goytisolo's adherence to the aesthetics of social realism. He does not produce a really personal version of recent Spanish history, his homosexuality remains rather implicit as a topic, and Arab or Islamic culture is completely absent. The main purpose of these novels and short stories is rather conventional: a critique of bourgeois society, exaltation of the working class, a cathartic process for the protagonists that results in their recognition of Marxist values, and a traditional scheme of narration and characters. It would appear that at this stage the author was numbed by traumatic experience, and avoided writing about it. This period in Goytisolo's evolution could be compared with the strategy of denial or repression described earlier. In effect, these novels show us that the abjection of Franco goes hand in hand with the identification with Arab culture and homosexuality: since the negative pole is not yet denounced openly (because of censorship and denial, I would venture), the positive pole is repressed, being either absent or, at best, only marginally present.[13]

---

[11] In the interview with Armada, the author says explicitly that these early works do not count for him, that he does not even look upon them as forming part of his oeuvre. Goytisolo himself states in that interview that he dates his work from *Count Julian*, but most critics agree that *Señas de Identidad* should also be considered part of this second period.

[12] According to R. Pope this third period starts with *Makbara*.

[13] Le Vagueresse 2000 analyses some of the implicit references to homosexuality in the earlier novels.

The acting-out experience: from Count Julian *to* Makbara

In *Count Julian*, by contrast, we find for the first time an extremely violent discourse, aiming at the destruction of Catholic and Franquist Spain, linked to values like heterosexuality and patriotism. In addition the literary canon (particularly the work of Lope de Vega, *el drama de honor*, the work of the generation of '98) and the essentialist, nationalist discourse through which it has often been interpreted, are all denounced.[14] Standard language and norms are also ravished: the liberation from oppressive ideology implies the violation of rigorous linguistic rules. Subversion resides in the creative use of language: linguistic innovation allows new thoughts to be expressed, and a new perspective on Spanish culture to be developed. The function of language in *Count Julian* can be formulated using Geoffrey Hartman's words: 'There is a trauma within the trauma and it is associated with language. The wound is also a wordwound, tied to a collective identity or cultural fate' (1996: 163).

The splitting of the protagonist and his destructive tirade seems to be an example of compulsive acting-out. The narrator relives the traumatic event in a dream, an oneiric fantastic discourse in which he tries to take revenge by all means. The last sentences of the novel insist on the repetitive character of the dream: 'the sleepiness disturbs your eyelids and you close your eyes : you know it, you know it: tomorrow will be another day, the invasion will start again' (1985: 304).[15]

The extremely violent act of rape which the protagonist commits at the end of the story, of the small child 'Alvarito', who stands for his own alter ego, and the murder of this symbol of his Catholic youth and education, can be considered as an attempt to silence the traumatic past. The narrator-protagonist sodomizes his own past, trying to forget it through a compulsive murder and a homosexual rape. The fact that Goytisolo qualified this novel on several occasions as a personal and national psychoanalysis, indicates its traumatic background. Geoffrey Hartman's characterization of trauma in literature fits *Count Julian* very well:

> The questioning of reference, or more positively our ability to constitute referentiality of a literary kind (with a symbolic or polysemic dimension),

---

[14] Cf. the famous passage about the '*textocidio*', in which the protagonist goes to the library of Tangier and crushes a handful of juicy insects between the pages of the canonical works praised by National-Catholicism, such as the 'drama de honor' by Lope de Vega, the poems about Castile by the generation of '98.

[15] 'el sueño agobia tus párpados y cierras los ojos : lo sabes, lo sabes : mañana será otro día, la invasión recomenzará'.

indicates the nearness of dream or trauma; negative narratibility *defines a temporal structure that tends to collapse, to implode into a charged traumatic core*, so that the fable is reduced to a repetition-compulsion not authentically 'in time'; *and the subjection of the subject, when it is not given an exclusively political or erotic explanation*, evokes what Lacan defines as *the 'fading' of the I before the Other*. This fading always indicates a disturbance vis-à-vis the symbolic order (Hartman 1995: 547-548; italics added).

Returning to the importance of cultural otherness, it is important to note the role which homosexuality and Arab culture fulfil in this novel: they stand in opposition to the normative Spanish values and operate as the positive pole in the story. We could say that Goytisolo is trying to cut himself off from his tradition, his culture, but in James Young's words, 'inasmuch as language and narrative are essential parts of any tradition [...] this desire to be "cut off" can never actually be enacted in writing' (1988: 97). Consequently, the criticisms that have been made of Goytisolo's way of representing the Orient are very pertinent. To the extent that the novel presents a wholly negative vision of the Occident and idealizes the Orient, Carmen Sotomayor's description of it as 'occidentalist' indicates very well the partiality and blindness of the traumatized narrator. We could perhaps draw a parallel with the first generation of postcolonial critics, like Edward Said in his early works, or Frantz Fanon, whose texts are clearly marked by the trauma of recent decolonization or the persistence of colonization. Like Goytisolo, they proposed an unequivocally anti-colonial perspective, a discourse directed against the metropolitan centre, which did not dream of hybridity or third-space histories: identity should be preserved by resistance, not by overture or syncretism.

Finally there is the apparently ingenuous confidence in the authority of the narrator's voice. *Count Julian* is written mostly in the second person, and the reader feels deeply involved and implicated in the story. However, this kind of personal testimony of a traumatic experience is exactly what will be questioned by his later novels.

Critical distance: 'working-through' strategies in Las semanas del jardín

Indeed, while the monologic voice of the narrator-protagonist of *Count Julian* tries to convince us in every way possible of the absolute evil of traditionalist ideologies, *Las semanas del jardín* employs a completely different strategy to deal with the Civil War trauma. On the cover of the book it is already indicated that a 'circle of readers' is to be considered as the author of this work. In the first chapter, the secretary of the circle informs us about the project: twenty-eight narrators/collectors – twenty-eight because of some calculations made on the basis of the cabbala – will write and read a novel about the life of the poet Eusebio, a victim of Civil War persecution. The only information we possess about the character Eusebio is contained in one particular novel by one particular author, in which this poet is said to have been interned in an army psychiatric hospital in Melilla after the insurrection of 1936, the beginning of the Spanish Civil War. The different narrators are staying in a beautiful garden, qualified as *'cervantino'* and *'borgesiano'* at the same time, and will each elaborate their own version of the further course of the protagonist's life.

The first chapter thus announces that this novel questions the value of the kind of personal testimony exemplified by *Count Julian*, proposing a rather 'postmodern' version of it. The concept of the author is completely undermined, the readers/collectors become the focal point of the story, and each one of them composes his own version of the history. 'The collectors decided to finish with the oppressive and all-embracing concept of the Author',[16] and are free to contribute to the story in any way they like: they can try different genres, different points of view: some respect linear chronology, while others decide to explore aspects which they consider to have been marginalized. It frequently happens that one narrator criticizes another for his supposedly 'apocryphal' version or 'Orientalist' perspective. In the closing chapter the secretary adds that the readers decided to invent an author for the story: after long deliberations they came up with a name, 'Goitisolo, Goitizolo, Goytisolo' (1997: 175), and finally they decide to keep the last one.

Another way in which the text questions the notion of the Author is through its intertextual composition. In the first chapter, the 'work whose Author I can't remember' is both a reference to the first sentence of *El Quijote* and to another novel by Goytisolo himself, *El sitio de los sitios*, in which the character of Eusebio was first introduced. Moreover, on the last page of the book, the secretary writes down the 'works read by the collectors of the Circle' and gives us a whole list of 'intertexts'.[17]

Then there is the relation between fiction and history. Even if the secretary assures us that the narrators' purpose is to write fiction, history

---

[16] 'Los colectores se proponían acabar con la noción opresiva y omnímoda del Autor' (1997: 12).

[17] It is important to note that most of Goytisolo's novels (including those which are not labelled by critics as being 'postmodern', like *Count Julian*) incorporate such a bibliography.

is always very present, not only because of the many literal references to the Civil War, the fascist ideology and discourse reproduced in the text, but also because of the narrators' attempt to write a kind of biography of Eusebio. In addition to this, at the end of the narrative we find a chapter written supposedly by the protagonist, in which he comments on and corrects the interpretations of his life presented earlier. The juxtaposition of all these different versions of Eusebio's life-story invites the reader to reflect on the factuality or referentiality of history; hence the novel has much in common with what has been labelled the 'new historical novel'. The insight it promotes is, in the words of Robert Scholes, that 'It is because reality [itself] cannot be recorded that realism is dead. All writing, all composition, is construction. We do not imitate the world, we construct versions of it. There is no mimesis, only *poesis*. No recording. Only construction' (quoted in Young 1988: 17).

However, *Las semanas del jardín* is more than just another example of postmodern fiction: in fact, the traumatic story of Eusebio's life is not limited to the problematization of historical referentiality. It avoids the scepticism resulting from the inaccessibility of history, and restores the political and ethical dimension of literature. In this novel we can find an example of 'founding trauma': the bond that unifies the 28 narrators consists precisely in their collective commemoration of an oppressive regime and ideology, a 'trauma that paradoxically becomes the basis for collective and/or personal identity' (LaCapra 1999: 724).[18] Or, to quote Kai Erikson, 'traumatic wounds inflicted on individuals can combine to create a mood, an ethos – a group culture, almost – that is different from (and more than) the sum of the private wounds that make it up. Trauma, that is, has a social dimension. [...] trauma can create community' (Erikson 1995: 185).

This means that besides the obviously traumatic experience of the protagonist Eusebio, rendered in different genres by the various narrators (letter written by Eusebio, testimony, parable, fictional story about Eusebio, etc.), and apparent from his PTSD symptoms (nightmares, hallucinations and schizophrenia), the narrators are themselves affected by these traumatic experiences. But unlike *Count Julian*, *Las semanas del jardín* is not so much an illustration of the compulsive repetition or acting-out of trauma in an oneiric and monologic discourse, but rather

---

[18] However, in this novel the 'founding trauma' does not have the mythological dimension attributed to it in LaCapra's definition.

exemplifies the working-through strategy through critical distance. This is why the collectors criticize each other's version of the story, thus dissolving the almost sacred bond between facts and narration maintained by many testimonies. Moreover, the humorous quality of the novel (see Adriaensen 2006) and its digressions on contemporary abuses (relating to immigration policies, xenophobia, etc.) contribute to a more detached view of the past, which, however, does not deny it through either repression (silence, taboo) or scepticism and relativism.

But what can we say about the relation between the Franco regime and cultural otherness in *Las semanas del jardín*? First, we see that the main scheme has not significantly changed: the negative pole is again represented by the ideology of Franco/the Falange, the positive pole by Communism, homosexuality and the Arab world. Even if the specific emphases vary, depending on the narrator, the basic structure is clearly maintained: Eusebio was imprisoned precisely for being 'red' and homosexual, and because of his strong preference for '*mojamíes*' or 'Muslims'.

However, it should be also mentioned that many elements of Arab culture are already intrinsic to the novel's conception. For example, the title of each chapter is a letter of the Arab alphabet, Ibn Arabi's mystical works constitute an important intertext, and the prominence of orality recalls the *halaiquís* (professional story-tellers) of Morocco. Moreover, if Goytisolo recognized that in *Count Julian, Juan the Landless* and *Makbara* he was much more interested in the Spanish reality than in the Moroccan décor and actors (see Goytisolo 1998), in *Las semanas del jardín* Arab culture receives much more attention. Some contemporary problems of Maghreb countries are dealt with, for example in the chapter 'AÍN/The Stork-Men' (which is based on an old Moroccan legend and mounts a vehement attack on immigration policy in Western countries), or in the story about the slave market, 'T'A', where the West's depiction of Morocco as a primitive country is criticized.

In conclusion we can say that *Count Julian* proposes a dualistic vision, in which a compulsive narration acts out a traumatic experience through the identification of the traumatized (Spanish) protagonist with Tariq, the eighth-century Berber invader of Spain. The violence omnipresent in this early novel becomes much more moderate in *Las semanas del jardín*, where the traumatic experience is represented in a very different way: through the polyphony of 28 narrators, history, factuality and the integrity of authorship/witnessing are questioned. Trauma is still linked consistently with violence and aggression, but humour and critical distance offered through the multiplicity of perspectives play an important role in the working-through process.

References

Adriaensen, Brigitte. 2001. 'The Representation of Arab Culture in Post-Franco Spain: Trauma and Cultural Difference in the Work of Juan Goytisolo' in *Entre Líneas* 1 (June 2001): 71-78.

Adriaensen, Brigitte. 2006 (forthcoming). *Arabescos para entendidos. La poética de la ironía en la obra tardía de Juan Goytisolo (1993-2000)*. Madrid: Verbum.

Armada, Alfonso. 2000. 'La mirada del que se sitúa a las afueras es más interesante que la del que está en el centro. Entrevista con Juan Goytisolo' in *ABC Cultural* (21 April 2000).

Caruth, Cathy. 1996. *Unclaimed Experience. Trauma, Narrative, and History*. London/Baltimore: The Johns Hopkins UP.

Castro, Américo. 1987 (1954). *La realidad histórica de España*. México: Editorial Porrúa.

Ericson, Kai. 1995. 'Notes on Trauma and Community' in Caruth, Cathy (ed.) *Trauma. Explorations in Memory*. Baltimore/London: The Johns Hopkins UP.

Felman, Shoshana & Laub, Dori. 1992. *Testimony: Crises of Witnessing in Literature, Psychoanalysis , and History*. London: Routledge.

Goytisolo, Juan. 1985 (1970). *Reivindicación del Conde Don Julián*. Madrid: Cátedra.

Goytisolo, Juan. 1989. *Count Julian*. Transl. Helen R. Lane. London: Serpent's Tail.

Goytisolo, Juan. 1995. *El sitio de los sitios*. Madrid: Santillana S.A.

Goytisolo, Juan. 1997. Un círculo de lectores [alias Juan Goytisolo]. *Las semanas del jardín*. Madrid: Alfaguara.

Goytisolo, Juan. 1998 (1981). 'De *Don Julián* a *Makbara*: una posible lectura orientalista' in *Crónicas Sarracinas*. Madrid: Alfaguara: 31-53.

Goytisolo, Juan. 1999 (1985). *Coto Vedado*. Madrid: Alianza Editorial.

Goytisolo, Juan. 1999a (1986). *En los reinos de Taifa*. Madrid: Alianza Editorial.

Hartman, Geoffrey. 1995. 'On Traumatic Knowledge and Literary Studies' in *New Literary History* 26: 537-563.

Hartman, Geoffrey. 1996. 'Holocaust Testimony, Art and Trauma' in idem, *The Longest Shadow: In the Aftermath of the Holocaust*. Bloomington: Indiana UP: 151-172.

LaCapra, Dominick. 1994. *History and Memory after Auschwitz*. Ithaca/London: Cornell UP.

LaCapra, Dominick. 1999. 'Trauma, Absence, Loss' in *Critical Inquiry* 25 (Summer 1999): 696-727.

Le Vagueresse, Emmanuel. 2000. *Écriture et marginalité*. Paris: L'Harmattan.

Moreiras Menor, Cristina. 2000. 'Spectacle, trauma and violence in contemporary Spain' in Jordan, Barry & Rikki Morgan-Tamosunas (eds) *Contemporary Spanish Cultural Studies*. London: Arnold: 134-142.

Pope, Randolphe. 1995. *Understanding Juan Goytisolo*. Columbia: University of South Carolina Press.

Sotomayor, Carmen. 1990. *Una lectura orientalista de Juan Goytisolo*. Madrid: Fundamentos.

Young, James Edward. 1988. *Writing and Rewriting the Holocaust: Narrative and the Consequences of Interpretation*. Bloomington: Indiana UP.

CHAPTER 4

KILLING AN ARAB?
GHOSTLIER DEMARCATIONS IN HAFID BOUAZZA'S
'SPOOKSTAD' AND 'ABDULLAH'S FEET'

Henriette Louwerse

And of ourselves and of our origins,
In ghostlier demarcations, keener sounds.
Wallace Stevens, 'The Idea of Order at Key West'

The collection of short stories *Abdullah's Feet (De voeten van Abdullah)*, with which the Dutch-Moroccan author Hafid Bouazza signalled his debut in 1996, caused a considerable literary stir in the Dutch-speaking world.[1] Unlike most migrant writers Bouazza was hailed as a serious author: 'one of the most interesting young writers of the moment' (Mulder 1996),[2] and the first migrant writer to produce 'real' literature rather than an amalgam of journalism and therapeutic self-expression. Here is an author who not only takes the phenomenon of literature seriously as an art form, but who also manages with his debut to carve out a special niche for himself as a wordsmith triumphantly working in the wake of authors like Borges and, especially, Nabokov: authors whose influence Bouazza has emphatically recognized on several occasions.[3]

In a review of the collection, Xandra Schutte characterizes the stories as 'malicious fairytales' (Schutte 1996). She believes that Bouazza does not offer the nostalgic side of Morocco that most readers expect to

---

[1] Bouazza 1996. In 2002 a new, revised edition of *De voeten van Abdullah* appeared with Prometheus (Amsterdam). The present discussion is based on the 1996 version, which was translated in 2000 by Ina Rilke (Bouazza 2000).

[2] See also Bakker 1996: 'the stories in *Abdullah's Feet* are so original and full of idiosyncratic and playful use of language, that they bode well for the the coming work of this young Dutch author' ('de verhalen in *De voeten van Abdullah* zijn zo origineel en vol eigenzinnig speels taalgebruik, dat ze verlangend doen uitzien naar het komend oeuvre van deze jonge Nederlandse schrijver').

[3] For appreciations of Bouazza's sophisticated craftsmanship, including his expressions of admiration for Borges and Nabokov, see e.g. Hoogervorst 1996, Bosman 1995 and Bakker 1996.

encounter; the writer does not feel homesick, and shows no melancholy yearning for his motherland: 'first and foremost, Hafid Bouazza plays a game with the autobiographical migrant story.'

Apart from commenting on the 'fairytale' or surrealist atmosphere, almost all critics pursue the line of reading the work as a reflection on the society of the author's childhood in Morocco, a country and a culture that he has left behind but which has greatly influenced his perception of the world.[4] The stories depict a staunchly religious and orthodox society in which people's main preoccupation seems to lie in finding the little space available to exercise their main, or even true, interest, which in the case of *Abdullah's Feet* is the interminable quest for sexual release.

Abdullah's Feet is a collection of eight short stories, seven of which are set (wholly or partly) in the same village somewhere in North Africa, presumably Morocco. The stories do indeed possess a fairytale-like quality: feet can think and talk, and so can trees. Yet the stories are far from idyllic: sexual aberrations rule, the spiritual leaders are as corrupt and degenerate as the rest of the people, stealing and cheating are the order of the day, and there seems precious little space for trust and honesty. Unlike in fairytales, there is no black and white characterization, no good and bad: under the merciless 'Moroccan' sun, everybody has a shady side.

The stories draw on common presumptions that exist in the Western perception of North Africa, ranging from the small currency of cultural cliché to the ruthless typecasting of racism. Playfully exploiting cultural expectations, the stories further appear to echo the one-dimensional views of the Arab world as both exotic and cruel, romantic and perverted, horrifying and fascinating, that are predominant in the West. A first reading might yield the impression of a writer who has freed himself from the restrictions his society of origin imposed on him. However, a closer inspection reveals that Bouazza is acutely aware of the pitfalls any exotic-native opposition harbours and that he uses the potential offered by this binary opposition to the full. He confirms what 'we' expect to read about a little village in Morocco, but inflates and emphasizes ele-

---

[4] For instance, 'Hafid Bouazza shows us the other side of a remote Moroccan village in his book. That world – half idyllic, half perverse and extraordinarily orthodox – does not leave the first-person narrator for one moment. Thought and deed are irretrievably recorded.' ('Hafid Bouazza toont met zijn boek de achterkant van de wereld in een afgelegen dorp in Marokko. Die wereld – halfidyllisch, halfpervers en buitengewoon orthodox – laat de ik-verteller niet los. Geen moment. Denken en doen zijn er voorgoed door getekend' (Meijsing 1996).

ments to upset the safe and recognizable, thus turning the experience of
his fiction into a rather unpleasant confrontation with one's own attitude
as a reader urged on by the ideological desire to make the stories 'fit'. At
first blush, Bouazza seems to side with the dominant; his observations
and descriptions suggest a measure of 'objective', if dismissive, detach-
ment and a more 'Western' viewpoint. Yet this first blush soon turns
into full-blown embarrassment: there is no comforting confirmation
here. Bouazza refuses merely to live up to expectations and instead exag-
gerates these preconceived ideas to the point of paroxysm: sexual perver-
sion, suppression of women, fake religious piety, superstitious silliness
and *Jihad* hysteria – the full arsenal of complacent cultural clichés framed
in a setting supiciously awash with local technicolour.

Thus, what seems to set out as a confident satire of the exotic and the
other quickly – develops into a discomfiting mockery of the native, the
reader, 'us' – a mockery that ultimately targets precisely 'our' ingrained
tendency to think of the relatively homogeneous cultural community of
Western eyes 'we' imagine ourselves to be, as the 'proper' readership of
this work. This cunning double-dealing seems to be one of Bouazza's
distinctive characteristics: he has his cake and eats it, leaving us hungry
for more of what is never quite the same. In what follows I shall illustrate Bouazza's cunning double-dealing by looking at two stories: the
opening story of the collection , 'Ghost Town' and the title story,
'Abdullah's Feet'.

'Ghost Town'

The opening story of *Abdullah's Feet* sets the tone for the entire collection. It consists of an unravelling network of overdetermined compo-
nents of cultural allegory shot through with disturbingly concrete intimacies and indiscretions recollected by the sinister I-narrator. The bare
bones of the story are as follows: an old and decrepit man reflects on his
relationship with his slave Sibawayh. The man bought Sibawayh when he
was still a young boy and he has used him to relieve his sexual desires.
But in the 'now' of his narrative activity, the narrator is blind and suffers
from a mysterious skin disorder, and the contrast between his old and
pustulating appearance and that of his younger servant, who entertains
women in the stable attic, is clearly very painful for the old master. Master and slave set out to visit a doctor whose attempts at curing the skin
disorder are bound to remain unrewarded (there is no cure for old age
and loneliness). On their way, the master is troubled by a beggar who

steals his precious slippers. Both men are now barefoot. In an uncomfortable mix of fatherly feelings and total disrespect for his serf, the old man muses on how he used to visit the local brothel (with Sibawayh) and on other trips the two have made. At the point at which he considers crushing everything, including the boy, he himself is attacked and presumably killed. The identity of the attacker remains unknown, but there is a strong suggestion that it may be Sibawayh exacting revenge.

The story contains one clear reference to Sibawayh's non-native origin. He refuses to wear the pretty slippers offered by his master and the narrator reads his tears whenever he was forced to put them on as symptoms of homesickness: 'No doubt he still felt the stony plains of his fatherland under the soles of his feet.'[5] Here, the text triggers an allegorical interpretation in terms of cultural identity. Sibawayh's status as a 'migrant' alerts the reader both to the numerous markers of cultural diversity in the text and to the equally important absence of any specific cultural identity for the narrator. The town which is the setting of the entire action and narration remains nameless throughout: the reader's initial reading of this setting is likely to be determined by the expectation that it will be Moroccan, but the text does not conclusively confirm this expectation. Instead, it abounds with references to the diverse cultures this 'ghost town' contains: the protagonist has tapestries on the walls of his home depicting scenes derived from Roman mythology (notably hunting scenes and portrayals of Venus), the keeper of the brothel holds a rosary in his fastidious hands (Bouazza 1996: 17), the somewhat suspicious doctor is a Jew, and the mosque, the house of Islam, takes on human dimensions when for unclear reasons, it has turned its back on the slave market (p. 11). The dominant presence of the mosque, together with a reference to the house of a pilgrim identified by its green door (p. 15), suggests that the town is located somewhere in the Arab World, but no further specification seems to be forthcoming: the only proper place name in the text, the mountain Tawbad, is probably imaginary. The composite picture, then, is one of a historically indeterminate place somewhere in the Muslim world inhabited by Christians, Jews, Muslims and slaves (like Sibawayh and the master's black parasol-bearer) of unspecified provenance, a place moreover that bears traces of the civilization of European antiquity.

---

[5] 'Onder zijn blote voeten voelde hij ongetwijfeld nog de stenige vlakten van zijn vaderland.' Bouazza 1996: 12; 2000: 11.

Interestingly, the old man himself is even less classifiable. He does not display any specific cultural or religious affiliation; yet he describes Sibawayh's rejection in terms of religious orthodoxy – Sibawayh is an apostate ('afvallige', Bouazza 1996: 9), who now invites 'infidel wenches' ('ongelovige deernen') into his bed (p. 14) – and displays an acute sensitivity to the blurring of social and cultural boundaries throughout. He is not just any bitter male at death's door who has fallen from wealth and power to become a blind, scabby, cruel old man living in a ghost town in an empty house complete with a 'defunct fountain' ('gestorven fontein'), crying out to be read as a fatally deflated phallus (p. 13). He is referred to as 'a blind elder, a couple of centuries old' ('een blinde ouderling, enkele eeuwen oud', Bouazza 2000: 9; 1996: 10), and the qualification 'a couple of centuries old' adds to the sense that we are dealing with a depersonified character implicated in a complicated allegorical set-up. The man is blind, yet he sees things he literally cannot see: he 'sees' future events, and he predicts that a mother will outlive both her sons (Bouazza 1996: 15). He laments,

> My days of noble pursuits are over, my pride is awash in threadbare purple, the fool has vanquished the king, my writing quivers, I live in a portable darkness, my bowel movements give cause for concern. My prose resembles the spectres of my memory: empty vessels, truncated epithets drifting soulless in a ghost town where even my language is dead (Bouazza 2000: 12).[6]

In his ghost town, language has deteriorated into 'truncated epithets', 'soulless' due to the rift between epithet and subject, like memories that have turned into one-dimensional renditions of past events. The words, like his memories, have become empty shells, meaningless, truth gone astray.

Here we touch upon one of the central paradoxes of the story: the 'Ghost Town' is not a deserted town – on the contrary, it is a place bustling with activity and thick with language, but to the old man's ears all is dead, offensive, ghostly. The old man, as the representative of a dead higher culture, is little short of a ghost himself. The symbols and rituals he employed to create an identity have crumbled or become meaningless, because they are no longer recognized and respected. His record of the

---

[6] 'Mijn dagen van adeldom zijn voorbij, mijn weelde doolt in versleten purper, de nar heeft de vorst verstoten, ik schrijf met beverige hand, ik leef in een draagbare duisternis, mijn stoelgang laat te wensen over. Mijn proza lijkt op de spoken van mijn geheugen: lege omhulsels, losgeslagen epitheta die zielloos dwalen in een spookstad waar mijn taal gestorven is' (Bouazza 1996: 16).

meeting with the beggar who eventually steals his slippers is significant in
this respect:

> I am repelled by beggars, particularly beggars whose rags belie their rhetorical
> skills. Here was a true poet of the wayside, a master if you will of mendicant
> eloquence who, glutted with inspiration, awaited with hungrily bated breath
> the passing of audible riches (Bouazza 2000: 13-14).[7]

Significantly, this beggar is explicitly characterized as a ghost:[8] an entity
that does not know its place, whose appearance does not correspond to
its behaviour, and that somehow crosses the boundaries the narrator
wishes to see intact. On closer inspection that is precisely the condition
of the town he now identifies as a 'ghost town': it is a markedly multicul-
tural place, where people, to the protagonist's chagrin, just do not know
their place.

It is not just the inhabitants who turn the town into a ghost town.
The setting, the town and its surroundings, the old man's house, all
congeal into a surreal geographical and cultural mix covered under a thin
layer of desert sand. On their way to the doctor, the master and slave's
first journey leads through the maze of the old man's house with its
elaborate corridors, staircases, empty rooms, a courtyard, a dysfunctional
fountain, yet more rooms and stairs. This is 'a cautious progress through
a languishing house, as smooth and perfect as a womb' (Bouazza 2000:
11).[9] The image of the womb does not represent the place of fertility, the
source of life but the very opposite, the womb as a locus of death, the
womb as tomb. Their second journey is through the town and the parallel is striking: oppressive alleys, steep roads, a square, yet more narrow
roads. It is a town with beggars and pilgrims whose religious efforts are
rewarded with 'a dishonourable death' (Bouazza 2000: 13) ('een onwaar-
dige dood', Bouazza 1996: 15).

And then there is the mountain Tawbad, an inescapable watchman,
whose presence looms over the town and is literally breathtaking

---

[7] 'Ik heb een afkeer van bedelaars, zeker bedelaars wier uiterlijke schamelheid in
het geheel niet strookt met hun verbale rijkdom. Hier was een ware dichter van de
weg, een meester zo u wilt van bedelaarswelbespraaktheid, die, verzadigd van inspira-
tie, hongerig op het voorbijgaan wachtte van hoorbare rijkdom' (Bouazza 1996: 15).
[8] 'Sibawayah verjoeg het spook' (Bouazza 1996: 15). Ina Rilke chooses to translate
the Dutch 'spook' as 'miscreant'.
[9] 'een omzichtige tocht door een zieltogend huis, glad en volkomen als een baar-
moeder' (Bouazza 1996: 13).

(Bouazza 1996: 18),[10] a stifling force set to inhibit the essential ingredient for life. At night demons raise their voices on its hillsides and in the cave of the Tawbad lurks a source which brings forth both monsters and prophets:

> There was a cave on the mountain of Tawbad, which backed the town, where a spring slumbered and monsters and prophets were born (Bouazza 2000: 13).[11]

These prophets (of indiscriminate religious affiliation) are not the familiar symbols of the messenger of the true faith. On the contrary, they are rather pathetic fools, ineffective and the butt of mockery:

> It was on that mountain that a leprous fool, a self-professed prophet, had sought refuge from the world – no prophet without a mountain. The hostile populace had pelted him with stones, which had moved him to put a curse on the town before he fled, broken and bleeding profusely. His sole companion was a donkey. He had not returned since – a farcical ascension to heaven (Bouazza 2000: 16).[12]

The description of this hapless prophet is clearly provocative. It contains references to Christianity (donkey, ascension), but the very act of ridiculing a *prophet* also links this passage with *the* prophet and thus with the Muslim faith. The house, the town and the mountain Tawbad figure as the ruins of oppressive cultural orthodoxy in general, showing up religion as a restrictive, suffocating institution which turns people into demons and human settlements into ghost towns.

At the close of the story, the narrator seems ready to echo the self-professed prophet's curse: 'What was there to stop me from grinding everything underfoot and having done with it?' (Bouazza 2000: 16).[13] Yet before he can act on his rhetorical question, he is quite literally stopped by his phantom attacker and felled to the ground where, 'instead of

---

[10] Ina Rilke opts for 'awesome' as a translation of 'adembenemend'.

[11] 'In de grot van de berg Tawbad, die achter de stad met ons mee liep, sluimerde een bron en werden monsters en profeten geboren' (Bouazza 1996: 15).

[12] 'Het was de berg waar een melaatse dwaas, een vermeende profeet, zich gebroken had teruggetrokken – geen profeet zonder berg. Het vijandige volk had hem gestenigd en hij, erbarmelijk bloemend, had zich nog verwaardigd een vloek over de stad uit te spreken. Zijn enige gezelschap was een ezel geweest en sindsdien was hij niet teruggekeerd – een klucht van een hemelvaart' (Bouazza 1996: 18).

[13] 'Wat weerhield mij ervan nu alles met een enkele beweging onder mijn hiel te vertrappen?' (Bouazza 1996: 18).

calling Sibawayh', he begins to vomit with petrified tongue. The curse on a composite culture is ultimately performed as inarticulate vomit.

'Ghost Town' can be read as an allegory of culture. Bouazza clearly tickles the reader into formulating a number of hypotheses, yet they fail to fall into place. This indeterminacy adds to the unsettling impact of the allegory: the story is haunted by the ghost of the clinching interpretation most readers aspire to. For what on earth is this tale about?

The two most obvious readings are as follows. First, the narrator can be seen as the oppressive guardian of a dying host culture, as a disciplinarian of dominant (though dead) language. In this set-up, the slave Sibawayh is the exploited migrant wreaking blind and speechless revenge. Yet this is precisely the xenophobic phantasm at the heart of all cultures identifying themselves as threatened by the migrants they have exploited and often continue to exploit, and it is hard to square this reading with the fact that the allegory is written by, precisely, a migrant.

The second option reads the sense of alienation and displacement suffered by the narrator as an indication that he, rather than Sibawayh, is the 'real' migrant. He lives the migration constitutive of culture as such, transposed into a culture transformed beyond recognition and robbed of the always imaginary cultural self-identity whose spectres now haunt him.

By refusing to cut the knot in which these two incompatible readings are entangled, Bouazza raises more ghosts than we may care to imagine. Neither of the two interpretations fully falls into place, and that is perhaps precisely what 'Ghost Town' is about. By confronting his reader with common clichés about the Arab world (and by pushing it just that much further by breaking into taboo grounds such as child abuse and bestiality), Bouazza arouses the reader's desire to make things fit. Yet the fulfilment of this desire is thwarted by a welter of unsettling elements that disturb the comfortable 'us-them' constellation. Bouazza plays with fixed conceptions by confirming, exaggerating and undermining them at the same time. The killing of the Arab thus turns out to involve the killing of the image, the myth of the Arab, as well as of the phantasmal homogeneous reading public.

'Abdullah's Feet'

'De voeten van Abdullah' introduces an unnamed teenage protagonist, presumably a younger version of the narrator. It tells the tale of the homecoming of a war hero, Abdullah, older brother of the narrator. However, only his feet have managed to return from the 'Holy War', yet the entire village is deliriously happy: the feet are worshipped by the imam and the older villagers, they are offered the best seat in the house, the best food money can buy and they attract all the parental attention. Then, one day, the feet simply disappear. The narrator and the other children are the implied culprits: 'Jealousy struck eventually' (Bouazza 2000: 30) ('jaloezie sloeg uiteindelijk toe' (1996: 34)). The parents are deeply upset at the loss of the remnants of their son: the father returns to his study of the Qur'an (notably the surah on Joseph, the favourite son) and the mother resumes her silence and castigation. This plot, which gives the story and the collection its title, is intertwined with anecdotes documenting the narrator's teenage obsession with sex, either as a solo performance inspired by the curves of his sisters' stooping bodies or in conjunction with his younger, innocent sisters in the privy.[14]

This arresting combination of private teenage sexuality and unleashed collective foot-fetishism is complicated even further by the emphatic textual presence of the older narrator looking back and commenting on his youth in a series of curious parabases which effectively amount to an oblique meta-textual commentary on the story's central events. The first of these parabases concerns the narrator's father: 'There sits my father [...] a Pinocchio in the dusty workshop of my memory' (Bouazza 2000: 19).[15] Not only does the narrator claim that his memory does not serve him well, he also reverses the generations when he as a Guepetto observes his handiwork, Pinocchio. The son has become the father of the puppet he creates and refers to as father, put together from fragments of a distant past in a dusty workshop. The principle of this reconstructive operation is of primary importance for an appreciation of what may be at stake in this uncanny tale of feet and fragments.

It is not just the 'dusty workshop of his memory' that prevents the narrator from writing an autobiographical, or factually correct, story. He freely admits that 'remembrance is biased, my own memory prudish, my rear–view mirror clouded' (Bouazza 2000: 21).[16] The subject matter is too close to his heart ('te hecht verbonden met mijn hart') for him to express himself without reservations: 'Shades of traditional shame haunt

---

[14] In good male tradition, the narrator suggests that the girls are not 'entirely unwilling' (Bouazza 2000: 30).

[15] 'Daar zit mijn vader [...] een Pinocchio in de stoffige werkplaats van mijn geheugen' (Bouazza 1996: 23).

[16] 'het geheugen is partijdig, mijn geheugen is preuts, zijn achteruitkijkspiegel besmeurd' (Bouzza 1996: 25).

me, intent on preventing me from writing an autobiographical story'
(Bouazza 2000: 19).[17] The events in question took place in the past, and
clearly under very different circumstances from the present: the narrator
claims to be separated from the landscape of his youth by 'a dark chasm'
('donkere afgrond'). He is almost as removed from his own youthful
experiences as his anonymous readers are and when he juxtaposes the
world of his youth with that of his audience, he clearly identifies with his
readers when he claims,

> It is not merely for the sake of literary convention that I would like to de-
> scribe my mother at this point, but also to satisfy my own curiosity and no
> doubt that of my readers too. [...] Here stands Fatima, my mother, face to
> face with me and the reader (Bouazza 2000: 21).[18]

The identification with the reader creating a clear distance between the
narrator and the circumstances of his youth has repercussions for the
text's uneasy operations in the multi-cultural context it cannot escape.
This becomes particularly apparent when the narrator goes on to high-
light the cultural category of 'the Arab' with all his enigmatic likes and
habits. The description of the mother is significant here:

> To be honest, not an exceptional woman: stout shaped by the exigencies of
> Arab Maternity. The wealth of her bosom and loins suggest a diva: the prodi-
> gious posterior harks back – rather literally – to black Africa. These distinc-
> tive charms are traditionally loved by Arabs: ostrich-down cushions for the
> spasmodic euphoria of manly release (forgive me Father) (Bouazza 2000:
> 21).[19]

So here we are confronted with a narrator at death's door ('aan dit uit-
einde van mijn leven', Bouazza 1996: 32) whose clouded memory is
busily but uneasily engaged in dishing out exotic truths about the country
and people of his youth. As he has already admitted to being a Guepetto,

---

[17] 'Schimmen van traditionele schaamte plagen mij, willen mij verhinderen een
autobiografisch verhaal te schrijven' (Bouazza 1996: 23).
[18] 'Niet alleen ter wille van literaire conventies zou ik op dit punt mijn moeder
willen beschrijven, maar ook ter bevrediging van mijn en ongetwijfeld van mijn lezers'
nieuwsgierigheid. [...] Hier staat Fatima, mijn moeder, en face met mij en de lezer'
(Bouazza 1996: 25).
[19] 'Om de waarheid te zeggen, een niet zeer bijzondere vrouw: lijvig, gevormd
volgens de antropometrische eisen van Arabisch moederschap. De weelde van boe-
zem en lendenen suggereert een diva; de omvangrijke billen wijzen – nogal letterlijk-
naar zwart Afrika. Deze geprononceerde charmes zijn van oudsher geliefd bij Arabie-
ren: struisvogeldonskussens voor de krampachtige euforie van mannelijke ontspan-
ning (vergeef mij, vader)' (Bouazza 1996: 25-6).

a creator of puppets that merely resemble the real thing, the reader had better be warned: the mummy-doll is no less a problematic construct than is papa Pinocchio.

There are a number of additional puzzling and contradictory elements in 'De voeten van Abdullah'. For instance, although the narrator claims to have a prudish memory and to be troubled by shame, he enthusiastically admits to using the privy as a private 'donor-bank', to groping his older sister(s), to having a sexual obsession with women 'performing certain sanitary acts' and 'to have free play' with his 'vulnerable and budding sisters'. Similarly, his very detailed descriptions of the events do not give the impression of springing from a particularly clouded mind. He remembers the exact date, 22 October 1977,[20] and his descriptions are confidently detailed. The narrator may well complain that he would like to write an autobiographical story but is prevented from doing so by the 'shades of traditional shame' – his actual textual performance, however, suggests that the straightforward narration of his life's story is not so much hindered by traditional reticence as by his uneasy awareness of the power of the imagination, which seems all too capable of summoning up the past at will. Like Guepetto who manages to create a being convincingly impersonating a living human son out of pieces of wood, the narrator conjures up a world of mystique out of snippets from a 'clouded' memory.

When the story thus far revolves around the somewhat suspicious transformation of fragments into a symbolic whole, it does not come as a surprise that the parents and villagers alike respond with great enthusiasm and gratitude when Abdullah returns. The fact that it is just his feet that have returned does not remotely spoil the party, the feet naturally and smoothly progress into the fully blown picture of the war hero, the symbol that appeals to the collective imagination as a living incarnation of their culture's truth: Pinocchio-power. The mother consistently refers to the feet as 'my son', the imam and the father call them 'Abdullah'. Only the children seem to be the exception here; they see two feet rather than a whole person and seem to have no qualms about making them disappear. The text suggests sibling jealousy may be to blame here (and the story of Joseph and his brothers clearly strengthens this suggestion), but that jealousy may perhaps also be read as a resistance to the danger-

---

[20] Notably the date at which Bouazza and his family arrived in the Netherlands.

ous facility with which a culture can wrest Holy Victory from the maimed bodies of its representatives.

In this sense, the return of the feet, and the great happiness it evokes, contains clear ridicule of religious fanaticism and hysteria, but Bouazza does not rest satisfied with this fairly complacent judgement from a comfortable critical distance. Indeed, the similarity between the villagers' reconstruction of the living reality of their culture from the ruined bodies of those sent out to defend it, and the narrator's reconstruction of the Moroccan village of his youth on the strength of a few clouded memories and a guilt complex, indicates a critical awareness on the part of the text of the workings of the imagination as a far from innocent ideological force.

Conclusion

Both 'Spookstad' and 'De voeten van Abdullah' can be said to exhaust the sinister potential of cultural stereotypes. They both blatantly recycle the received image of the Arab, kill it, and continue to flog it. The ghosts conjured up in this exercise, which derives its avowedly problematic authority from its author's ethnic origin, appear to lift the spell of demarcation between host and guest with which cultures accord themselves an image of self-identity. But lest we rejoice prematurely in the spectral company of post-self-identical culture, the violent vomiting on which 'Ghost Town' closes reminds us that the loss of this image may be harder to stomach than is realized in the wishful multi-cultural fantasies we nonetheless must entertain.

References

(14 July 1996).
Meijsing, Doeschka. 1996. 'Het ledigen der lendenen. Vreemde verhalen van Hafid Bouazza' in *Elsevier* (22 June 1996).

Mulder, Reinjan. 1996. 'Mijn geheugen is preuts. Weelderig debut van Hafid Bouazza' in *NRC Handelsblad*, (7 July 1996).

Schutte, Xandra. 1996. 'Witgetulband en wildgewingerd' in *De Groene Amsterdammer* (5 June 1996).

CHAPTER 5

CAST IN CELLULOID:
IMAG(IN)ING IDENTITIES IN SOUTH AFRICAN CINEMA

Jacqueline Maingard

This chapter focuses on how South African identities are constructed in the cinema based on images selected from three key 'moments' in South Africa's cinema history. These images are used to illustrate and discuss how (national) identity is variously framed in different films, against the backdrop of colonialism and apartheid. The first set of images is drawn from the film *De Voortrekkers* (1916) that reflects a desire for Afrikaner identity to be paraded as *the* national identity. Branded on its release as 'South Africa's National Film', it presents an alliance between British and Afrikaners while constructing black people as either barbarous or servile. A second set of images is drawn from films made by white entrepreneurs about black identities after the National Party took power in 1948. In *Jim Comes to Joburg* (a.k.a. *African Jim*) (1949), the city plays a central role in the representation of black and white identities: it is both a place where black servant is pitted against white 'boss', and where a new black identity is possible, primarily through the black jazz of the period. In *The Magic Garden* (a.k.a. *Pennywhistle Blues*) (1951) images of poverty and deprivation alongside the feisty community spirit of the inhabitants, represented through the music of the time, is the milieu within which characters and their identities are positioned, framed by an observational, satirical docu-drama. A third set of images is from recent films made by both black and white anti-apartheid filmmakers. They extend and politically re-align elements of images seen in earlier films. *Mapantsula* (1988) is set in the urban spaces of Johannesburg and Soweto. The images toy with individual stereotypes in the divided urban milieu of apartheid South Africa, where the stakes are high for shifting identities. In *Fools* (1998), primarily located in a Soweto neighbourhood, a plurality of identities is represented. Each set of images, located within a specifically key 'moment', constructs, positions, imagines and images identity in complex and sometimes problematic ways. The interrelationship of these constructions of identity with questions of national identity (and national cinema) is broadly the subject here.

South Africa may be seen as a laboratory for the study of identity fraught as it has been (and is) by constructions of identities wrought in its colonial and apartheid histories. It follows then that South African cinema is a fertile space for investigations of representations of identity, for exploring how these might be bound into the histories of the country's development, for understanding how these histories determine cinematic representations and how cinematic representations interpret history. In this chapter I am concerned with how images in South African cinema history have fixed identities. Specifically I examine how black identities have been represented in cinematic images from early cinema through to contemporary cinema. I do this by selectively examining three key 'moments' each located in a different period in South Africa's history and in the history of the cinema in that country. The first is 1916 where the exemplar is De Voortrekkers; the second is the late 1940s and 1950s with Jim Comes to Joburg (1949) and The Magic Garden (1951); and the third is the late 1980s into the 1990s with Mapantsula (1988) and Fools (1998).

My concern with the relationship between image and identity is framed by a broader project on South African National Cinema (see Maingard 2006). Thus the inflection of the national in the films I select is significant and following that, questions of national identity. Definitions of identity and especially of national identity are significantly determined by official or hegemonic positionings of those identities. In the South African apartheid context, race is primarily significant and it is conceptualizations of race and their concomitant representation in the cinema that I focus on here. Having said that, it is also impossible to ignore strands of other identity positions: class, gender, and so on. And often these are not so much positions with the connotations of fixity that are attached, but rather a more loose, unstable, open kind of positioning. Something like Stuart Hall's proposal that 'we should think ... of identity as a 'production', which is never complete, always in process, and always constituted within, not outside, representation' (1989: 68). My interest in identity, while rooted in South African experience with all its discrete definitions of identity in officialdom at least and beyond, centres around questions of plurality. It is from within this framework that I seek 'moments' in South African cinema, where the extent to which identities are represented as fixed, may be explored.

Identity in South Africa is *both* unproblematic (since so much of its formation can be easily traced within apartheid ideology) *and* complex, that is extremely problematic. The notion of the 'in-between', through Homi Bhabha's delivery of the Third Space and Trinh's concern with in-betweenness (Bhabha 1989; Trinh 1996), has been formative in my deliberations over identity and its definition. South African experience is arguably a constant movement within the 'in-between', and taking this notion further, within multiple layerings of in-betweennesses, which is a multi-plurality of identity (Maingard 1997). Thus while this paper seems to propose some interconnections between image and identity in apparently simple ways, in effect this is deeply complex terrain. I have purposely selected three key 'moments' that differ very strongly from each other so that some of these complexities or problematics can be opened out.

White supremacy and De Voortrekkers *(1916)*

The first key 'moment' in the trajectory of black identities in the cinema that I am creating is 1916 and *De Voortrekkers*, released under the English title of *Winning a Continent*, reflecting the sweeping colonial aspirations of its makers.[1] The focus of this specific 'moment' is the particular view that was developed to inscribe national borderlines and boundaries and to construct a certain history and national identity, predicated on erasing other histories and identities. Crucially one of the most important reasons for considering it exemplary in writing about identity in cinema is that the film's producers marketed it as 'South Africa's National Film'. Contrary to the inclusivity of identities that such a strategy connotes, it is a story of colonial conquest set in 1838 representing the migration of Boers (literally farmers) northwards into Zulu territory and the subsequent encounter with Dingane,[2] the Zulu chief. The ideological perspective is that of the Boers, an epic cinematic tale from the colonizer's point of view. Thus Dingane is represented as a barbarous, murderous villain who engages in infanticide, indeed commands the murder of his own son on a whim, while the Boers are endowed with righteousness. The core of

---

[1] The film has been compared with D.W. Griffith's (in)famous and epic film *The Birth of a Nation* (1915). For example, Gaines calls *De Voortrekkers* its 'South African equivalent' (2000: 298). The links go further than this since the film's director, Harold Shaw, was himself from 'an old Kentucky family' (*Edison Kinetogram* (15 May 1912): 16). He also reported that 'the colonial always appeals to me' (Shaw 1916: 2).

[2] This is the correct spelling, whereas the film uses the incorrect 'Dingaan'.

the conflict is deflected away however from this most obvious opposition (Boers vs. Zulus) to the influence of the Portuguese traders
stereotypically named Diaz and Pereira and slyly whispering into
Dingane's ear that the white man (sic) will come and take his land. They
play on Dingane's supposed tribal supremacist perspective: 'we come to
ask what laws you have for men who desert their tribe?' They pursue the
point: 'hundreds ... are at this moment trekking towards Zululand ... we
warn you that ... they will take your country, rob your cattle and despise
your people'. The 'blame' for the ensuing bloodshed is therefore very
neatly placed outside the conflict between the Boers and the British.
Indeed, they are seen to be working hand in hand in negotiating with
Dingane: a hand-clasping that suitably expresses the conjoining of Afrikaner and British interests in 1916 when the film was made, as one critic
has asserted (Tomaselli 1986). Diaz and Pereira's whisperings act as a
complex and ironic parallel to the position occupied by the character of
Sobuza.[3] One of Dingane's soldiers, he falls under the influence of the
English missionary, who persuades him to renounce violence as embodied by Dingane. Images that caricature Sobuza as idiotic represent his
musings over the words of the missionary. In 'tribal' dress he points to
the spear he carries apparently repeating the missionary's words. Shortly
after this he deserts Dingane and swears allegiance to the head of the
Boers, Piet Retief, assuming the position of servant in a verbal outpour-
ing of commitment that excessively crosses the boundaries of his former
identity:

> Henceforth thou art my Father and my Chief
> And Thy people shall be my people.

Yet ultimately it is he who kills Dingane. Thus the film reiterates the
notion that violence in the name of colonial conquest is not violence.

In the final frames of the film we see the church that has been built
to fulfil the promise made by the Boers in their prayers to win the battle
over Dingane's army. Sobuza is seated outside the church door, now
dressed in plain westernized trousers and shirt, excluded from the pro-

---

[3] The name 'Sobuza' has some interesting historical connotations, and I am grateful to Carolyn Hamilton for pointing these out. The choice of this name has historical
weight following the view that it was in fact a Swazi group that killed Dingane and
that it was Sobuzha I who established what became Swaziland. Gaines notes more
specifically that Preller's (the film's writer) 'own history spells the name 'Sopuza' and
identifies the figure as a Swazi chief who was ... said to have killed Dingaan around
1840' (2000: 314 n.2).

ceedings on the interior, yet apparently happy in his subservient role. Indeed, in the frame of the film's ideological positioning he could not be included for this would be tantamount to proposing, against the film's ideological stance, an integration of black and white people. Thus the film makes clear its position on national identity in this emblematic image that represents what was to be played out through most of the century as the exploitative expediency of white Afrikaner nationalist identity. This subservient positioning then, with Sobuza colluding and complying with his given identity, is represented as the rightful one within the film's ideological statement. Sobuza occupies the proper place for black identity whereas Dingane as murderous villain does not. Meanwhile inside the church the nuclear family is given central status. The penultimate image of the film is a full-frame shot of a man and woman with a small child on her lap, while the inter-title reads:

> ... and in keeping our covenant we shall, on every Sixteenth Day of December, render thanks to Thee, Almighty God, for our safe return and *the preservation of our Race and Country* [emphasis added].[4]

This focus on family, as key to the future of the white identity proposed in the film, is hinted at through the film itself by presenting a love story sub-theme between the daughter and son of two Voortrekker families, Johanna Landman and Willem Faber (who appear as the couple with a child in the church at the end). On the other hand, no such intimacies are revealed in relation to the Zulus. In an uncharacteristic moment though, that takes the camera into the interior of one of the Zulu dwellings, we see a number of Zulu women making their way out, with the camera positioned behind them. On first view it seems as if the camera/film is contradicting its ideological frame: a point-of-view interior shot from within the enemy's camp? But within the film's spectrum of identities and their positionings, it becomes clear that this shot is a(nother) comment on Dingane's construction as barbaric and 'savage',

---

[4] It is tempting to read these words as a conscious claim to the nation on racial grounds, but as Hees advises the use of 'race' in the English translation of 'volk' (literally 'people'), which is how it appears in the equivalent Afrikaans inter-title, is a reflection of the use of language at the time (2003: 58). Backed up by reference to Dubow (1995) this use of 'race', while apparently totalizing, is not necessarily what it may seem, and rather refers to the more limited boundary of the Afrikaner people (or race) as against the British (race). Nevertheless, the broader sense of the term, given the interrelations between Boer and British that the film supports, is still invoked to some measure.

for these women represent his wives, and therefore his polygamous nature. And in relation to the focus on romance and family in the Boer camp, where the monogamous nuclear family is revered, it becomes clear that there is no contradiction in the shot of Dingane's wives. Thus the thematics around family make it possible for the film to remind audiences, in the interior shots of the church, of the nuclear family as the backbone of white Afrikaner identity. Indeed, the focus on family and white procreation was to become a major ploy of the Nationalist government after it came into power in 1948, with laws protecting white identity. Thus in the final frames of the film the relationship of Boer to Zulu, white colonizer/settler to black colonized, is cast in celluloid - a relationship that is reiterated in precisely this form in history, as we now know.

There are two further ways that the film fulfils its white supremacist ideological approach: the use of a biblical-style linguistic register in ascribing words to various characters in the inter-titles and, linked to this, representations of gender, especially masculinities. On the linguistic register, a complex set of signifiers is at play here. Being 1916 and therefore pre-sound in the cinema, the film is silent. But in line with the conventions of its cinematic counterparts in other parts of the world and also its epic scale, it uses and indeed relies on inter-titles – so critical to the film's meanings that they might be seen as inter-images in the form of words. Similar to the linguistic register of the words ascribed to Sobuza, the 'faithful servant', when he 'defects' to Piet Retief, note the peculiar biblical ascription to the following words after two unsuccessful Zulu attacks on the Boer camp, as one of the Zulus comments to his fellow soldiers,

> Would ye return to your King defeated by a mere handful of white men? I call ye cowards, cowards all!

These kinds of biblical appropriations that sit uncomfortably both with the subjects to whom they are ascribed and the period depicted, suggest an engagement with the notion of Afrikaners as a 'chosen people'. While Giliomee asserts that this was 'by no means a mainstream doctrine or a source of common inspiration' (2003: 178) it may well have suited Gustav Preller's ideological projections in De Voortrekkers, for which he wrote the screenplay. It is significant here that he was a key figure in promoting Afrikaner identity and Afrikaans as an official language. I.W. Schlesinger, owner of African Film Productions that produced De Voortrekkers, probably had sympathy with this kind of sensibility in his own right. He grew up in a Jewish-Hungarian immigrant family in the United States, where (amongst other things) his father established a bank for fellow Jewish immigrants. Schlesinger relocated to South Africa in the early 1900s, eventually establishing himself as 'one of the greatest entrepreneurs in the country's history' (Kaplan 1986: 149) primarily through insurance and property business interests but also through the entertainment industry.[5] The use then of 'ye', 'thou' and 'thy' in biblical style in *De Voortrekkers*, especially in Sobuza's comments to Piet Retief that incorporate the phraseology 'thy people shall be my people', neatly matching the film's epic narrative, elevates its historical significance far beyond the ordinary. This is pertinent too for how the battle between Boers and Zulus is perceived. For this is no local battle (remembering the English version title of the film: *Winning a Continent*), rather it is a battle of not only national but continental proportions, on which rests a war of larger universal significance, the colonial domination of Africa. Incorporating and ascribing this linguistic mode entirely inappropriately in relation to the Zulu characters effectively erases the existence of any other languages or styles of language in indigenous culture. In relation to the film's ideological project, however, this epic universalization acts to underscore the apparently powerful and potentially superior character of the Zulus in war. This is a clever plot on the part of the filmmakers because ultimately it is the Boer that in their view has to be represented as especially superior. This is borne out by Harold Shaw, the film's director, when he writes that the film will '... for the first time, bring home to everybody with full force the hardships, sufferings, and stupendous difficulties that faced the early South African settlers' (1916: 2). Thus by constructing the Zulus as exceptionally difficult to defeat, the superlative heroic abilities of the Boers in ultimately defeating them are deeply underlined. This kind of construction is summarized in the inter-title following the defeat of the Zulu army, where the battlefield is described as 'unequal':

> Having left thousands of their dead on the unequal battlefield, the demoralized Zulu army return to report its defeat to Dingaan.

This notion of inequality embodies a number of connotations: the Zulu army constructed as potentially superior is now defeated by the Boers who are thus ultimately more powerful. The film's representation of the

---

[5] I am especially grateful to Benedict Anderson for opening up these aspects of my thinking (at the workshop on 'Narrating and Imaging the Nation', held at SOAS in November 2001).

Boers as ultimate heroes, with all its epic repercussions, turns vitally and virtually entirely on this play with where the superiority, or indeed inequality, might lie. Ultimately the power to win the supremacy of white Afrikanerdom rests on this battle. At no point is there a connection made between winning the final battle and the power of the gun. The place of the bullet in colonial conquest is erased and the battle is fixed between the colonizer/settler represented as victim against the apparent force of the Zulu. Linked to this is another connotation of the notion of inequality and that is the depiction of the mass strength of the Zulus, by numbers of bodies, versus the apparently small number of Boers. Hence the filmmakers create a further opportunity to depict the potential power of the Zulus against the Boers, and the ultimate superiority of the Boers in defeating them. This is where the second element noted earlier comes in: representations of masculinities.

There is a great deal to be said about representations of masculinity in this context where Zulu men's bodies are represented *en masse* and near-naked, thus eroticized, whereas Boer men's bodies are represented more ordinarily, at times even as weak, puny, bandaged and wounded. Despite the fact that they are within the frame of the *laager* (formed by linking the ox-wagons into a large circle) they are disembodied from a mass. This is true too precisely because they are *in* the *laager*, whereas the Zulu soldiers literally swarm over the countryside, as if they 'own' the landscape, an 'ant-like mass' according to Davis (1996: 133). Here a set of complex readings becomes possible. The Zulu soldiers in a sense embody a familiarity with the terrain that the Boers do not, bound within the apparent safety of the *laager*. This could be read by audiences as depicting the Zulus as the rightful owners of the land. The fact that this is apparently not the case suggests that the 'safety' of the film's ideology relies in part beyond itself and certainly on a pre-existing set of values and beliefs. It thus can be seen at some levels as reiterating an already-developed supremacist stance and not only as constructing or inventing one. Indeed the uses that the film was put to suggest that it was a long-awaited piece of representational propaganda that Afrikaner nationalist organizations used to celebrate their dominance over black South Africans. According to reports, the film was shown to audiences across the country every year on 16 December, the day commemorating the victory of the Boers (called the Day of the Vow and later the Day of the Covenant in recognition of the covenant they made with their God to build a church and to mark the day for eternity if they won the battle).

Looking beyond this particular period to the 1930s, a strong inter-
textual relationship can be, and should be, made between these cinematic
images and their representation of masculinities and those of the sculptural friezes in the Voortrekker monument in Pretoria. Here the ideological principles on which the film was made in 1916 are entrenched in
excess.[6] But in relation to representations of masculinity the ways in
which a similar dichotomous positioning of masculinities in the figuring
of the Boer men's bodies and the Zulu soldiers' bodies is at work, is of
particular interest.

This section on *De Voortrekkers* is a comment on the skewing of
national identity, on a cinematic attempt to entrench particular perspectives of Afrikaner identity, and more broadly white identity, in short, to
represent it exclusively as *the* South African national identity.

Conscious representations of black identity: Jim Comes to Joburg *(1949) and*
The Magic Garden *(1951)*

Moving on now to the second 'moment' selected: while films made by
black people were virtually absent from South Africa's cinema history
until the major political shifts of the 1990s and new national film policy
introduced after the first democratic election of 1994, many and perhaps
most cinema practices and the images they produce, from the first films
onwards, open up questions of black identity in critical ways, as I have
shown in the example of *De Voortrekkers*. There are however key moments that foreground black identity from a (variously) black point of
view in unique ways. One of these is the period of the late 1940s to the
early 1960s when a small number of films were made that engage specifically and consciously with representations of black people, to the extent
that one critic has proposed that this was a development towards a black
cinema in South Africa (Davis 1996). There is some debate to be had
about the specific films made in this period and their production contexts. The broader socio-political context is critical too. The new, white,
national party government had come into power in 1948 and with it a
plethora of laws enforcing apartheid. This was a period of rising resistance and defiance on the part of black organizations.

---

[6] Preller's screenplay for *De Voortrekkers* arguably 'invented' Afrikaner iconography
(see Hofmeyr 1988) which was also inspirational for the sculptural representations in
the Voortrekker Monument.

I shall comment here on two films directed by a small group of liberal, white filmmakers, independently of the monopolistic African Film Productions. The first of these films, *Jim Comes to Joburg*, tells the story of a young man who leaves his rural home to seek work in the city. Note the choice of the name 'Jim', erasing his given name rooted in his African identity, and universalizing his personal identity. He gets mugged on his first day in the city, is fired from his first job as a domestic worker, then finds work in a nightclub. His singing voice is discovered and he is offered a recording contract by the (white) 'boss' who initially fired him. The story of Jim in the city is woven around the central city, black nightclub that did not, and indeed could not, exist in reality and was constructed specifically for the film, setting up a Hollywood-like *mise-en-scène* with an African-derived decor.[7] This setting makes it possible for the filmmakers to incorporate music, specifically black music, in ways that had not previously been seen in South African cinema. This was, for example, the first time that Dolly Rathebe, who later became a famous singer, was seen on screen. Thus the film, because it is based in a liberal sensibility, accomplishes some remarkable strides while at the same time retaining a conservative perspective in representing black identities.

Where the city is the locus of *Jim Comes to Joburg*, in the next film made by the same director Donald Swanson, called *The Magic Garden*, the city is differently used, this time as a framework. The striking feature of this framework is that the filmmakers choose the figure of a white, male tourist, dressed in a safari suit holding a map, looking bewildered in amongst the hustle and bustle of the city centre, as the central 'character'. Thus an observational, satirical approach sets the scene for the opening framework. Interestingly, it sets the scene for the remainder of the film too, even though the tourist falls away after the opening. In some ways the filmmakers are themselves tourists, looking from the outside in. Indeed, the character of the tourist they create at the beginning may well be representative of themselves and their own experience of Johannesburg city. It also establishes the relationship they have beyond the city centre to the locale of the remainder of the film. Thus I have chosen the notion of a framework very specifically because this beginning is in the form of a mini docu-drama primarily set in the central city that leads into the film's narrative proper after some minutes (seven in all), which takes

---

[7] Davis (1996: 23) describes the origin of the setting as 'of course Hollywood films'.

place in a black township called Alexandra some miles from the centre. It is the story of forty pounds, stolen from the church by a local thief, who upon being chased hides it under a cabbage in a woman's garden. She finds it, believes it to be a miracle and proceeds to use it as credit in the local store ... and so the forty pounds takes on a life of its own, helping various characters through their scrapes, until it is eventually returned to the church and the thief is caught.

Like *Jim Comes to Joburg* and most of the other films in this small cluster consciously focusing on black identity in this period, music is a central feature. Thus, for example, the pennywhistler is a central motif in *The Magic Garden*. And like the inter-textual or generic references to Hollywood, the relationship between the development of black music in the 1940s and 1950s with its counterpart in the form of black jazz in the USA, is close. In some ways the film acts as a conduit for representations of black music where at times the narrative itself loses prominence, much like the genre of the musical. Indeed, the musical elements and the chase sequences both pay allegiance to their counterparts in Hollywood cinema. While doing so however, the film operates entirely within the geography of the township that makes its setting. Thus it is as if, once beyond the city itself, black township people live independently of the broader socio-political context, where the unsuspecting viewer's perceptions of reality would be delimited by the film's selective framing. This was later replicated in films made for black township audiences in the 1970s, where historical realities were delimited by narratives set within black townships with no whites present, a practice which one critic described as a 'structuring absence' (Gavshon 1983).

Returning to the opening docu-drama, there are a few points to be made that reflect upon the way the film itself works as a film, as a text, *and* the elements of that text in relation to identity (in a nutshell) as a complex process of authentication. This happens primarily through the documentary nature of the opening section. It looks as if the camera has filmed reality as lived, as experienced, and that the voice-over has been added as an explanatory commentary. But in fact the sequence is carefully scripted, albeit using the 'real' ambience of the city. Because documentary is *seen as* real, however, and it has a special claim to reality, the comments in the voice-over gain a heightened sense of reality too. Thus the comments that describe life in the city and, a little later, life in Alexandra seem true, indeed in this context could be taken to be unequivocally so.

This commentary raises a number of problematics and I shall briefly focus on two. First, the narration uses a white, male voice suspended beyond the frame itself with the accompanying omnipotent authority with which such a voice is imbued.[8] It has a patronizing air that matches the notion of the tourist mentioned earlier. This tends towards a perception of black experience that has the accoutrements of authenticity but that in effect operates from within white, middle-class liberalism. This is borne out by a newspaper article written many years later (1986) by one of the (white) people associated with the film where he nostalgically and mythically represents Alexandra: 'It was somehow stirring and beautiful in its rude exuberance, savage and squalid, but so alive ...'. He goes on, '... now it is a place of fear and violence ...', and then in reference to the film itself, 'there in the vaults in Pretoria[9] is Alexandra *as it was*' [emphasis added] (*The Argus*, 22 February 1986), acting as further confirmation of the film's rootedness in perceived reality. Second, the commentary over-generalizes, for example making reference to 'all the tribes of Africa', as if Alexandra is representative of the entire continent.[10] But at the same time as it does this, it describes black identities in over-discrete ways. To explain: once the city centre has been described the image of a bus leaving the centre is used as a lead into the next section of the docu-drama that takes place in Alexandra, where the film's narrative will unfold. Here the filmmakers focus individually on a number of different people, each dressed and adorned in different traditional attire representing what the voice-over calls 'tribes'. One part of the problematics here is the conservative distinction between different groups, made all the more strong by using the conventions of the expository documentary film mode, devoid of personalization and objectifying and exoticizing the subject. But beyond this, although linked to it, another part of the problematics is that the film's broader narrative is in no sense related to this notion of 'tribal' identity. Apart from the descriptive opening we never see this purportedly major feature of Alexandra again. It is as if the filmmakers are proposing that despite all these 'tribal' differences everyone is in it together. Here again we see the mythical view of life in a black township. Indeed,

---

[8] For useful discussions of voice-overs as omnipotent and authoritative see Nichols 1983, and 1991: 34-38.

[9] A reference to the National Film, Video and Sound Archives in Pretoria.

[10] This could also be a touch of self-aggrandizement on the part of the filmmakers, that their film is representative of all of Africa, an interesting notion in relation to my earlier comment about the English title, *Winning a Continent*, of *De Voortrekkers*.

the characters in the film, performed by non-professional actors, are represented as ordinary people all relatively equal to each other. Difference is marked by particular roles, for example priest, teacher, shopkeeper, policeman, and to a lesser extent by class, where some individuals have easier access to money. Thus the experience of township life is naturalized, as if this could be anywhere in the world.

As with *Jim Comes to Joburg* we are given a view of the world that is engaging, where some significant features of South African and especially black identity are explored, notably in the musical elements, on an ethnographic, documentary level. The same is true of the setting itself where Alexandra, as it was then, is exploited as the film's mise-en-scène. Combined with the non-professional acting, the film therefore has a 'slice-of-life' quality portrayed as an apparently realistic view of black identities. But ultimately, for the reasons raised here, the film reflects an unresolved perspective of the identities it portrays. It presents itself as a film made from within black experience, which it achieves in part, but retains a view exterior to that experience. This is represented by the all-knowing, white eye and voice as evidenced in the docu-drama and continued through the text by setting up a mythologized perspective upon black identity. In the next key 'moment' in the line of black identities that I am tracing it will become apparent that this move to focus consciously on black identity in the early 1950s is given an intimate, subjective turn at the point where apartheid is crumbling, towards the end of the century.

Black subjectivity: Mapantsula *(1988) and* Fools *(1998)*

The third key 'moment' I wish to focus on here is rooted in the apartheid period of the late 1980s and the post-apartheid period of the 1990s. The most significant film here is *Mapantsula* made in 1988 by a white filmmaker, Oliver Schmitz, in close collaboration with a black writer, Thomas Mogotlane, who plays the central role of Panic in the film. In brief, the film focuses on Panic as 'gangster' uncharacteristically transformed by the end of the film into taking a political stand. The story set in this way is a strong political statement in itself, but the chief point to be made here is that the film's significance lies in its entrenchment of a black point-of-view. For the first time in a fiction film in South Africa made for general release, audiences see through the eyes of a black subject. Thus where earlier films might have been made within the context of black life and experience this film has the additional value of ideologically locating itself within black subjectivity. It is thus an interiorized point of view. Where *The Magic Garden* has the perspective of outsider looking in, this film is located on the inside looking out. The camera is used in sophisticated ways to achieve this. One example is when Panic takes a bus ride from the city centre to the white suburb where his lover, Pat, is a domestic worker. The camera is positioned to look through the window at the high walls and large gardens that the bus passes by and in a slow pan left incorporates Panic into the image as if what the camera sees is what he sees. Thus we are given his personalized point-of-view of this apartheid landscape. Similarly, when he and Pat are in her room on the property of her white employers, the camera is positioned behind Panic looking through the window at the silhouette of the employers through the kitchen window of their house.

This divide that is set up throughout the film, reflecting the apartheid 'barrier' between black and white experience, is most acutely portrayed in the moment when Panic, having been chased off the employers' property, throws a stone through the front window of the house and shatters it. Here the camera is positioned on his side of the window. But the same image is used later in the film and is especially pivotal in Panic's re-creation through flashbacks of the events leading up to his detention and torture in prison. When he is forced to hang out of the window, reminding audiences of the many deaths from high windows of political detainees, as his head hangs over the edge of the window, the film cuts to a flashback of the same stone-throwing scene. But this time the camera is placed on the inside of the window, positioned within the house itself. This does not however re-position the subjective identity of the film away from Panic, rather, precisely because the film is so closely positioned as Panic's point-of-view, this inverted shot of the stone smashing through the window underlines the fact that Panic is looking at himself smashing the window, thereby remembering the significance of this act for his life's trajectory. Thus the film not only positions the camera alongside and with the black subject who is central to the narrative, but it also positions itself on the interior of his visual and mental perceptions of himself. Audiences are therefore intimately bound into his point-of-view, with this kind of layering of strategies to secure the point of view as located without any doubt within a black subjectivity.

The film is not without its flaws however. For example, we see less through the eyes of Pat, Panic's lover, while he inhabits her space and comments through it on her exploitation as a domestic worker in a white suburb. Furthermore, in this scene he acts abusively towards Pat in ways that evoke sympathy with her against him (Maingard 1994). This is useful for the portrayal of his character in the narrative and could be seen as a move to represent his behaviour towards women authentically within the character type he portrays. At the same time the message beneath his abuse is significant since it is about her exploitation. This is even more complex because it is not strictly speaking Pat's space, but rather that of her employers where she lives during the week. And every other aspect of her life beyond this space makes it clear that she herself has no sense of it as hers. Yet in the film's narrative it is a crucial feature since it makes possible the representation of the divide between black and white identities, by showing the geographical differences between the Soweto neighbourhood where Panic lives, and the white suburb where Pat works. This lends itself at times to a categorization of identities in stereo-typical ways that suggests the divide more excessively than in (some) lived experience. But because the divide is a core element of the film it fixes in the minds of viewers a geography of identities based on race and class that acts as the framing feature for the story of Panic's transition from gangster to taking a political stand against the apartheid state. Thus despite the film's flaws it is deeply representative of a black subjectivity, albeit a particularized one, that is layered and complex, and contextualized in the broader socio-political structures of South Africa under apartheid.

The second film I wish to mention briefly is *Fools*, made more recently in 1998, based on a story of the same name written by a black South African author and academic, Njabulo Ndebele, set in a fictitious Soweto neighbourhood in the 1980s. The film is both written and directed by black filmmakers, Bekhizizwe Peterson and Ramadan Suleman. As with *Mapantsula*, the filmmakers use the geographical context to comment upon black identity, but this time it is located almost entirely in Soweto without the comparative imperatives set up in *Mapantsula*. Here the film's characters are imbued with a magnitude that engagingly surpasses the narrative line,[11] from the world war two veteran who lives literally in the street itself and, wearing his war helmet, intermittently

---

[11] I borrow the term 'magnitude' from Bill Nichols (1986 and 1991), who uses it to describe the ideological space a documentary film might occupy to lift it beyond the miniaturizing effect of filming a subject, and more importantly to give it the 'full dimensionality of the world in which we live' (1986: 107). In the present context it connotes the way in which the film exposes contexts far broader than the local neighbourhood streets where, in the main, the narrative is played out.

cries out 'Father, forgive them!', to the gang leader who is dressed in the 'uniform' of black, male domestic workers, and drives an old BMW. Matching this kind of magnitude is the *mise-en-scène* of the neighbourhood street scenes that is deeply textured revealing a multi-plurality of identities. One example of this is the sequence where the teacher, the film's central character, leaves his house and walks along the street first greeting women selling fruit and wares at roadside stalls. At the same time a wedding is in progress and people are gathering and singing, some of the women traditionally dressed as Xhosas, while the bride and groom process through the streets with an entourage of guests and locals joining in the festivities. Features of these street scenes and the multiple view of identities they entrench include vignettes such as a wood and coal merchant on donkey-drawn cart passing by in the background of a shot, someone in a wheelchair pushing themselves along the edge of the frame, and a young boy rushing down a street pushing an old supermarket trolley. The narrative line itself, teacher rapes student and flails about in his guilt and shame, is also played out in the close/closed confines of the neighbourhood, never taken beyond this space, never into official legal machinations. This is a powerful statement on the interiorizing of violence in South African experience and the abhorrence for official (apartheid) state legislation and its practices. At the same time, it sets up a deep ambivalence about justice with regard to the nature of violence and abuse in neighbourhoods like this one, located as it is so essentially within black township experience. For while it remains confined within, locked into an interior world and perspective, its existence cannot be framed more broadly in moves to shift the imbalances of apartheid and to resist the perpetuation of divisions between South Africans.

Conclusion

My purpose here has been to excavate from a broad possible range of films made in South Africa through the twentieth century, three 'key moments' as I have called them, that make it possible to examine how identities, especially black identities, have been both imagined and imaged. In the knowledge that South Africa's particular colonial and apartheid history has created starkly divided identities, my intention here has been to trace a line through time that shows how representations of black identities have shifted through the century. The first 'key moment' is 1916 when *De Voortrekkers* was made. This film is an aberration against the black voice and the black body, promoting a white supremacist view.

The second moment in the line stretches beyond the virtual propaganda
of the first towards a liberal framework that alongside its conservative
conventionalism, opens up a space for representing black identities and
contributes historically significant ethnographic material to the archive of
celluloid images of black experience. In the third 'key moment' two films
exemplify how representations of black identity have moved into the
realm of the interior in complex ways. The first of the two examples
engages the tools of the cinema, namely the camera and its positioning,
to construct an interiorized, black, subjective point-of-view. In the second example, the filmmakers locate the narrative in the interior space of
a black township and use the opportunity this provides for an outpour-
ing of multiple identities within the close/closed confines of neighbourhood streets. This process of tracing how identities have been cast in
celluloid reveals itself as complex and difficult. For celluloid, that is the
cinema, by its very nature fixes images and thus too identities. This paper
shows that some South African filmmakers have begun to explore how
the machinations of the cinematic might be used to erase earlier reduc-
tive, hegemonic images/imaginings of identity to imag(in)e identities
beyond apartheid.

References
Argus (22 February 1986).
Bhabha, Homi. 1989. 'The Commitment to Theory' in Pines, Jim and Willemen,
    Paul (eds). *Questions of Third Cinema*. London: BFI: 111-132.
Davis, Peter. 1996. *In Darkest Hollywood: Exploring the Jungles of Cinema's South
    Africa*. South Africa: Ravan.
Dubow, Saul. 1995. *Illicit Union: Scientific Racism in Modern South Africa*. Johannes-
    burg: Wits University Press.
Edison Kinetogram (15 May 1912).
Gaines, Jane. 2000. 'Birthing Nations' in Hjort, Mette and MacKenzie, Scott
    (eds). *Cinema and Nation*. London and New York: Routledge: 298-316.
Gavshon, Harriet. 1983. 'Levels of Intervention in Films made for Black South
    African Audiences' in *Critical Arts*, 2(4): 13-21.
Hall, Stuart. 1989. 'Cultural Identity and Cinematic Representation' in *Framework*
    36: 68-81.
Giliomee, Hermann. 2003. *The Afrikaners: Biography of a People*. Cape Town: Tafel-
    berg.

Hees, Edwin. 2003. 'The Birth of a Nation: Contextualizing *De Voortrekkers* (1916)' in Balseiro, Isabel and Masilela, Ntongela (eds). *To Change Reels: Film and Film Culture in South Africa.* Detroit: Wayne State University Press: 49-69.

Hofmeyr, Isabel. 1987. 'Popularising History: The Case of Gustav Preller' in *Journal of African History* 29: 521-535.

Kaplan, Mendel. 1986. *Jewish Roots in the South African Economy.* Cape Town: C.Struik.

Maingard, Jacqueline. 1994. 'New South African Cinema: *Mapantsula* and *Sarafina*' in *Screen* 35(3): 235-243.

Maingard, Jacqueline. 1997. 'Transforming Television Broadcasting in a Democratic South Africa' in *Screen* 38(3): 260-274.

Maingard, Jacqueline (forthcoming 2006). *South African National Cinema.* London and New York: Routledge.

Nichols, Bill. 1983. 'The Voice of Documentary' in *Film Quarterly*, 36(3): 17-29.

Nichols, Bill. 1986. 'Questions of Magnitude' in Corner, John (ed.) *Documentary and the Mass Media.* Great Britain: Edward Arnold: 107-122.

Nichols, Bill. 1991. *Representing Reality: Issues and Concepts in Documentary.* Bloomington: Indiana University Press.

Shaw, Harold. 1916. 'Filming "The Voortrekkers"' in *Stage and Cinema* (30 December 1916): 2.

Tomaselli, Keyan. 1986. 'Capitalism and Culture in South African Cinema: Jingoism, Nationalism and the Historical Epic' in *Wide Angle* 8(2): 33-43.

Trinh, T. Minh-ha (in conversation with A. Morelli). 1996. 'The Undone Interval' in Chambers, Iain and Curti, Lidia (eds). *The Post-Colonial Question: Common Skies, Divided Horizons.* London and New York: Routledge: 3-16.

CHAPTER 6

BLACK SKIN, BIG HAIR:
THE CULTURAL APPROPRIATION OF THE 'AFRO'

Angeline Morrison

Figure 6.1: Contemporary Afro. In *Untold* 13 (July/Aug. 2000): 122.
Photograph by Mark Mattock. Copyright: Untold Publications UK Ltd.

After more than three decades in style wilderness, the originally black hair configuration known as the 'afro' or 'natural' is finally enjoying a fashion comeback. The British popular culture magazine *Heat* recently declared it 'the hottest hairdo of the summer' in their style barometer (25

June/1 July 2005: 77). This accolade was partly inspired by the fact that
no fewer than three of the contestants in the 2005 UK version of the
television game show *Big Brother* (Channel 4) were identifiable by their
'afro' hair. One of these was a Turkish man (Kemal), whose very curly
hair was teased out into a fluffy afro cloud, one a black British man
(Science), whose 'afro' was regularly groomed, styled, combed out and
braided. The third and most notorious 'afro' was worn by Makosi, a
young woman from Zimbabwe. Hers was the most fascinating because it
did not at first seem subject to the same hair etiquette as Science's.
Makosi's 'afro' appeared to require no grooming, combing or braiding. It
very soon became apparent that the superhuman, gravity-defying bounce
and glossiness of Makosi's 'fro was entirely down to the fact that it was
actually a weave, or treated nylon hair, sewn on to the wearer's own hair,
which is usually braided tightly down against the scalp. Presumably she
chose this option because she thought it would be easier to groom.
Whatever her reasons, it is fascinating to note that the 'afro' has now
become such a desirable fashion accessory that someone who actually
has a natural head of 'afro' hair will spend time and money acquiring a
false one to wear over their own. The 'afro' in weave form suggests that
this style is now fast approaching an equality with straight hair in terms
of popularity.

    If it seems inappropriate to speak of a natural ethnic characteristic in
terms of fashion, that is precisely the point. Ethnic African hair is perhaps the most powerful signifier of our difference as black subjects in
the West, and has a history of having been 'worked' by various black
writers, and by visual artists such as David Hammons, with his 1970s
series of sculptures made from clippings of black (diaspora) hair (Jones
1998). As Kobena Mercer writes,

> hair functions as a *key ethnic signifier* because, compared with bodily shape or
> facial features, it can be changed more easily by cultural practices such as
> straightening. Caught on the cusp between self and society, nature and cul-
> ture, the malleability of hair makes it a sensitive area of expression (Mercer
> 1994: 103).

This chapter will explore the subject of 'afro' hair from the starting point
of hair as Barthesian signifier or identity text; a highly coded symbol
worn on the body, that also signals a belonging, in terms of shared beliefs. This particular morphology of hair can actually be situated within a
highly specific context. The time was the late 1960s, the place North
America and the mood revolutionary. Wearing an 'afro' was a clear state-

ment of pride in one's black identity, a powerful signifier of refusal to buckle under the dead weight of white society's beauty myths. The argument here is that the high-velocity dilution of the style's original political significance can be directly related to white society's ravenous appropriation of the 'afro' as a fashion accessory. At the height of the Civil Rights Movement, the political and social stance symbolized by the 'afro' posed a direct threat to white society as it was. This 'threatened' society unconsciously co-opted the style and put its own mark upon it, recasting it as 'fashion', and therefore domesticating the perceived threat. Eventually, as an accompaniment to the 'radical chic' look, the 'afro' was to become no more eloquent or relevant than a thick-soled shoe.

Straightening your 'fro

Few hair discussions are shot through with such political, historical, cultural and ethnic significance as those that surround the straightening of naturally curly African hair. These conversations are highly emotive, peppered with issues of black consciousness, so-called black 'authenticity', accusations of 'selling out' and so on. 'Natural heads' believe they should be allowed to go natural without ridicule, and without the bullying from hairdressers that frequently accompanies this choice. Others believe – more reasonably, I think – that straightening is simply a personal style choice, rather than a compliance with an oppressive and inappropriate white beauty myth, and that one should straighten without guilt. Unsurprisingly, the internet is buzzing with sites devoted to these discussions (e.g. www.nappyhair.com). A typical pro-natural debater is 'MM' from 'Philly', who writes,

> Why are we the only people on God's earth who must apologize for our natural [...] hair? We are the only ones who are forced to hide our natural beauty with scarves, wraps and chemicals (Hair Matters 2005).

'MM' also touches on the issue of the energy expended by the diaspora subject in *hiding* the lengths gone to in order to mimic straight hair (ibid.). The debate has since become even more complex because of the widespread acceptance of 'artifice' in hair ornamentation in both white and black beauty-cultures. Almost as many white female celebrities now adorn themselves with long hair extensions as black female celebrities wear long, straight weaves. The discussion changes as constantly as fash-

ions change, and it is therefore difficult (or inadvisable) to attempt a
single fixed position on the subject.

The intellectual position that all the artifices of beauty should be
embraced by people of the African diaspora, simply enjoyed and played
with, is tempting. It is particularly so when we consider first the obvious
artifice of *all* beautifying practices, and also that within the African aesthetic of hair adornment, skilful artifice features heavily. Judith Wilson
observes that,

> Where western culture generally condemns most forms of body adornment
> or alteration as vain, deceitful, grotesque, tasteless, or at best merely frivo-
> lous, Africans tend to view *failure* to supplement, transform, or otherwise
> improve on nature as a lapse of character or a breach of decorum (Wilson
> 1994:13).

This understanding remains in the vast majority of African diaspora
women in the west. The 'curved African follicle' (Smith 2000) in its
natural or unprocessed state is tacitly understood to be a foe that must
be tamed, or colonized. It is sometimes considered a source of shame
and embarrassment, almost as though a woman stepping out without
'doing' her hair may just as well have left the house barefoot in a dressing
gown. The stylistic 'norms' therefore tend to involve either disguise, or
chemical alteration. Oprah Winfrey drew a pertinent parallel when she
once remarked that black women spend their lives fighting their hair in a
way comparable to that in which white women spend their lives fighting
their bodies.

Whilst one can agree with Kobena Mercer (1994; see also Turning
Heads 2001) that the 'all straightening is wrong' thesis is too extreme and
lacking in subtlety, it is also true that there are popular black styles which
can be identified as belonging to a white beauty aesthetic. These styles
are generally seen worn by famous, beautiful and successful black
women, and the associations that these images generate help to perpetuate tantalizing beauty myths amongst diaspora subjects – particularly
women – that will never fit. However, things are not quite that simple.
There are also styles which are characteristically and identifiably black,
but which require straightening to create. Also, walk down any Western
shopping street today and you will see styles, worn exclusively by white
women, which are clearly inspired by the bone-straight, sleek artificiality
of chemically relaxed Afro hair. Can these styles, then, be said to belong
to a black aesthetic? Or will any attempt to trace a style's provenance be
doomed before it begins by the endless hybrid conversation that is cul-

ture? In any discussion of black hair, the variables are abundant, and include the parody and satire of the white aesthetic that can be found in certain black hairstyles. Perhaps, ultimately, the issue of black hair style choice is irresolvable. However, the debate does set up areas of anxiety and tension – and it is in these areas that some of the most valuable discussions can take place.

The 'afro' and Africa

> The hair follicles of women of African descent emerge from a slanted or oval shaft, which causes the hair to fold over and curl into a tight or loose spiral as it grows out (Faison et al. 2000).

Black hair is unique; apparently the continent of Africa is the only place in the world where this particular hair type occurs. A wide variety of stylistic idioms exist throughout the continent, each style variation its own little world of meaning. For example, amongst the Rendille people of the northern desert of Kenya, the women form their hair into a sort of coxcomb or quiff, created by adding a mixture of mud, animal fat and ochre. This is a sign that the woman has given birth to her first son.

It is highly unusual, however, to find examples of the 'afro' style discussed here in indigenous African societies, as the style tends to be associated with the West. This is so much so that the Tanzanian Government banned the wearing of the 'afro' in the 1970s, because it was considered to be a badge of pro-Western revolutionary sentiment. Recently, *Guardian* journalist Hannah Pool wrote of a trip to her birthplace, Eritrea, where she was reunited with her birth family. She was surprised to find that her 'afro' was not received in quite the way she had hoped. She was told that her father '...wants to know why your hair is like that...Why is it not "done"? He says you look like a bandit.' Pool herself considered the irony of how

> the Afro that I (and lots of other black adults in the diaspora) wear thinking it is an outward signifier of how in touch we are with our roots actually screams the opposite (*Guardian Weekend* 9 July 2005: 20; extract from Pool 2005).

The style can however, be found in some of Africa's cities or commercial centres, where western fashions are more common. So we can see that the 'afro', where ethnic hair is left untroubled by anything more sophisticated than a comb, is a specifically diasporic style formation. The

signified of the 'afro' is the Africa of the imagination, a homeland that is
on the bodies and in the hearts and minds of diaspora people.

Black girls and the white beauty myth
For some time now the only remaining 1970s style that has remained
mildly ridiculous is the 'afro'. We have seen the gradual mainstreaming of
flared trousers, elongated shirt collars, the ubiquitous platform sole. Until
now, however, the 'afro' has failed to catch on the second time around.
African American recording artists like Macy Gray and Erykah Badu
have helped to popularize what has been called the 'Afro Bohemian'
look, and this look can be seen in high fashion publications and in adver-
tising images (see Figure 1). At street level the style is now largely a signifier of affiliation to the Hip-Hop community, and does tend to be considered a more acceptable option for men than for women.

It is more usual to see public black figures associated with success,
talent and – most importantly – beauty, wearing elaborate straight weaves
or a combination of chemically relaxed hair and a straight weave or hair
extensions. Black British model Naomi Campbell, and African American
singer Beyoncé Knowles, are notable examples of this trend. The point is
that the institutionally-approved images of black beauty, those dispersed
and endorsed by the fashion and music industries, still clearly favour the
white beauty aesthetic of long, flowing, shining, straight or gently curling
so-called 'good' hair. The Rapunzel myth of magical locks of improbable
length, golden colour and heavy, soft malleability has – wittingly or otherwise – been instilled into generations of little black girls. Whilst many
of these girls are now magazine-buying adults, they still find that everywhere the most beautiful and successful black women appear to have
this unattainable Barbie-hair. The more we continue to see these images,
the more we work ourselves up into a lustful feeding-frenzy. We must
get that Barbie-hair, at any cost to scalp or purse.

The folk myth of long, soft, golden locks as an immediate signifier of
desirability lurks of old in the unconscious of the dominant white beauty
aesthetic for women. In European folk or fairy tales, for instance, it is
common for the heroine's hair to be described as 'flaxen'. In *Twa Sisters*
(also known as *Cruel Sister* or *Binorrie*), a folk song found in different
versions in England and Scotland, things get even worse. Blonde and
dark are directly opposed – the fair-haired sister (beautiful, good, desired
by the prince) is also an innocent victim. She is actually drowned by the
dark-haired sister (older, uglier, evil-minded, jealous as can be) (in Child

2002). The white myth of the innate beauty of the long-haired woman remains as deeply scored on African diaspora consciousness as it does on the white. This accounts for the diaspora terms 'good hair' and 'bad hair'. As may be imagine, 'bad hair' is the most African type of hair – thick, tightly curled or 'kinky', short and puffy, dry and scratchy and utterly parched. 'Good hair' is the most European-looking – the softest, longest, most loosely-curled or even straight, swinging-in-the-breeze hair.

If white, Western society reads long, straight hair as a powerful signi-fier of feminine beauty, attractiveness and (hence, of course) value, it is hardly surprising that slave women and their daughters, cut off from the African beauty-myths of their ancestral cultures, were left with an ill-fitting western paradigm that was both alien and powerfully alienating. Many slaves became proficient at styling and caring for their white mas-ters' hair, and hairdressing became a popular occupation for freed slaves in the United States. Kitchen beauty parlours and salons were common, with herbal recipes handed down orally in slave families forming the basis of treatments. An early self-made American millionaire was in fact a black woman, a freed slave named Sarah Walker, who made her fortune selling 'Madame Walker's Wonderful Hair Grower'. This pomade was designed to repair black hair damaged by over-processing. She also sold various skin lightening preparations, and patented the revolutionary hair-straightening 'hot comb', still in popular use today as a temporary straightener, originally designed for black women who had no access to running water in their own homes. Sarah Walker went on to become an active patron in the Harlem Renaissance movement (Madame Walker 2005).

Slaves with 'good hair', often the result of sexual congress forced by white slave-owners on black slave women, would frequently be put to work inside the master's house where they would be more visible. Their hair was considered more 'tame', more 'white', and therefore less un-sightly than their less mixed counterparts. Not only were these lighter-skinned, softer-haired black people considered easier on the white eye, but the 'good hair' was a signifier of white ownership and power. By permitting these slaves with 'good hair' the visibility and proximity to the white 'master-family' that working in the house offered, the slave-owner was also showing the absolute control he had over the bodies of his female slaves. He was involved in a territorial display of the bounds of his authority, marking the fact that his ownership of the slaves was abso-lute. This ownership stretched to the sexual use of their bodies, and thus, even to their genetic make-up (Henriques 1974; Hyam 1990; Young 1995).

As far as extremely curly, or 'wild-looking' hair in the white imagination, is concerned, the nineteenth century is full of telling examples. Charles Darwin made some explicit connections between hair type and mental state, with a particular patient of whom he wrote, 'the state of her hair is a sure and convenient criterion of her mental condition'. A typical maniac could be diagnosed by the hair 'that rises up from his forehead like the mane of a Shetland pony' (Darwin 1872: 297). Hair phrenology seemingly enjoyed great popularity in Britain as a sort of pop-science, with some predictably essentialist results. In 1912 one Professor R.W. Brown, a self-styled phrenologist of some repute, gave regular lectures in Britain on the subject of how to tell character from hair. He espoused the essentialist belief that the rougher the hair, the coarser the mental and moral nature of the person.

If these ideas persist, the position of the black woman wishing to look attractive in white society is highly problematic. What's a girl to do? Irie Jones, the mixed-race protagonist in Zadie Smith's novel, *White Teeth*, embodies the experience of so many girls who would give almost anything to get that elusive Rapunzel/Barbie hair. Irie's traumatic first visit to a black hairdresser will, she feels, allow her finally to snare the boy of her dreams. Irie is 'intent upon transformation, intent upon fighting her genes' (Smith 2000: 275). Smith symbolizes this doomed fight beautifully with Irie's mantra of desire. At any cost, she must get 'straight straight long black sleek flickable tossable shakeable touchable finger-throughable wind-blowable hair. With a fringe' (ibid.).

The politics of beauty
In America, by the late 1960s, the mood amongst African American women was beginning to change with relation to their hairstyles. A virulent body of opinion against chemical straightening emerged. This was a direct response to Malcolm X and the Cultural Nationalists of the 1950s, who had spoken out very clearly against straightening. In his biography, Malcolm X had written with explicit shame and regret of the days when he was known as 'Detroit Red', during which he wore the straightened 'conk' hair style with a reddish colour. Malcolm X wrote that straightening his hair was,

my first really big step towards self-degradation: when I endured all that pain, literally burning my flesh to have it look like a white man's hair ; I had joined that multitude of Negro men and women in America who are brainwashed into believing that the black people are 'inferior' and white people are 'superior' – that they will even violate and mutilate their God-created bodies to try to look 'pretty' by white standards (Malcolm X 1991: 52-3).

Marcus Garvey also unequivocally encouraged black people to stop straightening altogether, stating that 'kinks' were not to be removed from the hair, but from the brain (Hair Matters 2005). W.E.B. du Bois wrote in *The Souls of Black Folk* in 1906 (1994) of the 'double consciousness' of the diaspora subject, in but not of the nation state. However, anyone who still stuck to straightening was seen as exhibiting not double but *false* consciousness; they were clearly ashamed of their blackness.

In 1966, African American lifestyle magazine *Ebony* carried an article entitled 'The Natural Look: New Modes for Negro Women'. The piece related the story of

a Frenchman, who had been in this country but a short time, was astonished to encounter on the street one day a shapely, brown-skinned woman whose close-cropped, rough-textured hair was in marked contrast to that of Brigitte Bardot – or any other woman he'd ever seen. Intrigued by her extraordinarily curly locks, he rushed up to her and blurted in Gallic impulsiveness: 'But I thought only Negro men had curly hair' (Natural Look 1966).

Perhaps the Frenchman's shock is easier to understand in terms of the extraordinary image shown in Figure 2. Painted in about 1405, this image shows the Queen of Sheba represented as a black woman. The artist has given her the deepest ebony skin tone, but her hair is clearly an absolute mystery to him. He has crowned his Black Queen with the only possible option in keeping with her royalty and renowned beauty – long, golden Rapunzel hair cascading down her body in elegant little waves. This image demonstrates the difficulty posed to the white imagination by the notion of African hair as not only 'beautiful', but also 'feminine'. As a signifier of power befitting a regal beauty, the choice for this artist had already been made.

Figure 6.2. The Queen of Sheba. De Bellefortis, 1405.
Copyright: Cosmic Illusion Productions Foundation, Amsterdam.

In 1967, just one year after the *Ebony* article, the *New York Times* carried reports of revolts on campus in the historically black universities. Whilst the primary motivation of these revolts was political, it was combined with an evangelical zeal for educating black students out of their obedient following of white fashion and beauty dictates. A representative of the Afro American Students' Union was reputed to have said that they want to celebrate their African heroes and their culture, and stop the self-hating practices of hair-bleaching and hair-straightening.

During the same period in radical white youth culture, hair also took on important significatory duties. Long hair was worn by white youths as a powerful sign of rupture from their parents' restricting culture, protest against the unjust war in Vietnam, and anti-conservatism in general. Natural, un-processed, African hair in the proud, round cloud of the 'afro', however, was inextricably associated with the political slogan, 'Black is Beautiful.' The 'afro' in the late 1960s became almost synonymous with the Civil Rights movement. The style was worn as a mark of defiance against inappropriate white beauty myths, signifying a rejection of the embedded beliefs that Afro hair was something to be intrinsically ashamed of. Many white youths who sympathized with the Civil Rights movement would also tease their hair into an 'afro' to show allegiance and support.

This was the first time in the history of African diaspora hair styles where what was foregrounded was not a particular style or design, but the *ethnic characteristic* of the hair itself. The 'afro' hair style drew attention specifically to the biological characteristics of African hair, making no apologies for the fact that it was radically different from European hair, and encouraging a feeling of pride and respect for Africa and the slave ancestors. The prouder the 'afro' stood out from the wearer's head, the more 'successful' it was considered. This demanded almost continual combing or picking out, which of course problematizes the notion of the style as something 'natural'. What was important about the 'afro', however, was that there was no way of hiding or disguising the hair type. The style set itself directly in opposition to the long, soft, straight locks of Europeans. The associations of the style amongst African Americans were specifically revolutionary, and radical black groups such as the Black Panthers wore the style almost as a part of their uniform.

Around eighteen months after the initial uprisings were reported, the image in Figure 3 appeared in British *Vogue* magazine. The white model wears an 'afro' style which is described as being 'in vogue' for that season. The leap has been made from genuine radical statement to fashionable so-called 'radical chic'. So we can see that in less than eighteen months the 'afro' had become, quite literally, in *Vogue*. Ironically enough, wigs, perms and other chemical treatments became common tools amongst fashion-conscious white women wishing to achieve the 'afro' look.

Figure 6.3. Photograph by Clive Arrowsmith from *Vogue* (15 September 1969: 162). Copyright: Clive Arrowsmith/Vogue ©The Condé Nast Publications Ltd.

What the *Vogue* illustration shows is the phenomenal speed with which white fashion appropriated this symbolic style. The association of the 'afro' with real uprisings against white society was becoming a problem. Absorbing the style into fashion meant that its political significance could, over time, also be absorbed; and as the style became more about adornment and decoration rather than rebellion, the feeling of actual political 'threat' could be proportionately reduced. In less than eighteen months, the 'afro' was, quite literally, *in Vogue*.

One of the most lasting black cultural embodiments of 'afro' chic was in the 'Blaxploitation' film genre, where male and female heroes frequently sported huge 'afros'. The forerunner of all Blaxploitation movies was also the first ever truly 'independent' movie, Melvin Van Peebles' seminal *Sweet Sweetback's Baadaass Song*, of 1971. In this film, the hero is not only identifiable by his good looks and 'fly' styling, but also by his proud 'afro' hair. It was quickly followed by Gordon Parks Snr's 1971 *Shaft*, and then by *Superfly*, directed by Parks Jnr, in 1972.

What is of stylistic interest in terms of Blaxploitation's two main survivors, *Shaft* and *Superfly*, is the oppositional hair styles of the protagonists. Crime-fighting detective Shaft sports an 'afro', indicating his unequivocal status as African American good-guy with political consciousness. This is notable because just four years after the original riots, mainstream Hollywood cinema could accept the styling of an American hero who wears his African ancestry like a crown. The process of appropriation into white fashion had, by this time, had enough time to be highly effective.

On the other hand 'Priest', the lead role in *Superfly*, could not be more different. Actor Ron O'Neal wears a bizarre straight toupée, with what looks like chemically relaxed hair underneath. The effect is that of shoulder-length, straight glossy locks. Not only was this an unusual style for a man, it was also unusual in a cinematic anti-hero. Priest's image is that of African-American dandy – it would seem that this image inspired rapper Snoop Dogg's styling as the character of Huggy Bear in Todd Phillips' 2004 film, *Starsky & Hutch*. Priest wears the clothes of a pimp and lives what another character refers to as 'the American dream', which presumably includes wearing white American-looking hair. The heroism of *Shaft* and the anti-heroism of *Superfly* are clearly signified in the identity texts of their hair.

Conclusion

Successful incorporation of the desired object into the desiring subject depends on the ingestion and eventual death of the object. Upon incorporation, the desired object ceases to be what it was originally, autonomously. Its new context demands much, and those doing the appropriating want the desired object as their own. A reconfiguration takes place – sometimes so subtle as to be undetectable at first – where the object is emptied of its original signifying power and filled with the signifiers of the appropriator.

In this case, the 'murder' was the trivializing of the original political implications of the 'afro'; what was desired was the silencing of these political implications. One of the easiest ways to domesticate and contain a threat is to absorb it into oneself – and the threat the 'afro' in its original form posed to white society was the very real threat of its own disintegration. So gradually, in a notable reversal of ethnic and cultural beauty myths, the 'afro' was de-semiotized until finally, the colonizing processes peculiar to fashion ensured its eventual status as an object of ridicule. Now, in accordance with the cycle, the style is again the height of fashion and desirability.

The cyclical process of appropriation that is fashion can be partly understood in terms of Nietzsche's dramatic theory of 'style' (Ehrenzweig 1975). The analogy is only partial because the Nietzschean style theory does not really allow for the revivals in the fashion process. Nietzsche suggested the oppositional forces of Dionysus and Apollo were entwined in perpetual battle. The Dionysian force is chaotic and destructive, bent on breaking up individual human existence. Conversely, Apollonian force weaves together the fragmentation caused by Dionysus, moulding the chaos into order and beauty. Over the course of many years, the works lose their emotion and pain (or in the case of the 'afro', their political significance), becoming in modern readers eyes embodiments instead of the sublimity and grace of 'classical beauty' (or again, in this case, retro cool).

Fashion's cyclical processes of shock, domestication, ridicule and revival can of course be said to occur with any radical sign. As the style is gradually disseminated into society at large and normalized, the initial feelings of disruption are forgotten. However, the example of the 'afro' hair style is particularly important. The 'afro' punctuated the battle against the personality of the African hair in diaspora culture in a very radical, even violent way – but only for a short time. To my knowledge, this was the first and only time that a natural ethnic characteristic was foregrounded as a meaningful stylistic symbol, set in a directly oppositional relationship, by a diasporic group, to the beauty myth of the dominant, oppressive culture. Instead of taking a style and applying it to the body, or wearing clothing tailored to create specific shapes, the 'afro' style concerned itself only with the natural character of African hair. This in itself was radical in terms of fashion; but in terms of the history of the African diaspora in the West, it is unprecedented. With the 'afro', untreated, unprocessed African hair took centre stage in fashion in a historically unique way. Similar 'naturalistic' styles such as dreadlocks have not really been bound up with revolutionary sentiment in quite the same way. In the case of the 'afro' of the late 1960s, the political implications of (un)conscious white appropriation were highly specific. Today, however, we can look back and see that this particular example of ravenous appropriation is as unique as the 'afro' itself. Appropriation of black styles by white people, and white styles by black people, appears to be continuous, and almost always goes both ways. Whilst black people continue to both straighten and curl their hair, white people continue to do the same. As a dance of desire and murder, then, appropriation can sometimes appear as aggressive. At other times it is subtle or beautiful, appearing harmless. If eternal shifting towards (and then away from) satisfaction characterizes any desire, then as desiring subjects, perhaps we too can never achieve a fixed 'conclusion' on this subject. However, it will be very interesting to see how far into the mainstream the contemporary version of the 'afro' manages to penetrate, and how much this new version will contain the old signifiers.

References

Child, Francis J. (ed.). 2003 [1882-98]. *English and Scottish Popular Ballads*. London: Dover Publications.

Darwin, Charles. 1872. *The Expression of the Emotions*. London: John Murray.

Du Bois, W.E.B. 1994 [1906]. *The Souls of Black Folk*. London: Dover Publications.

Ehrenzweig, Anton. 1975. *The Psychoanalysis of Artistic Vision and Hearing*. New York: Braziller.

Faison, Nakesha, et al. 2000. 'African American Skin and Hair: What Makes the Difference?', in *Guide to Exploring African American Culture*, Penn. State College. On line at: http://condor.depaul.edu~mwilson/divided/ chptthre.html (accessed 20 May 2000).

Hair Matters. 2005. 'Hair Matters'. On line at: http://www.endarkenment.com /hair/ (accessed 30 August 2005).

Henriques, Fernando. 1974 [1953]. *The Children of Caliban: Miscegenation*. London, Secker & Warburg.

Hyam, Ronald. 1990. *Empire and Sexuality: The British Experience*. Manchester: Manchester University Press.

Jones, Kellie. 1998. 'In the Thick of it: David Hammons and Hair Culture in the 1970s' in *Third Text* 44 (Autumn 1998): 17-24.

Madame Walker. 2005. 'Madame C.J. Walker: Entrepreneur, Philanthropist, Social Activist'. On line at: http://www.madamecjwalker.com (accessed 30 August 2005).

Malcolm X (with Alex Haley). 1991 [1966]. *Autobiography of Malcolm X*. London: Penguin.

Mercer, Kobena. 1994. 'Black Hair/Style Politics' in Mercer, Kobena (ed.) *Welcome to the Jungle: New Positions in Black Cultural Studies*. London: Routledge: 97-130.

Natural Look. 1966. 'The Natural Look: New Modes for Negro Women' in *Ebony* (Dec. 1966).

Pool, Hannah. 2005. *My Father's Daughter: a Story of Family and Belonging*. London: Hamish Hamilton.

Smith, Zadie. 2000. *White Teeth*. London: Penguin.

Turning Heads. 2001. 'Turning Heads: Conks, Curls and Identity Politics'. On-line at: http://www.jolique.com/hair/turning_heads_conks_curls.htm (accessed 2001).

Wilson, Judith. 1994. 'Beauty Rites: towards an Anatomy of Culture in African American Women's Art' in *International Review of African American Art* 2(3).

Young, Robert. 1995. *Colonial Desire: Hybridity in Theory, Culture and Race*. London: Routledge.

NATIONAL AND REGIONAL IDENTITY

CHAPTER 7

REPUBLICS, TRIBES AND NATIONAL IDENTITIES

Paul Gilbert

If nations are, as Benedict Anderson has famously expressed it, 'imagined communities' (Anderson 1991: 6), then national identity consists in membership of such a community and depends upon how this community is imagined to be. This chapter distinguishes two styles in which national communities may be imagined, and draws some conclusions about the contrasting types of national identity to which they lead.

I shall start by asking, 'How many communities are there in the North of Ireland?' One answer, by far the commoner, is 'Two' – Protestants and Catholics, or loyalists and nationalists, thought of as having 'opposing national and cultural identities ... together with conflicting aspirations' (Kearney 1997: 71).This answer would be that returned overwhelmingly by the Protestants in question, but also increasingly by Catholics. It conforms, apparently, to current practice in the individuation of communities, enjoying the legitimation afforded by anthropology, albeit an anthropology rooted in colonial classifications of subject peoples. It is not, however, the only possible answer. Another is that there is, at least potentially, only one community in the North.[1] And just as the Protestant and Catholic communities identified in the first answer can be thought of as parts of wider British and Irish ones respectively, so, in the second, people in the North are thought of as part of a single Irish national community. This, I take it, is an answer that chimes in with a tradition of sociological thought older than that implicated in current practice.[2] It identifies communities not in terms of religion, culture or, indeed, any self-conscious identities or 'aspirations' at all, but rather in terms of their possessing a certain desirable kind of unitary social character.

---

[1] Classically expressed in Wolfe Tone's ambition 'to unite the whole people of Ireland ... and to substitute the common name of Irishman in place of the denominations of Protestant, Catholic and Dissenter' (Butler 1996: 32).

[2] Specifically that tradition stemming from Montesquieu which accords primacy to political rather than cultural factors (Aron 1965: 17-62).

Both answers are to be found in the Good Friday Agreement[3] on the constitutional future of Ireland, incompatible as they would seem to be. Its text constantly vacillates between them, now speaking of two communities in the North, now of one, albeit one with two sections. Such sleight of hand is not surprising given the disagreements between the signatories on how to count the relevant communities. The disagreement in the answers is not, though, a disagreement about how many there are on the basis of an agreed criterion of community. It is a disagreement about how to count communities, arising from different conceptions of what a community is. What I want to ask now is how these different conceptions arise, and what their implications are for the notion of a national community.

I begin with Saint Augustine, on whom I shall blame the inception of cultural nationalism nearly 1400 years before Herder.[4] But, as readers may remember, Augustine starts his discussion of community in *The City of God* by quoting from Cicero's *De Republica*:

> In the case of music for strings or wind, and in vocal music, there is a certain harmony to be kept between the different parts, and if this is altered or disorganized the cultivated ear finds it intolerable; and the united efforts of dissimilar voices are blended into harmony by the exercise of restraint. In the same way a community of different classes, high, low and middle, unites, like the varying sounds of music, to form a harmony of very different parts through the exercise of rational restraint; and what is called harmony in music answers to concord in a community, and it is the best and closest bond of security in a country. And this cannot possibly exist without justice.[5]

Augustine goes on to quote Cicero's definition of a people or community as 'an association united by a common sense of right and a community of interest.'[6] It is a classic statement of the republican conception of a political community. People with common interests arising from their shared situation associate together under a system of justice, on which

---

[3] Concluded on 10 April 1998 through multi-party negotiations in Belfast and implemented by the British and Irish governments following its ratification by referenda in the two parts of Ireland.

[4] Following a hint from Carl J. Friedrich (1959: 7-8). Friedrich sees the 'decisive change in the conception of community', which I go on to elaborate, as one from 'a legal and rational basis' to an 'emotional and spiritual' one. This is at most one aspect of a more far-reaching change.

[5] *De Republica* I 25, quoted in *City of God* II 21 (in the quotations that follow I have used Henry Bettenson's 1972 translation: Augustine 1972).

[6] Ibid. (Augustine treats 'people' and 'community' synonymously since *populus* means a people united in a political community).

they agree as advancing their common interests rather than some sectional interest. Thus, as Augustine goes on to observe, Cicero denies the title of community to people living under a tyrant, a faction, or an oppressive majority, for here there is 'no bond of justice', and hence nothing to fashion people who do have common interests to pursue into a single body fitted to pursue them.

It is this feature of Cicero's republican definition of community that Augustine draws upon later in the book to reach the more radical conclusion 'that commonwealth never existed because there never was real justice in the community' (Augustine 1972: II 21). What are Augustine's reasons for denying the existence of republican communities? They are that *real* justice is to be found only among a community of Christian believers, for

> justice is found where God, the one supreme God, rules an obedient City according to his grace, forbidding sacrifice to any being save himself alone; and where in consequence the soul rules the body in all men who belong to this City and obey God, and the reason faithfully rules the vices in a lawful system of subordination; so that just as the individual righteous man lives on the basis of faith which is active in love, so the association, or people, of righteous men lives on the same basis of faith, active in love, the love with which a man loves God as God ought to be loved, and loves his neighbour as himself. But where this justice does not exist, there is certainly no 'association of men united by a common sense of right and by a community of interest'. Therefore there is no commonwealth; for where there is no 'people', there is no 'weal of the people' (Augustine 1972: XIX 23).

One of the things Augustine is doing here is denying, in a manner reminiscent, as we shall see, of contemporary communitarians, that there can be a system of justice whereby a community's affairs could be regulated irrespective of its members' religions or other cultural attachments. And, furthermore, he is asserting that only the Christian conception of the good life will yield a system that can properly be regarded as a system of justice at all. But this high redefinition of justice leaves Augustine with a problem. For he is not wanting to deny that we can distinguish people or communities in *some* sense from 'any and every association of the population', and he accepts that the Roman state 'certainly was a commonwealth to some degree, according to more plausible definitions' (Augustine 1972: II 21-22). His task, then, is to provide such an alternative definition.

The definition Augustine offers is that 'a people is the association of a multitude of rational beings united by a common agreement on the

objects of their love.' 'It follows,' he continues, 'that to observe the character of a particular people we must examine the objects of its love', and
he concludes that 'by this definition of ours the Roman people is a people and its estate is indubitably a commonwealth.' The same goes, he
comments, for the Athenians or other Greeks, the Assyrians 'or indeed
... any other nation whatsoever' (Augustine 1972: XIX 24). All these
count as communities on the alternative definition, although – as examples of 'the city of the impious' – they are specifically contrasted with the
City of God, which would alone exemplify community as understood on
Cicero's definition. It is, I want to suggest, in this alternative definition of
community that cultural nationalism has its roots; for, instead of locating
what we can think of as the national community in terms of a type of
organization to secure common interests, it identifies it on the basis of
the common character of its members, and this, in turn, is conceived of
as the sharing of values – values which mark out the various nations
from each other. It is here that we see the origins of the dichotomy
between the republican and the cultural nationalist conceptions of community.[7] How exactly does the dichotomy between republican and
cultural nationalism arise? The crucial difference between Cicero and
Augustine is that the former confidently identifies communities in terms
of an *objective* standard. He asks whether their social structures conform
to principles of justice which enable them to pursue shared interests.
Augustine by contrast, in his alternative definition, employs a *subjective*
criterion: do their members agree upon what to value? And this is taken
to be not just a matter of what is observably manifest in their behaviour,
but of how they identify themselves – specifically, perhaps, by the gods
they worship, devotion to which unites them as this or that people. Augustine's criterion is subjective because it is, one might say, a confessional criterion.

　　Why did Cicero and Augustine differ in this way? Cicero maintains a
Stoic conception of justice as recognizable by reason and thus applicable
in any polity, whatever its cultural make-up. Augustine, on the other
hand, rejects the claims of human reason to deliver such an understanding, as a result of the benighted condition of humanity after the Fall:
revealed religion alone will disclose true justice, which can therefore be

---

[7] Throughout this chapter I do not *contrast* republicanism with nationalism as many
authors do, but regard republican nationalism as one possible form of nationalism to
be contrasted with cultural nationalism. For a defence of this position see Gilbert
1998: 81-82.

pursued only by those who possess the appropriate values. This is an historical explanation of the difference between them. It has important repercussions when the Augustinian approach is taken up into Protestant ideas of nations with a mission to pursue the values of the righteous[8] – ideas not yet entirely dead everywhere – and, via an optimistic generalization and secularization of these ideas, into the German Romantic view of nations as forming communities, not through forms of organization which rely on principles common to all human beings, but through forms specific to particular cultures with their distinctive values. This, I suggest, is the history of the dichotomy.

Recent critics like Martin Thom (1995) and Maurizio Viroli (1995) have wanted to emphasize the rupture that occurred around the end of the eighteenth century between an Enlightenment vision of the rational objects of political allegiance and a Romantic dream of its historically sanctioned and culturally compulsory ones – between, that is to say, the civic republicanism rooted in Ciceronian thinking and the cultural nationalism of Herder and Fichte. Not least important in this transition from one form of allegiance to another, differently founded one was a change, noted in particular by Thom, from one type of entity as eliciting allegiance – from the city to the tribe, as Thom calls it. The significance to attach to that change is that under civic republicanism a group is identified in terms of its territorial situation and the shared life which being thrown together with others in that situation brings. Republicanism then sets out an agenda whereby that group can lead a good life together, namely by forming and sustaining a political community in which people are motivated by pursuit of the common good to act justly towards each other. Allegiance essentially consists in having this motivation *vis à vis* the group. Under cultural nationalism, by contrast, the group to which one owes allegiance is picked out as those people whose sharing of values already makes them a community. Allegiance consists in keeping faith, in not departing from the values adherence to which makes it the group it is and departure from which, on any scale, would destroy its collective existence. The change from the city to the tribe as the focus of allegiance is momentous precisely because it imposes preconditions on those with whom one should associate in pursuit of a common good, preconditions which were absent under republicanism. And these preconditions arise

[8] For a discussion of the English case see Adrian Hastings 1997, especially 55-65, 80-95.

from the way the culturally national group is constituted, by contrast
with the potentially republican one, namely by a pre-existing agreement
in values.

So much for these contrasting images of the national community. Let
us now return to Ireland, where, as we can see, it is a republican conception – and not only in the capital 'R' sense – that yields the answer 'One'
to the question of how many communities there are in the North, and,
indeed, in the island of Ireland as a whole; a cultural nationalist conception yields the answer 'Two'. The identity that the North's inhabitants
acknowledge, in the sense in which this is thought relevant to their political organization consists, as I have said, in their membership of one or
other of these supposed communities: a single community conceived in
the republican style, or one of two conceived in cultural terms. Yet to
draw the contrast in this way is potentially misleading. It suggests that it
is only on the cultural nationalist conception, as I have termed it, that
national identity is culturally constituted, and not on the republican one.
This is far from being the case. It is rather, as I shall now set out to
illustrate, that culture itself, as constitutive of politically relevant identities, is thought of differently under the two conceptions.

Under the cultural nationalism that burgeons in the German Romanticism of thinkers like Herder, culture is conceived of as essentially con-
sisting in the manifestation of values which mark out as distinctive a
particular way of life. These values are internalized by individuals as their
national character, and cultural practices and productions are viewed as
reflections of this character. Such a so-called Reflection Theory is widely
recognized to be inadequate, neglecting as it does the fact that cultural
practices and productions are, indeed, just that – things done and made,
and as such subject to the same sorts of explanations as other human
performances, not the mysterious mirrors of tribal affections. The point
is well made, but it is made in the context of what is generally thought of
as a purely academic debate between Reflection Theory (Corse 1997:
Ch.1) and a Social Constructionist view of culture. What I want to claim
is that such apparently academic issues are not politically innocent, and
that Reflection Theory, to start with, belongs together with a particular
view of political identity, the cultural nationalist one. As such it nourishes
certain political claims, particularly partitionist ones, as in Ireland. For if
cultures reflect distinct characters, then 'the mingling of various nations
and human types under one sceptre', as Herder describes it, can only

result in 'a fragile and lifeless contrivance between the separate parts of which no mutual sympathy is possible' (Zimmern 1939: 165). The republican view of culture is completely different. Rather than reflecting a common character that springs from shared values and which thereby makes living together possible, culture, on the republican conception is shaped by people as a means of allowing them to live together amicably. It is what, in the musical image of Cicero quoted earlier, produces a certain harmony ... between the different parts. The laws which provide the community's sense of justice are themselves a prime example of such a culture. For laws on the republican conception, are transparently man-made, unlike the God-given objects of love that bind together the inhabitants of Augustine's City of God or, more generally, the values prior to and presupposed by collective choices that shape the cultural nation.

Yet living under common laws, it will be objected, even laws that are in some sense one's own, can scarcely confer a shared cultural identity. Quite so; more is required, and republican thought acknowledges that a much richer cultural identity needs to be shared for effective membership of a common polity. But what it is for this identity to be shared is not just that cultural characteristics should coincide. Indeed, in many areas of life they may diverge, most notably in the area of the values that characterize religion or personal morality. The republic's members may, as in Cicero's Rome, worship at many altars, not just at one as in the City of God. Rather, then, what is required is that there should be a sharing in the construction of the republic's culture, so that no group that has a part in contributing to its common good is excluded from the building of the shared culture in terms of which this good can be recognized and celebrated.

To illustrate the point, consider the construction of an Irish national culture in the century or so leading to independence. Unlike the Protestants in the North today, the Protestants in Ireland found themselves in a small minority despite their political and economic dominance. Yet they played a key role in seeking to shape an inclusive cultural identity, most particularly in the field of literature, and, towards the end of the period, resisted, successfully as it has turned out, the imposition of a tribal identity that would have excluded them as members of a group no longer dominant in Irish life.

It is, of course, Anglo-Irish writers like Yeats and Synge with whom this cultural movement is particularly associated. Its essentially republican roots lie much earlier in the thought of another Anglo-Irishman, Edmund Burke. It will no doubt seem shocking, in view of Burke's denunciation of the revolution that heralded in the French republic, to describe him as republican. Certainly he often attacked the idea of founding a polity upon abstract rational principles which most republicans, in Ciceronian style, have held. But this idea is not essential to the republican conception as I have introduced it. Under that conception Burke counts as a republican precisely because he thinks of communities as constituted by shared occupation of a particular place under laws designed for the common good (Mehta 1999: 160). Thus in his 'Tracts on the Laws against Popery in Ireland', Burke condemns 'a law against the majority of the people' as 'a law against the people itself' and, as such, 'not particular injustice but general oppression'; for, Burke goes on to affirm, 'in all forms of government the people is the true legislator' (Hampsher-Monk 1981: 71). It is only when the laws can be viewed by this objective test as so originating in popular will that Burke grants them the validity of a system of justice; and this is surely a republican conclusion.

What goes for laws goes for customs generally. Indeed, notoriously Burke rests the authority of law on its basis in the customs of a people. Therein lies his conservatism. It follows that a nation as a community brought together under laws must have a history. For 'a nation is not an idea only of local extent, and individual momentary aggregation' (Mehta 1999: 188). But a national history of this sort is not a static reflection of unchanging character, as Orange parades, for example, are simply continual re-enactments of the same revelatory events of 1689 and 1690. Rather, a republican history narrates what the community has done politically in response to altered circumstances and changed relationships, in struggling for instance against injustice and oppression. And the story is not only one of what is man-made and thus open to further development: it is itself a man-made story, emphasizing some things at the expense of others to tell a narrative with which each member of the community can supposedly associate, and as such it is itself subject to their changing contributions.[9]

It is this requirement that brings us back to the Anglo-Irish writers of the early twentieth century, like Yeats, who sought precisely an historical and literary narrative of the island of Ireland that all its inhabitants could

[9] And this should, of course, despite the gendered appearance of 'man-made', include women.

acknowledge as their own in their present political circumstances. As he enjoined,

> Sing the peasantry and then
> Hard riding country gentlemen,
> The holiness of monks and after
> Porter-drinkers' rowdy laughter ...[10]

A nation cannot exist, he claimed, without 'a model of it in the mind of the people' (Lyons 1979: 49), but this is a model not of a single national character but precisely of a set of relationships between people of very different characters which is formed through a shared history. Thus, Yeats continues,

> Cast your mind on other days
> That we in coming days may be
> Still the indomitable Irishry.

It is a vision in stark contrast to President de Valera's dream of 'a people who value material wealth only as a basis of right living, of a people who were satisfied with frugal comfort and who devoted their leisure to things of the spirit' (Moynihan 1980: 466). And this exemplifies the contrast between the republican and cultural nationalist conceptions of culture.

I have emphasized, perhaps over-emphasized, this contrast. Yet however robust it may be analytically it is, I fear, quite fragile politically. The republican conception, for all its virtues, is always under threat, so that the images produced under it rigidify into those whose reflective function a cultural nationalist could endorse. Even in Yeats we see this happening, so that around the same time as he celebrates diversity and dynamism in the lines just quoted he sees the Easter Rising simply as re-enacting a mythic Gaelic past:

> What stood in the Post Office
> With Pearse and Connolly?
> What comes out of the mountain
> Where men first shed their blood?
> Who thought Cuchulain till it seemed
> He stood where they had stood?[11]

---

[10] 'Under Ben Bulben'.
[11] 'The Death of Cuchulain'.

Here, certainly, it is the supposedly recurrent 'splendour of the Gael' that
is eulogized, rather than 'the first-born of the Coming Race' whom
Yeats's fellow Anglo-Irish poet, George Russell, 'would gladlier hail'.[12]
Russell hails new members of the community because they can initiate
change in 'the image of their communion',[13] in which Russell, anticipat-
ing Benedict Anderson, locates the existence of a nation. And in the Irish
case they can stop that image ossifying into an exclusively Gaelic tribal
one.

  Yet it is because control over cultural production is not straightforwardly vested in each new member of the national community as in the
existing ones that its culture can harden into patterns to which all are
expected to conform, and thereby lose its republican character. It does
so, we may say, because of imperfections in the workings of the puta-
tively republican community itself in which some gain power at the expense of others and maintain it through installing their image of the
community as an homogenizing and unchangeable one. When there is a
contest for dominance then this may become associated with competing
images around which antagonistic identifications build, particularly if, as
in the North of Ireland, they became linked to cultural differences that
elsewhere remain in the private realm. Then conflict can be an easier
option than harmony, partition than integration, and cultural nationalism
develops from the decay of a republican ideal in which even Northern
Protestants once shared.[14]

References
Anderson, Benedict. 1991. *Imagined Communities: Reflections on the Origin and Spread
  of Nationalism*. London: Verso.
Aron, Raymond. 1965. *Main Currents of Sociological Thought I*. Harmondworth:
  Penguin.

[12] We would no Irish sign efface
     And yet our lips would gladlier hail
     The first-born of the Coming Race
     Than the last splendour of the Gael.
       'On Behalf of Some Irishmen Not Followers of Tradition'.
[13] Anderson 1991: 6. Cf. Russell 1937: 183: 'A nation exists primarily because of its
own imagination of itself.'
[14] For example in Wolfe Tone's United Irishmen (see note 1 above).

Augustine. 1972. *Concerning the City of God against the Pagans*, transl. Henry Bettenson. Harmondsworth: Penguin.

Butler, Hubert. 1996. *In the Land of Nod*. Dublin: Lilliput.

Corse, Sarah M. 1997. *Nationalism and Literature*. Cambridge: Cambridge University Press.

Friedrich, Carl J. 1959. *Community*. New York: Liberal Arts Press.

Gilbert, Paul. 1998. *The Philosophy of Nationalism*. Boulder: Westview.

Hampsher-Monk, Iain W. (ed.). *The Political Philosophy of Edmund Burke*. London: Longman.

Kearney, Richard. 1997. *Postnationalist Ireland*. London: Routledge.

Lyons, F.S.C. 1979. *Culture and Anarchy in Ireland 1890-1939*. Oxford: Oxford University Press.

Metha, Uday Singh. 1999. *Liberalism and Empire*. Chicago: University of Chicago Press.

Moynihan, M. (ed.). 1980. *Speeches and Statements of Eamon de Valera 1917-1973*. Dublin: Gill and Macmillan.

Russell, G.W. 1937. *The Living Torch*. London: Macmillan.

Thom, Martin. 1995. *Republics, Nations and Tribes*. London: Verso.

Viroli, Maurizio. 1995. *For Love of Country*. Oxford: Clarendon Press.

Zimmern, Alfred (ed.). 1939. *Modern Political Doctrines*. London: Oxford University Press.

CHAPTER 8

'PAR LES YEUX PARLER À L'INTELLIGENCE':
THE VISUALIZATION OF THE PAST
IN NINETEENTH-CENTURY BELGIUM

Tom Verschaffel

The practical use to which history can be put is advanced in almost every handbook on the subject. Every author who has pronounced about the way history should be written and read has underlined that history should aim at *utilitas*, and that utility is held to be realistically obtainable, providing of course that the history is written and read in the correct manner. According to traditional ideas expressed throughout the early modern period, but also reaching back to antiquity, what one finds in history books has been thought to be useful. In its simplest form, this means that the reader is capable of applying the lessons of history in his or her own life. If s/he finds himself in a given situation, he should think of an exemplary historical figure who has been in the same circumstances ('dans les pareilles conjonctures') (Dufresnoy 1713, 3). Depending on the way, good or bad, in which the 'example' acted, the reader should decide how s/he should act. This implies that the history consumer can only be interested in a limited number of very specific parts of history and of history writing at any one time. Ideally there should be many different histories, for many different readers.[1] It also implies that the only persons really interested in history are those confronted in their own lives with situations comparable to the ones in the history books. Thus, if princes are the main characters in history, princes should also be the main readers. It has been said that history is meant in the first place for current and future kings. They, more than anyone else, have to learn history's lessons.[2]

---

[1] Bolingbroke 1752, 46: 'We ought to apply, and, the shortness of human life considered, to confine ourselves almost entirely in our study of history, to such histories as have an immediate relation to our professions, or to our rank and situation in the society to which we belong'.

[2] E.g. Bossuet 1961, 665: 'quand l'histoire serait inutile aux autres hommes, il faudrait la faire lire aux princes'.

In the course of the history of history, its ideal and real audience has changed, and therefore the definitions of its utility, as well as the means believed necessary to achieve the goals, have had to be adapted to new situations and contexts. In the eighteenth century, the reading public was 'a widening circle' (Darnton, Fabian & McKeen Wiles 1976). Should the 'new' readers be excluded from 'consuming' history then? Of course not. So the theoreticians of the *Geschichtsdidaktik*[3] had to safeguard their utilitarianism by pointing out that in fact everybody had a function in society and thus in politics (as was argued in England),[4] or by pleading in favour of the thematic diversification of historiography. Not only princes and high-ranking officials should read history fruitfully, not only magistrates and bishops, but also ordinary priests, teachers and others, and even fathers and mothers; 'en un mot tous ceux qui ont quelque autorité sur les autres' (Rollin 1732, 5). In fact every citizen can become a better citizen by reading history.

The public scope and the functions of history shifted even more, and certainly more fundamentally, in the nineteenth century. History was no longer meant only for individuals, but also for the nation and its members. In the new-born nation states of the nineteenth century, such as Belgium, which had become independent as the result of its revolution in 1830, history was of course the *national* history. It had to legitimate the existence of the nation as an independent state by developing the argument that in fact the country had always existed as an entity and a unity. The revolution and independence was not the beginning of Belgian history; on the contrary, it was the end of it, its glorious conclusion, its culmination point. The whole national view of the Belgian past was determined by the fact that independence was the 'goal' (the *telos*) of the past. This history was therefore considered as one long struggle against foreign occupations and for freedom, a struggle that began with the first occupation by the Romans and Julius Caesar who wrote of the *Belgae*, with whom the modern Belgians identified, and which came to an end in 1830. Then – at last – the Belgians obtained what they had pursued for about nineteen centuries. History as a social actor was meant to inspire

---

[3] Pandel 1990, especially p. 25: 'Geschichtsdidaktisches Denken ist integraler Bestandteil der theoretischen Reflexion der Fachhistorie'.
[4] E.g. Bolingbroke 1752, 49: 'The sum of what I have been saying is, that in free governments, the public service is not confined to those whom the prince appoints to the different posts in the administration under him; that there the care of the state is the care of multitudes'.

the Belgians with this idea of their history, with identification with the forefathers, and with pride for what the Belgians *themselves* had been able to do in the past. In short: history was intended to propagate patriotism. The history consumers thus were addressed *as* Belgians. The lessons of history did not consist of what was specific for the reader's social and the individual position, and thus could not be different for different readers. Now history's meaning and message was essentially the same for all readers, at least for all those who belonged to the nation, since it was exactly in this capacity that they were addressed. Not only the meaning of the national history, but also its importance, was equal for every member of the nation. So literally every Belgian, every citizen, had to be reached by historiography.

Clearly historiography needed to be interpreted in a broad sense of the word. For the eighteenth century English writer Lord Bolingbroke, useful history should be within the reach of 'every man who can read and think' (Bolingbroke 1752, 4). Neither in the eighteenth nor the nineteenth century did this mean literally everybody. But to fulfil its nineteenth-century mission, history needed to reach literally everybody, including those who did not read history books, or could not read at all. The national interpretation of the past therefore had to be presented in other forms than 'real' history writing, in other forms that were noticeable and comprehensible to a larger audience. History and its messages had to be presented in texts other than historiographical ones: in historical novels for instance, but also in non-written, *visual* forms.

All kinds of cultural and artistic production were summoned to come to the aid of the nation and its drive towards the generalization of patriotism, this 'grande entreprise de glorification nationale' (Dasnoy 1948, 169; see also Ogonovszky-Steffens 1999). Artists were stimulated by the authorities, by cultural institutions, and by poets and journalists to serve their nation (Etlin 1991). 'La patrie a droit au pinceau de ses enfants, comme à la lyre des poètes', Alexandre Pinchart wrote in his *De la peinture historique en Belgique* (1845, 5). Every artist was urged to illustrate the national history. It was his mission. The visual arts partly took over the role of historiography (Flacke 1998; and especially Koll 1998). And according to their potential, 'la puissance de l'art',[5] they might not only reach an audience that did not read history books, but also might be more effective and impressive than texts could be, at least for an audience that was

---

[5] Charles Rogier (1848), quoted in Album 1849, 11.

more or less 'illiterate'. Patriotism was believed to be a religion: 'cette religion qui s'appelle l'amour de la patrie' (Fetes 1848, v). Visual representations of the national past then could be considered a kind of 'biblia pauperorum'.

Throughout the Romantic works of art a large but specific iconography was developed, an ensemble of visualization of the past with a national, patriotic and educational programme, and with suitable strategies and rhetorics. These visual rhetorics were to a certain extent specific for the genres, such as the statues that were erected in large quantities, and the enormous historical paintings that were so admired at the time.[6] I shall concentrate here, however, on book illustrations, engravings that were made for historical publications from around the middle of the century. These images were thus reproduced in books, and therefore meant to be seen by people who did indeed read historical texts. However they are in themselves valuable sources for the research concerning the rhetoric of images. The iconography of these engravings reflects, sometimes in a rather explicit way, images that have been 'invented' by the history painters. They can be considered a form in which their work is reproduced, distributed, sometimes slightly transformed and adapted to be used in a slightly different context, but at the same time standardized in a way which enabled them to consolidate their place in the collective memory of the nation. They had to be created in large series, for some of these history books had to have hundreds of engravings, and therefore they had to be created by large numbers of draughtsmen and engravers, not all of whom could possibly be 'great' or even inspired artists. The engravings often seem to be mere variations on other examples, and thus seem to be standardized or even in a sense mechanized. These ensembles of illustrations thus reveal, even better than individual paintings, the mechanisms that make these images work.

These works were 'Romantic' – Romanticism then being, as Martin Meisel (1984) has put it, 'the art of effect'. Romantic art wanted to influence, to convince, to change the audience, using national historical culture to make its 'consumers' more patriotic than they were before. The spectator therefore gets no choice. He is expected to identify himself

---

[6] Some of these paintings, with subjects such as *The September Days* (an episode from the Belgian Revolution) by Gustave Wappers, *The Battle of Woeringen* and *The Battle of the Golden Spurs* by Nicaise de Keyser, *Les têtes coupées* (the last tribute to Egmont and Hoorn) by Louis Gallait, or the allegorical *La Belgique couronnant ses enfants illustres* by Eduard de Biefve, made tours, even abroad, and were seen by many people.

with the historical individuals or groups that are presented to him. And he actually did so, because he was indeed impressed by the possibility of seeing the past; he was manipulated by the artist, who was giving his public not just a place in historical scenes, but a particular place (Verschaffel 1987, especially 47-64).

In every traditional visual 'scene', the spectator has a point of view. This point of view is chosen and fixed by the artist, and cannot be changed by the viewer. This point of view is to be understood literally: it is the position of the viewer in the represented scene, the spatial relation, the short distance between the eyes of the spectator and what he has to focus upon. The choice of this point of view is of course a means of creating an involvement concerning the meaning of what is shown and seen. The spectator is impressed by the nearness of the past, of kings and heroes, but there are many other, more specific, feelings at stake. The viewer is intended to admire the heroes he sees, who are so close that he can almost touch them. He is to be excited by the fact that he is present at important or even crucial events in the glorious history of his country, present at moments and in places where it is in fact impossible to be, not only because the evoked past has gone for good, but also because no-one else besides the main characters was actually present at the occasion. The spectator attends secret meetings and confessions, and is always there at the right moment. He attends murders and conspiracies, and is there exactly when it happens. Thus the spectator is not only present, and a privileged witness; he even is a participant in the historical events. The nineteenth-century Belgian, looking at the visualizations of the history which he is intended to consider to be his own, is taking part in what has been happening. He is in the middle of the battle scenes. And he is not only near the historical characters, but also with them, on their side. An oft-recited episode in Romantic Belgian history is the one in which Klaas Zannekin, the leader of a popular rising in Western Flanders in the fourteenth century, managed to enter the enemy army's camp, disguised as a fishmonger. The spectator knows who the fishmonger is; the soldiers to whom he is talking do not. The spectator is not going to betray the hero, for he is his accomplice (see Figure 1).

Verschaffel

Figure 8.1. Nicolaas Zannekin disguised as a fishmonger in the enemy's camp. Source: From *Fastes militaires des Belges*, vol. III (1835).

If there is an opposition in the image, if there are Belgians on one side, and enemies on the other, the spectator is located clearly on the Belgian side (Figure 2). He is shooting with his countrymen, fighting with them. Even when they are victims, the spectator shares their fate (Figure 3). For example, when the Viking marauders are returning to their ships, carrying off the Belgian chattels, leaving a murdered corpse and his distraught wife, the spectator stays 'here', watching the villains disappear (Figure 4).

Figure 8.2. A scene from the crusades: the siege of Arsuf. Our viewpoint is the hill occupied by compatriot-crusaders; the enemy is on the 'other' side. Source: T. Juste, *Histoire de Belgique*, 3rd ed., vol. I (1850).

Figure 8.3. The battle of Turnhout (1789), part of the Brabant Revolution against the Austrian Emperor Joseph II. The viewer shares the position of the revolutionaries. Source: *Les Belges illustres*, vol. I (1844).

Figure 8.4. The Vikings leaving the country, after a raid. The spectator is left behind with the Belgian victims. Source: H.G. Moke, *Abrégé de l'histoire de Belgique*, 15th ed. (1887).

The explicitness is characteristic of this kind of national Romanticism. The importance of the 'meaning' and the 'message' drives the artist towards what we now see as melodrama, over-acting, and an excess of theatricality. Many book illustrations seem to show a opera stage, filled with stage properties, and populated with 'actors' who, well aware of the fact that they are being watched and have to make things clear, express their feelings with almost ridiculous exaggeration. Sometimes the images seem to depict a scene from a stage-play enactment of a historical event, rather than the event itself.

Illustrators have an undeniable preference for sumptuous events, such as coronations and abdications, and for episodes in which death (in its many forms) plays an essential part. These are considered to have a self-evident emotional impact, and therefore to be 'impressive' and 'effective'. If one sees the national history passing by in a long series of illustrations, that history appears as extremely violent, as an endless sequence of murders, battles and sieges, bouts of single combat, executions, mornings-after on the battlefield where the corpses of the famous are discovered, mourning session at death-beds, and funerals. The impact of these scenes is amplified by the choice of the moment at which the episode, the event, is 'frozen' and represented. As a critic wrote in 1841,

La peinture n'est pas comme l'histoire, qui raconte les faits tels qu'ils se sont succédé et nous place sous les yeux une suite d'événements. Moins heureux, le peintre ne peut fixer sur la toile qu'un seul fait et il est de la plus grande importance, pour le succès de son oeuvre, qu'il sache faire son choix avec discernement et avec goût (Voisin 1841, 20-1).

Figure 8.5. The crusaders take Jerusalem. The moment represented is the one in which the 'first' Christian sets foot on the city walls. Source: T. Juste, *Histoire de Belgique*, 3rd ed., vol. I (1850).

Figure 8.6. Clovis killing Alarik, King of the Visigoths, at the battle of Poitiers (507 AD). The axe is about to fall. Source: *Histoire de la Belgique en images* (1894).

The artist had to try to represent an episode, a story, a certain duration, by showing only one 'moment', by fixing only one glance. It was a problem of 'uniting picture and narrative, the moment and its significance', of combining 'a temporal subject and an atemporal medium' (Meisel 1984, 18-19). In order to recognize and to understand the event, the spectator is of course assisted by his previous knowledge (the stories he already knows), by the texts the images are intended to illustrate, and by the titles they sometimes have. Moreover episodes can be recognized by the combination of various types of personages, attitudes, attributes, and gestures. These elements are deliberately chosen by the artist, to make obvious what the story is and what it means. The body-language of the main characters normally reveals what is happening; the time-frozen gesture is what is going on. The moment chosen to 'stop' the action is often the emotional climax. The death of a historical character can be represented by the moment at which he is not yet dead, but is just about to die. The axe is in the air, just about to fall, just about to kill. It is the tensest, the most thrilling moment of the action, which is the clash between the two protagonists in the middle of a large mêlée of simultaneous action; at the same time, it is the second in which a larger episode, which is the battle, or even the war, is condensed. The decisive, the crucial moment of the battle is represented (Figures 5 and 6). Everything is intended to thrill the spectator, to invite or even to force him to have certain feelings, to share the fear, the excitement, the pride, the courage and the resoluteness he recognizes in the heroes, who are representatives of his own people and nation; in short to empathize with his forefathers in action.

This also was the purpose of another expression of this Romantic historical culture, namely the historical cortege (Verschaffel 1996). This form was especially popular in nineteenth-century Belgium. History, and sometimes the national past as a whole, was represented in a limited number of scenes or *tableaux vivants*, sometimes staged on big wagons, and by a large number of actors, personifying historical characters. It was a form which, unlike the history book, was not meant for individual consumers, but for an audience of masses, and therefore specifically 'popular'. Edmond de Busscher, who was responsible for the content and the composition of one of the first corteges, in Ghent in 1849, defined the genre as, tableaux vivants des pages les plus mémorables de nos chroniques, cette narration sommaire doit se graver facilement dans la mémoire, et par les yeux parler à l'intelligence: c'est de l'histoire en action (Busscher 1849, 4).

De Busscher explicitly stated that these corteges were meant to educate the people of all classes of society.

History represented in a cortege did impress, not only because it was spectacular, but also because it showed history as real and living. The nineteenth-century audience was not used to modern illusory effects, and the viewer could get the illusion that the past was present, that he could actually see and even touch it. For a moment the susceptible viewer could get the illusion of being in the past. A journalist, enthusing about a cortege of 1856, wrote, 'n'êtes-vous pas en plein moyen-âge?'[7] This living history was, on the other hand, not much more than an illusion, and photographs, as well as more critical descriptions of the time, make clear how easily the illusion could be shattered (Verschaffel 1996).

The images of the national past, in book illustrations but also in the scenes of corteges and stage plays that belonged to the same tradition of Romantic iconography, have proven to be enduring, even without the texts they were intended to accompany and to illustrate. The engravings were often used subsequently in books other than the ones they first appeared in, and many of them eventually ended up in *L'histoire de la Belgique en images*, a collection of historical images, without accompanying text (not even an introduction), and obviously intended for use in schools.

We can conclude with the consideration that the idea of the effectiveness of images, and of their power in providing a large and historically untrained audience with historical illusion, has led to their use in instruction and education, and to the belief that the use of images is a suitable means of reaching children and providing them with impressions of the peculiarity and the strangeness of the past. Illustrations in the books that were used until quite recently in primary education, and the large school posters showing scenes from life in the old days, or of episodes of the great events of the national history, reflect the iconography that was developed in the Romantic era.

History handbooks still are illustrated of course, but the modern way of doing so is by showing visual source material by means of photo-

---

[7] In *Le Bien Public* (25 July 1856).

graphs: by displaying what has been found, and what there still is to see. The visual reconstruction of the past, of historical characters and scenes in images and *tableaux vivants,* is no longer practised in an academic or educational context. The historical illusion now is left to the imagination of the onlooker or pupil. The re-enactment of the past is channelled towards the domains of folklore and entertainment. At least, that was the case within the context of modernism; perhaps the postmodern will reallow certain kinds of reconstruction, even including the presentation of history as virtual reality.

References

Album. 1949. *Album du salon de 1848 par une société d'artistes et gens de lettres.* Brussels.

Bolingbroke, Lord [Henry St. John]. 1752. *Letters on the Study and Use of History.* London: Millar.

Bossuet, J.B. 1961. *Discours sur l'histoire universelle,* in *Oeuvres,* ed. Abbé Velat & Yvonne Champallier. Paris: Gallimard.

Busscher, Edmond de. 1849. *Description du cortège historique des comtes de Flandre.* Ghent: De Busscher.

Darnton, Robert, Bernhard Fabian & Roy McKeen Wiles. 1976. *The Widening Circle: Essays on the Circulation of Literature in Eighteenth Century Europe.* Philadelphia: University of Pennsylvania Press.

Dasnoy, Albert. 1948. *Les beaux jours du romantisme belge.* [Brussels: JaRic.]

Dufresnoy, Nicolas Lenglet. 1713. *Méthode pour étudier l'histoire, où après avoir établi les principes & l'ordre qu'on doit tenir pour la lire utilement, on fait les remarques necessaires pour ne pas se laisser tromper dans le lecture.* Paris: Gandouin.

Etlin, Richard A. (ed.). 1991. *Nationalism in the Visual Arts.* Washington: National Gallery of Art.

Fêtes. 1848. *Les fêtes de septembre illustrées, ou description historique et pittoresque du grand cortège national, suivi du compte rendu des fêtes et cérémonies publiques. XVIIIe anniversaire de l'indépendance belge.* Brussels: Jamar.

Flacke, Monica (ed.). 1998. *Mythen der Nationen. Ein Europäisches Panorama.* Berlin: Deutsches Historisches Museum.

Koll, Johannes. 1998. 'Belgien. Geschichtskultur und nationale Identität' in Flacke, Monica (ed.). 1998. *Mythen der Nationen. Ein Europäisches Panorama.* Berlin: Deutsches Historisches Museum: 53-77.

Meisel, Martin. 1984. *Realizations: Narrative, Pictorial and Theatrical Arts in Nineteenth-Century England.* Princeton: Princeton University Press.

Ogonovszky-Steffens, Judith. 1999. *La peinture monumentale d'histoire dans les édifices civils en Belgique, 1830-1914.* Brussels: Académie Royale de Belgique.

Pandel, Hans-Jürgen. 1990. *Historik und Didaktik. Das Problem der Distribution historiographisch erzeugten Wissens in der deutschen Geschichtswissenschaft von der Spätaufklärung zum Frühhistorismus (1765-1830)*. Stuttgart/Bad Cannstatt: Frommann-Holzboog.

Pinchart, Alexandre. 1845. *De la peinture historique en Belgique*. S.l.

Rollin, Charles. 1732. *De la manière d'enseigner et d'étudier les belles lettres, par rapport à l'esprit & au coeur*, vol.3: *De l'histoire*. Amsterdam: Aux dépens de la Compagnie.

Verschaffel, Tom. 1987. *Beeld en geschiedenis. Het Belgische en Vlaamse verleden in de romantische boekillustraties*. Turnhout: Brepols.

Verschaffel, Tom. 1996. 'Het verleden tot weinig herleid. De historische optocht als vorm van de romantische verbeelding', in Tollebeek, Jo, Frank Ankersmit and Wessel Krul (eds), *Romantiek en historische cultuur*. Groningen: Historische Uitgeverij: 297-320.

Voisin, Auguste. 1841. *Abdication de Charles-Quint, par M. Louis Gallait. Légende historique et description*. Ghent, second edition.

CHAPTER 9

THE SCHIZOPHRENIA OF AN ICON:
THE IMPACT OF *THYL UYLENSPIEGEL* ON NATIONAL
AND GENDER IDENTITIES IN BELGIUM IN THE
NINETEENTH AND TWENTIETH CENTURIES[1]

Marnix Beyen

Figure 9.1. Book cover, Frans Notelaar, *Uilenspiegel* [1944].

Shortly after the liberation of Belgium from Nazi occupation in 1944, at least three different books with anti-German jokes or anecdotes appeared in Flanders with very similar cover illustrations. They all show a jester-like figure, mocking the German soldiers or even aiming kicks at

---

[1]   Unless otherwise stated, the information contained in this chapter is taken from Beyen 1988, where extensive bibliographical references can be found.

Hitler himself (Figure 1). This jester figure represents Thyl Uylenspiegel, a legendary folk-hero who was thought to symbolize the Belgian spirit of resistance against the Germans. This association was not surprising for during the occupation several illegal resistance newspapers had used the name of that same Uylenspiegel as the title, or as the *nom de plume* of the editor. Among the Belgian exiles in London, too, Thyl Uylenspiegel had been lauded as the 'Belgian national hero, always mischievous, always gay, always ready to fight for liberty.'

Figure 9.2. Poster, 'De asche van Claes', 1942.

Yet this same Uylenspiegel had also appeared during the Second World War in entirely different contexts and shapes. On a poster which adorned the Flemish streets in the autumn of 1942 he was depicted with his typically medieval clothes, but this time as an heroic and stern-looking figure, rather than as a jolly jester (Figure 2). The background, formed by the logos of the SS and the Flemish heraldic lion, clearly informs the message written underneath: 'Uylenspiegel summons you too for the Waffen-SS', recruiting soldiers to fight the Bolsheviks on the eastern front. The extreme right-wing and collaborationist Flemish nationalist parties had supported that campaign since the summer of 1941.

We are therefore confronted with two similar images referring to two identities diametrically opposed to each other – an observation which is all the more striking since neither was a singular or marginal case. Thyl Uylenspiegel as the resistance hero and Thyl Uylenspiegel as the collaborationist were both quite widespread and therefore recognizable icons – and they both were the logical outcome of pre-war developments. The case of Uylenspiegel therefore seems to underpin the view that images are empty boxes that can be filled at will by diverging ideologies, and that they can be manipulated freely in order to construct identities. In this essay, I shall sketch a genealogy of the Uylenspiegel theme in the Belgian political and cultural landscape of the nineteenth and twentieth centuries, and move towards the conclusion that the role of images in the shaping of identities is not necessarily a merely passive and instrumental one, but that it can also be creative and dynamic.

A volatile national hero

The birth of the Uylenspiegel figure as a jolly jester goes as far back as the fifteenth century at least, and took place in the north of Germany, where to this day Uylenspiegel has retained his primarily farcical character (e.g. Janssens 1998). Next to - and only partly derived from - this buffoon Uylenspiegel, however, a more serious and militant Uylenspiegel grew up, the one that would become both a resistance fighter and a collaborationist, but which at an earlier stage had already been a powerful revolutionary icon in Soviet Russia. The roots of this particular Uylenspiegel are not to be found in late medieval Germany, but in nineteenth-century Belgium.

The spiritual father of the political Uylenspiegel was Charles De Coster, a Francophone Belgian journalist and writer who belonged to the leftist Liberal political and literary *avant-garde* of Brussels.[2] In these progressive milieus, the Uylenspiegel figure was already in use before De Coster took him up, serving as the spokesman of good-humoured, anti-bourgeois satire. Even if Uylenspiegel was often labelled in this context

[2] For a biography of De Coster, see Trousson 1990.

as a 'national' figure (embodying a humorous frankness considered to be
typically Belgian), this satirical use of the figure was not a Belgian monopoly, since it appeared also in Dutch liberal circles of that time. That
was to change drastically at the end of 1867, when De Coster's *magnum
opus*, the *Légende d'Ulenspiegel* appeared.[3] Originally, De Coster had wanted
this book to be a mere literary adaptation of the old folkloristic tale, but
while writing it, he had come under the influence of the tumultuous
political events of his time. Not only had the tension between Catholics
and liberals suddenly increased because of the Papal encyclical *Quanta
Cura* and the *Syllabus Errorum*, but the imperialist politics of the French
Emperor Napoleon III had also given rise to a widespread fear for the
survival of Belgium as an independent state.

Impressed by these events and obviously inspired by a political pamphlet in which Uylenspiegel was staged as the spirit of national resistance
against French imperialism (Beyen 2003a), De Coster steered his work in
a firmly political direction. The *Légende d'Ulenspiegel* starts off as a
folkloristic tale about Uylenspiegel's well-known jests, but in the course
of the *Légende*, he gets involved in the renowned sixteenth-century revolt
of the Netherlands Provinces against the Spanish ruler, Philip II. He
evolves into a dauntless hero for freedom, against Catholic obscurantism
and political tyranny. Although the book was a literary masterpiece much
more than a political pamphlet, it was clear to all that Philip II stood for
Napoleon III, and that the rebellious Seventeen Provinces represented
poor threatened Belgium. No less obvious were the parallels between the
struggle depicted in the *Légende* and the ongoing disputes between Catholics and liberals in late nineteenth-century Belgium (Strikwerda 1997).

A source of many of the later ambiguities resided in the fact that De
Coster called his hero 'the spirit of Flanders'. With that term, he referred
not to the Dutch-speaking part of Belgium (as was becoming common in
De Coster's own lifetime), but to the older Duchy of Flanders, which in
medieval European history had played such a prominent role. Most of
all, however, De Coster's use of the word Flanders was symbolic: it
represented, as it did for many Belgian intellectuals at that time, the
principle of freedom which had been the main key to the historical great-
ness of the Low Countries, and which since 1830 had been embodied in
independent Belgium. In that perspective, Flanders and Belgium were

---

[3] On the gestation of this novel, which has often been considered the birth of
Belgian national literature as such, see Beyen 2003.

THE SCHIZOPHRENIA OF AN ICON

synonymous. De Coster's vision was not very different from that of the so-called Flamingants, who at that moment wanted to protect the Flemish language and culture in order to support Belgium by stressing its non-French identity.

By the last decade of the nineteenth century, when the *Légende d'Ulenspiegel* was finally discovered on a larger scale, this identification between Belgium and Flanders had become more problematic. The first Flemish adaptations of the theme, written by liberal Flamingants around the end of the century, were not as yet overtly anti-Belgian, but they did nevertheless suggest a certain resentment against a Belgian state unwilling to listen to Flemish demands. In the first place, however, they contained anti-clerical complaints against the Catholic Church, which was judged responsible for the backwardness of Flanders.

Shortly after these liberal versions, however, the first Catholic adaptations of the theme appeared, in which Uylenspiegel preached the traditional message of Catholic Flamingantism, as it had existed since the mid-nineteenth century. The quintessence of that message was that Flanders had to maintain its Flemish character in order to keep out the French secularizing tendencies. Obviously, in this clerical narrative, Uylenspiegel could not be staged as a hero of the anti-Catholic rebellion of the sixteenth century. He was therefore transferred to the late eighteenth century and made into a hero of the conservative struggle of the peasants against the French Revolutionary armies. Apart from that transposition, however, the framework of De Coster's story remained intact. Unlike De Coster's original, which figured on the Papal Index until the mid-1950s, this Catholic version of the story became immensely popular in Flanders before and during the First World War.

Not surprisingly, the Uylenspiegel theme gained momentum considerably at that time. The German occupation of Belgium offered an obvious parallel with the Spanish domination of the Low Countries in the late sixteenth century. The same author who had conceived the Catholic Uylenspiegel as fighting the French revolutionaries - Jan Bruylants, *alias* Auctor - now transferred his hero to the trenches of Flanders, fighting Prussian soldiers (Figure 3). And yet, the war circumstances also engendered a totally different Uylenspiegel. In a small group called the Activists, who believed they could liberate Flanders from the Belgian yoke by collaborating with the German occupier, De Coster's *Légende* was eagerly read and Uylenspiegel was discovered as the symbol *par excellence* of the Eternal Flanders for which they fought.

Figure 9.3. Illustration, Jan Bruylants, *Tijl Uilenspiegel aan het front
en onder de Duitschers*, 1921.

This anti-Belgian appropriation of De Coster's Uylenspiegel was not
confined to the liberal Flamingants. Catholic Activists, too, discovered –
in spite of the papal interdict – De Coster's *Légende* through German
translations. The anti-clerical aspects of the book were considered acceptable in the light of its strong Flemish-national potential, thus demonstrating that only during the First World War did a genuine Flemish
nationalism come into being, in the sense that only then did the Flemish
aspirations prevail over more general, ideological allegiance. Moreover,

these Flemish aspirations were for the first time overtly directed against the Belgian state.[4]

Notwithstanding the fact that the Activists consisted initially of a marginal group, they set the tone for the large-scale radicalization of Flemish nationalism during the interwar period. Not only was the anti-Belgian character of Flemish nationalism reinforced; it also became heavily imbued with anti-democratic, right-wing tendencies. Even if the ecclesiastical authorities protested against this evolution, right-wing Flemish nationalism found its advocates first and foremost among Catholics, who grafted their traditional anti-modern resentments onto this new, anti-Belgian and anti-democratic form of nationalism. Flanders, for them, was the heart of sound and Catholic mores, and was to be protected against the onslaughts not only of French secularization, but also of Belgian democracy.

Figure 9.4. Poster, Paul de Bruyne, 1952.

[4] On the complex story of nation-building in Belgium, see e.g. Vos & Deprez 1998.

Thyl Uylenspiegel, too, followed this evolution of Flemish nationalism. Time and time again, he was staged at Flemish national events and
electoral campaigns, and gradually he was invested with other elements
of the Flemish national imagination. One of the most elaborate versions
of this nationalist Uylenspiegel was presented on a drawing dating from
as late as 1953 (Figure 4). The hero is represented against the background of the IJzer tower – the most monumental *lieu de mémoire* of
Flemish nationalism - inscribed with the telling words, 'All for Flanders,
Flanders for Christ', with the Flemish lion on his chest, and surrounded
by other Flemish national symbols. De Coster's hero of tolerance and
liberty had become the symbol of an essentialist and therefore intolerant
and exclusivist nationalism – as had also been made clear during the
Flemish nationalist electoral campaign of 1939, when Uylenspiegel was
shown chasing away not only Communists, liberals, and the Francophone bourgeoisie of Flanders. Thus the SS Uylenspiegel of the occupation period was far from being a sudden or unique derailment.

Figure 9.5. Rally Poster, Flemish Communist Party, 1939.

During that same 1939 campaign, however, Uylenspiegel figured in a very similar way on a Communist placard, where he was chasing away the fascists of the Flemish national party (Figure 5). It is not improbable that this Communist use of the story was conceived in response to the 1937 directive from Moscow to adopt a pro-Flemish profile. That Uylenspiegel was employed in this context was hardly surprising, for ever since the 1920s De Coster's *Légende* had been quasi-officialized as an anti-capitalist and revolutionary Bible by Russia's new rulers. This Communist use of Uylenspiegel would also last until well into the 1970s.

Next to these evidently ideological uses of the Uylenspiegel story, a more liberal version of Uylenspiegel was safeguarded, not so much by a political party as by Belgian intellectuals, mainly of Liberal, but also of social-democratic or even Catholic signature. These intellectuals presented themselves as the true heirs of De Coster, and rejected the Flemish nationalist and – to a lesser degree – Communist versions of Uylenspiegel as perversions of the original message proclaimed by the nineteenth-century author. The only *real* Uylenspiegel, they claimed, was the fighter for freedom and tolerance shaped by De Coster, and they railed against the shameless, ideological misuse of an image they considered to be pure and noble.

In reality, this charge of misuse was not entirely legitimate. It cannot be denied that the right-wing, Flemish nationalist Uylenspiegel was the carrier of a political message as far removed from De Coster's explicit views as possible. However, *La Légende* itself contained some of the germs of this later evolution. For as well as being Belgian-patriotic, anti-clerical and to a certain extent anti-capitalist, the *Légende d'Ulenspiegel* was first and foremost Romantic. The connection that was made by De Coster between the nation and liberty brought to mind Schiller and Mazzini more than eighteenth-century Enlightenment thought. The nation was not considered a contract between citizens, designed to safeguard basic human rights, but an eternal principle – or at least a historical continuum - embodying the principle of liberty. De Coster's Uylenspiegel was shaped as the perfect personification of this principle. At several places in the book he is presented as 'eternal' or even 'eternally young'. That characteristic becomes most manifest in the last pages of the book. Uylenspiegel, considered dead, is being buried, when suddenly he wakes up, saying, 'Can one bury Uylenspiegel, the spirit of Flanders? He too can sleep, but die? Never!' What Ernest Gellner once called the Sleeping

Beauty motif of Romantic nationalism is illustrated here in a most striking way.

The idea that Uylenspiegel was the carrier of eternity, and therefore
of historical continuity, was also conveyed by his recurrent battle-cry,
'the ashes of Claes beat on my chest'. Claes was Uylenspiegel's father,
who was burned at the stake by the Spanish Inquisition. Uylenspiegel had
filled a little bag with his ashes, which he hung on a string around his
neck. His particular battle-cry therefore suggested that his struggle was
incited to a large degree by feelings of revenge, and of respect and loyalty
towards his father. At a metaphorical level, Claes represented the long
line of forefathers, which made up the Flemish and therefore the Belgian
nation. The struggle for national freedom was, in the view of De Coster
and many of his contemporaries, not so much a rational option towards
a better future as a necessary act of piety towards the forefathers. It was
precisely this Romantic and backward-looking view of the nation that
would deliver the core of the integral nationalism which reigned during
the first half of the twentieth century, whereby the sense of historical
continuity would increasingly be complemented or even replaced by a
sense of biological, racial continuity. Combined with the inherent ambiguities of the term Flanders as used by De Coster, and with the fact that
this intransigent form of nationalism was adhered to by many Catholics
for mainly anti-modern reasons, the evolution of Uylenspiegel from a
liberal Belgian patriot to a Catholic and reactionary nationalist was far
from illogical. Not surprisingly, the sentences about the ashes of Claes,
and those about Uylenspiegel's eternity, were the ones most often repeated by the Flemish nationalists. Even the Waffen-SS referred to this
theme in the poster in Figure 2, in the hope of gaining new recruits from
Flanders.

During this process, Flemish nationalists and more moderate Flamingants alike seem to have been manipulated by Uylenspiegel at least as
much as he was manipulated by them. Or, to be more precise, Uylenspiegel as shaped by De Coster articulated, visualized and therefore reinforced the largely pre-reflexive ideas of many nationalists about the essence of the nation. It was, of course, not the image of Uylenspiegel that
created the idea of an eternal and therefore exclusive nation, but it certainly did contribute to the persistence and to the broad popularity of
that idea. Uylenspiegel had, in this respect, the additional advantage of
his folkloristic and popular roots – and of the fact that this folkloristic
image persisted along with the more political one. Thanks to that

equivocity, Uylenspiegel remained a ready-at-hand hero, not monopolized by a sectarian group of extreme nationalists, but accessible to all people who considered themselves Flamingant. The image of Uylenspiegel contributed therefore not only to the radicalization, but also to the dissemination and 'banalization' of an integralist form of nationalism (Billig 1997). During World War II, Uylenspiegel was ubiquitous in the everyday Flamingant culture of that time. The fierceness of this attachment was (and is still) attested among other things by the small wooden statues of Thyl and his beloved Nele adorning thousands of Flamingant chimneys, or by the equally numerous stained-glass windows representing the same idyllic couple. Right up to the 1960s, many Flamingants were undoubtedly familiar with the image of Uylenspiegel and the connotations it bore, as much as with explicit concepts of Flemish history or Flemish identity. In this case, therefore, image seemed to precede identity.

Gender purism

The determining character of the Uylenspiegel image also became manifest in another, more surreptitious way. For the image of Uylenspiegel appears to have produced – or at least strengthened - not only national but also gender identity (Beyen 2001). The Flemish nationalist Uylenspiegel was not only the purest of Flemings, but also the purest of all males. Iconographically, he was usually represented as a tall, muscular figure, with stern, masculine facial traits. This seemed to be in contradiction to De Coster's vision which, in accordance with the folkloristic tradition, had represented him as a rather small and clown-like figure – a representation that would remain common in the more Belgian-patriot iconography. And yet, here again, one might say that the association between Thyl and masculinity found its deepest roots in *La Légende*. In the book, De Coster had created a girlfriend for Uylenspiegel with the name Nele. Even if De Coster, as a progressive liberal, was an advocate of the liberation of women, the relationship he depicted between Thyl and Nele was deeply influenced by a Romantic vision of the fundamental difference between man and woman. Nele was called the heart of Flanders, implying that she stood for emotional rather than for intellectual values. Moreover, she appeared as a passive type, faithfully waiting for her Thyl who, for his part, did not seem to be concerned too much about faithfulness or chastity. Nele appeared as the principle of purity, whereas Thyl was the principle of activity.

This duality was gradually magnified *and* simplified in the consecutive Flemish national and Catholic discourse. Even in the strongly moralizing discourse of the Catholic youth movements, Thyl and Nele were staged as ideal role-models for boys and girls. In the course of this process, national orthodoxy and gender-orthodoxy almost became synonyms: being a real Fleming implied acting according to one's gender codes. Illustrative of this interwovenness is the imagological evolution of the third main character of *La Légende d'Ulenspiegel,* Lamme Goedzak. This fat and gourmand pal of Uylenspiegel was described by De Coster as a somewhat weak-hearted figure, not only in the struggle for the Low Countries, but also in his relationship with his bossy and unfaithful wife. In that sense, Lamme was the one who did not correspond to the 'natural' role-model, who did not live up to his masculine duties. This weakness did not prevent De Coster from showing a marked sympathy for this figure. But in Flemish national rhetoric, Lamme became the symbol of all those half-hearted Flemings who did not dare to take up the fight against Belgian national democracy. National impurity and gender impurity appeared to be related phenomena.

Even more than the evolution of Uylenspiegel towards a national symbol, this process of 'gender streamlining' seemed to be guided less by active manipulation than by a dialectical dynamic in which the search for identity and the inherent features of the image itself affected each other reciprocally. Hence, the figures that the progressive and 'feminist' liberal Charles De Coster created could 'naturally' - or at least without being abused - evolve into some of the strongest icons of a radically right-wing and masculine ideology. Once an image is handed over to society, it seems, it becomes virtually uncontrollable, with serious consequences both for the image itself *and* for society.

References

Beyen, Marnix. 1998. *Held voor alle werk. De vele gedaanten van Tijl Uilenspiegel.* Antwerp & Baarn: Houtekiet.
Beyen, Marnix. 2001. 'Zuiver geest in zuivere lichamen. Het literaire trio Tijl-Nele-Lamme en de genderende kracht van de natie' in Wils, Kaat (ed.) *Het lichaam (m/v),* Leuven: Leuven UP: 209-230.
Beyen, Marnix. 2003. '1867. Parution de *La Légende d'Ulenspiegel* de Charles de Coster. Autour de la difficile naissance d'une littérature nationale' in

Bertrand, Jean-Pierre, et al. (eds) *Histoire de la littérature belge francophone, 1830-2000.* Paris: Fayard : 107-116.

Beyen, Marnix. 2003a. 'Un Tijl Uilenspiegel patriotique au Parlement belge. Louis Defré *alias* Joseph Boniface (1814-1880) et l'aspect romantique du libéralisme' in Herman, Jan, et al. (eds) *Littératures en contact. Mélanges offerts à Vic Nachtergaele.* Louvain: Louvain UP: 31-46.

Billig, Michael. 1997. *Banal nationalism.* London: Sage, 2nd ed.

Janssens, Jozef. 1998. 'De wereld op zijn kop omstreeks 1500. De merkwaardige lotgevallen van een Nederduitse schalk' in *idem* (ed.), *Uilenspiegel. De wereld op zijn kop.* Louvain: Davidsfonds : 15-58.

Strikwerda, Carl. 1997. *A House Divided. Catholics, Socialists, and Flemish Nationalists in 19th century Belgium.* Lanham, Maryland: Rowman & Littlefield.

Trousson, Raymond. 1990. *Charles De Coster ou la Vie est un Songe.* Brussels.

Vos, Louis & Kas Deprez. 1998. *Nationalism in Belgium. Shifting Identities, 1780-1995.* Basingstoke: Macmillan.

CHAPTER 10

ON BEING CHINESE

Adrian Chan

Our image of a people whose culture and language are very different and distant from ours is generally derived from our own experts on that people. From those experts, and from the mass media and entertainment, we form an image which in time becomes, for us, the identity of that people, though there may be distortions in this process. So what most of us know of the Ancient Romans comes from our school texts, the media, cinema and television. It is in this way that we gain our knowledge of the Chinese and their culture – though most of us will have met a Chinese or tow in our local take-away or restaurant. To most of us, the image of the Chinese and their culture is informed by experts called sinologists, and the mass media and entertainment. In addition, we might meet a Chinese (but not a Roman). From these sources we gradually create our impressions of the identity of the Chinese.

However, I suggest that in fact the popular identity of the Chinese in the West is the result of centuries of moulding and reshaping Chinese culture to make it more like Western culture. This process of distortion was begun by the pioneers of sinology, and still continues today. The effect has been to make Chinese culture appear as 'an integral part of European material civilization and culture' helped by a 'supporting vocabulary', a process Edward Said called Orientalism (Said 1995: 2). Because this is a controversial assertion, this study will mainly restrict its attention to sinology in English – the most common language in Chinese studies – to show how the pioneers and their successors tried to make Chinese culture appear Western. By translation and interpretation, they tried to invalidate those aspects of Chinese culture that are different from those in the culture of the West. In so doing, they distorted the image and identity of the Chinese and their culture. While modern sinologists would deny being Orientalists, this study intends to show that most still maintain the position of the pioneers, the Christian missionaries. Sinology was Orientalist long before Said raised that term to our consciousness, and

he is too generous in exempting the post-1960 East Asian specialists
from Orientalism (Said 1995: 301).

Defining being Chinese

To some, being Chinese is like being Jewish, but instead of a maternal
lineage the Chinese call for a paternal one. That was how the Taiwan
regime defined Chineseness until 1999, when it required both parents to
be Chinese. But since that regime prefers not to regard itself as part of
China but as a separate political entity, its idea of being Chinese is really
irrelevant.

To some, including many sinologists, the Chinese tend to show a
Central Kingdom Mentality – a tendency to be ethnocentric, to regard
China as the centre of the world and the Chinese as the only civilized
people. But those who identified this syndrome in the Chinese have also
located China in the Far East without any sense of irony. If China is in
the Far East, one may logically assume those who made that observation
have to be in the Centre – the Centre marked by two copper strips embedded in a footpath in Greenwich, a London suburb. Those who have
identified the Central Kingdom Mentality in the Chinese should perhaps
share the self-perception and worldview of the Chinese, for both regard
themselves as being in the centre of the world – the Chinese are told so
by the British, and the British are so by an application of their own logic.

Some define Chineseness in cultural behavioural terms as if acquired
characteristics can be inherited. An example is S.G. Redding, a British
Professor of Geography at the University of Hong Kong, and one-time
Visiting Professor at the Australian National University. He claimed
Chinese capitalist entrepreneurs in Hong Kong are 'basically Confucian
in nature' (Redding 1995). This is a strange observation in the light of
Confucius' dictum, 'If one's action is guided by profit, one will incur
much ill will' (Lau 1979: IV/12). A 'capitalist Confucian' is therefore an
oxymoron, though many modern sinologists share Redding's view (Chan
1996).

Some problems of definition

Today, concern about Chineseness has been an expanding niche in sinology and the publication of a volume entitled *The Encyclopaedia of Overseas
Chinese* (Pan 1999) shows this concern has come of age and is now a
world wide enterprise. Yet one wonders if this search for attributes of
Chineseness by scholars using languages other than Chinese misses the

point. To a Chinese or British person, being Chinese or British is not being distinctive but being natural. But as questions on the nature of Chineseness are continually raised, this seems to indicate a methodological problem in the study of China, sinology. This is so, I suggest, because there is no Chinese equivalent for the term sinology. For this study, I will define it as the study of China in languages other than Chinese. Those who try to understand China while expressing their knowledge and problems in languages other than Chinese are in a comparative enterprise, though few sinologists are aware of this or admit to it openly. This unacknowledged problem is not peculiar to sinology but is shared with other cross-cultural endeavours. The problems of such comparative enterprises may be overt, as when comparing the philosopher-king in Confucius and Plato. More problematic are implicit comparisons that involve the unexamined assumptions and the cultural baggages of the investigators. The lack of awareness of these assumptions has been the root problem in defining being Chinese, since the time of the pioneers.

Whether we are non-Chinese, or ethnic Chinese using a language other than Chinese, we achieve our understanding of China through our own distinctive individual frame of reference produced by our cultural inheritance. Furthermore, modern sinologists are burdened by the works of their predecessors, who distorted Chinese culture and the cultural texts they translated to make them appear part of European civilization. The pioneers of sinology had the Orientalist approach defined by Said, with the best motives of course, from their own perspective. Modern sinologists may not be conscious of it but have to negotiate this foggy professional legacy. This study will explore this legacy to show how it impacts on our knowledge of being Chinese.

The origins of the problem

It is not s question of malice on the part of the pioneer sinologists. One of the earliest in this category was the Jesuit Matteo Ricci. Few would not acknowledge that he was a great pioneer in his field, and his work enabled Chinese culture to spread to parts of the world where it was shrouded in mystery. But to do his task more proficiently, as he saw it, he resorted to distortion. As he recalled,

> I make every effort to turn our way the ideas of the leader of the sect of *literati,* Confucius, by interpreting in our favour things which are left ambiguous in his writings. In this way our Fathers gain favours with the *literati* who do not adore the idols (cited in Rule 1986: 1).

As a Christian missionary, Ricci naturally saw the opportunity to spread the Christian message and save Chinese souls as the prime reasons for being in China. For him, that end would justify most means. There was, however, one aspect of Chinese culture that Christian missionaries had to reject, and that was its cosmogony or theory of the origin of the universe. In China's cosmogony the beginning is a *hun-dun* condition, which may be described as an amorphous cosmic mass. Its mythic logic and the cosmogonic tradition have never transformed the puzzle of origin into a one-off event needing a causal presence of an individual, or a hero of creation, outside the created order. That is to say, it has no Creator-God. Instead of a prime mover, the Chinese perspective has a prime movement, continuing from the primary resonance to now. Without a Creator-God, the Chinese language has no word for sin, for there is no one to sin against.

The Christian missionaries had to insist that the Chinese cosmogony be rejected and that theirs was the only universally valid one. Any culture whose cosmogony does not acknowledge the universality of the Christian cosmogony had to be invalidated and denied. That was understandable, for if they accommodated the Chinese cosmogony, they would be denying the Christian cosmogony as the only universally valid and true one, and also denying the very rationale of their vocation and reason for being in China. They would have to reject their Creator-God and tolerate evil. Theirs was in reality a totalitarian system, though proclaimed to the Chinese as a Message of Love. To reject their Message of Love is to court eternal damnation, as Lucifer had done to his eternal pain, so Christian mythology advises. From another perspective, the missionary's insistence that their cosmogony was the only universally valid one was really an expression of ethnocentrism premised on the faith that one's own belief is universally true. If the Chinese held a comparable belief, it would inevitably be dismissed as an expression of their Central Kingdom Mentality.

Since the time of Ricci, Christian missionaries, especially the English-speaking Protestants, have been much more explicit in their rejection of this aspect of Chinese culture. They not only denied the validity of China's cosmogony but also rejected much of her cultural and moral values, and cast aspersions on those Chinese who tried to defend them. The tragedy is that today many sinologists, acculturated to regard China as in the Far East, still maintain this missionary position, and condemn the Chinese who resisted Christianity as victims of their Central Kingdom mentality, or anti-foreign. This is not simply an attack on non-Chinese sinologists, because many ethnic Chinese scholars also share this perspective. Nor should this be seen as anti-Christian or anti-missionary, but rather it is meant to be a statement that many modern sinologists remain trapped in the early Christian missionary's outlook, unwittingly and not necessarily with malice. They seem unaware of being engaged in comparative enterprises, and so have not given due care to their choice of the framework of reference as they make their evaluations of Chinese cultural expressions. This lack of awareness has impacted on the identity and image of the Chinese in both scholarly and popular understanding.

A case in point was missionary-sinologist James Legge, arguably the most influential of the type, and the first to translate Chinese cultural texts on a systematic basis. The way he divided the Chinese texts into chapters and verses in imitation of the Bible is still in use, as are many of his assumptions and judgements. Today many sinologists still observe Chinese culture through the Orientalist prism created by Legge nearly 150 years ago. Legge's work was sponsored by Joseph Jardine of the Jardine Mathieson mercantile empire, the largest English importer of opium to China. Legge recalled that Jardine had said, 'We make our money in China, and we should be glad to assist in whatever promises to be of benefit to it' (Legge 1971: iv). On becoming Professor of Chinese at Oxford University, Legge's translations became authoritative, so much so that in 1948 the General Assembly of the new United Nations Organisation recommended its Education and Scientific Commission, UNESCO, to re-publish his works as among the 'most representative of the cultures of certain member states ... of Asia' (Legge 1988: v). As the UN was about to deny China membership, it was nonetheless happy to tell the world what it should know about the Chinese.

In his translations, Legge replaced the cosmogony in China's culture with the Christian one, thus effectively practising Said's Orientalism by making the Orient as 'an integral part of European ... civilization.' While this article is not a discussion on the cosmogony of China, we should recall that leading sinologists as Bodde (1961), Needham (1951), and Mote (1972) agreed with the scholar John Major that China's cosmogony 'has no first cause or creator, and the only eternal principle, *Dao*, was functionally equivalent to change itself' (Major 1978). We have noted that the origin or cosmogony of China is a condition called *hun-dun,* which may be described as an undifferentiated and amorphous cosmic stuff. As their cosmogony has no Creator-God or sin, the Chinese have other ways to define goodness and authority. It is secular and political, and their cosmogony informs them that nothing happened that is not always happening, and hence that the most important duty in their existence is to maintain harmony with this constantly changing cosmos.

This leads to two distinctive results. First, if 'nothing happened that is not always happening' seems hard to reconcile with constant change, it was explained by Xun Kuang (d. 312 BCE) the most lucid of the classical Confucians, who explained in his *Xunzi* there are now more people to share this finite and constant world. Operating in this cosmogony, China's social theorists saw it as their duty to propose solutions to maintain social harmony in this ever-changing world. While sinologists have commented on the Chinese preoccupation with harmony, they have not tried to explain the reasons for it. Secondly, with no personalized or external evil that humanity has to combat and reject, we have to choose to be good or bad.

As a Christian missionary, Legge had to reject China's cosmogony and replace it with the Christian one because the rationale of his vocation demanded it. He did so by translation, and made Chinese culture into an integral part of European civilization by giving Chinese culture the Christian Creator-God. The Chinese words are *di,* which means king, emperor, or ancestors of kings; and *shang,* which means high, superior, senior, or ancestor. In his Preface to the *Shu jing* (Book of Poetry), the oldest of China's cultural texts, Legge admitted he knew that in some classical texts these terms referred to the mythic kings Yao and Shun. He also knew that Antoine Gaubil SJ, Interpreter-General at the Chinese Court, had rendered *di* as 'le Seigneur', and *shang di* as 'le Souvergain Maitre' while Medhurst, a contemporary from the USA, had rendered them as 'the Supreme' and 'the Supreme Ruler'. Yet Legge declared,

> more than twenty-five years ago I came to the conclusion that *di* was the term corresponding in Chinese to our 'God' and that *shang di* was the same, with the addition of *shang* equal to supreme. In this view, I have never wavered, and I have rendered both the names 'God' in all the volumes of the Chinese classics thus far translated and published (Legge 1988a: xiii).

God may or may not be an Englishman, but the Chinese god was a gift from an Englishman!

That Legge should act in this way is understandable because without a creator-god, the Christian message he brought to China would have been irrelevant to the Chinese. Besides, without a creator-god in her culture, and no word for 'sin' as understood in Legge's English, the rationale for the vocation of the missionary is untenable, for it is premised on sin, so a sinless culture must be denied. But to give Chinese culture a god does not really solve the problem of a language with no word for sin. So the missionary-translators adopted the word *zui* for sin, which actually has a very different meaning. To commit *zui* is to commit a crime or to transgress against temporal authorities. While *zui* is also transgression in Buddhism but as Buddhism also has no creator-god, to commit *zui* is to transgress against one's conscience or the Buddhist transcendent nature, not against the Christian God.

Of the three Abrahamic traditions, those of the Jewish and Islamic religions who came to China for refuge rather than for proselytizing had maintained long and quite harmonious relations with their hosts, while practising their faiths. The Christian missionaries who to went China however, especially those who went in the nineteenth century, came from societies intoxicated by imperial conquests, and were confident that their countries' military strength and material wealth were rewards from their God. So they not only insisted on the universality of their cosmogony but also regarded the Chinese one as wrong and morally inferior.

This was best exemplified by the Rev. Griffith John, the first Protestant missionary in Hankou, today's Wuhan, a thousand kilometres upstream on the Chang Jiang (the Yangtse River). He arrived in China shortly after the 1858 Treaty with Britain and France, which the Chinese called The Second Opium War Unequal Treaty, and which forced China to open the interior to trade and Christian endeavours. In 1858 John remarked,

> Protestant missionaries have come to your China ... over 50 years preaching the Holy Way ... the people ... should all have repented and believed in the Lord. But ... the believers are few and unbelievers many ... an obvious sign of human depravity. Hence, you Chinese, according to the laws of God, are all truly sinful (Cohen 1963: 54).

The Chinese were damned as criminals, people with *zui*, for rejecting a moral code their own moralists regarded as repugnant.

While Ricci seemed to show some awareness of certain moral preferences of the Chinese moralists, many later missionaries and modern sinologists seem so confident of the universality of their culture, including its cosmogony, that they showed little awareness of the fundamentally incompatible aspects in the two cultures, including their concept of morality. This can best be illustrated by comparing their respective modes on moral improvement. The way of the Chinese moralists is best exemplified by Confucius himself. His goal in life was the pursuit of moral perfection: 'At seventy [I hope] what I want to do will coincide with what I ought to do' (Lau 1979: II/iv). To achieve this required a life-long struggle which he began at fifteen. To the Christians, one must admit one cannot arrive at moral perfection by one's own effort but has to accept the free gift of a Saviour. So we have an impasse because the Chinese moralists must condemn the Christian way as moral cowardice. To the Christians, the Confucian way is spiritual pride, and must be rejected if one is to be saved.

The problem persists

Paul Cohen, a modern sinologist specializing in the history of Christian missions in China, wrote in 1963 that the Confucian literati were leaders of the anti-Christian movements in mid-nineteenth century, and claimed that opposition was an expression of the innate conservatism of the Confucian tradition or of 'anti-foreignism', rather than of the incompatibility of the moral systems of the two cultures (Cohen 1963). This omission was presumably due to Cohen's inappropriate use of the framework of reference in the comparative enterprise of sinology. It was the result of ethnocentrism premised on the faith that one's own experience is universal. Christian missionaries regarded the godless Chinese culture as something to be utterly rejected, and so we need not be surprised when frustrated missionaries confessed that the Chinese had no 'correct idea of sin' (Wolferstan 1909: 75).

While modern translators would not be as blatant as Ricci or Legge, it would unfair to regard the pioneers as dishonest because they thought they had a higher calling. Like Joseph Jardine and Legge over two hundred years later, Ricci probably thought what he was doing was for the benefit of the Chinese. Today, an appropriate term for their endeavours is Orientalism. It is posited here that from its beginnings, with a few notable exceptions, the Orientalist mode has remained the dominant mode among modern sinologists (though none admits to it). In our age of secular modern science, this persistence – even if out of habit – deserves little charity.

Missionary-translators went on to give a new trinity to Chinese culture. Having donated sin (*zui*), and god (*shang di*), to Chinese culture through mistranslation, the new trinity was completed with the gift of Heaven by the mistranslation of the word *tian*. It can mean the sky – what we see when we look up – or more abstractly fate or providence. In the culture of the centre whence came the missionary-sinologists, Heaven written with a capital letter has a specific meaning. Given China's cosmogony, to render *tian* as *Heaven* is Orientalism, a supporting vocabulary for discourse, as Said advised. This effort of the pioneering missionary-sinologists still persists today. In the most commonly available translation of the *Analects of Confucius*, the sage is made to say, 'When you have offended against Heaven, there is nowhere you can turn to in your prayer' (Lau 1979: III/13). Given China's cosmogony, a more appropriate rendering, with less violence to the original text, might be: 'One can expect no help if one goes against providence.' With this translation-induced Trinity, Chinese culture is mutated to be part of European civilization, the first of Said's two characteristic attributes of Orientalism.

The roots of the problem

One may regard these matters as problems of translation because the study of translation theories has not been particularly vibrant in sinology, despite a great volume of translation in recent years. So, a brief detour into translation theory is required, to cast some light on this problem in sinology.

If sinology is defined as the study of China in languages other than Chinese, it becomes an interlingual and cross-cultural enterprise. Thus much of its activity will be concerned with translations, such as Legge's works. The famous paper by Roman Jakobson distinguished three types of translations: interlingual, intralingual and intersemiotic (Jakobson 1971). Sinology is obviously interlingual, which he called 'translation proper', and defined as 'an interpretation of verbal signs by means of some other language.' While one should equate translation with interpretation only with care, all self-respecting translators do aim for the highest degree of fidelity possible. But what that fidelity means is disputable especially in translating sensitive texts between the languages of disparate cultures, for example from classical Chinese to English. In practice, the translator chooses between literal or free translation. The former conceives the intention of the source text as its extension, and attempts to render this extension as faithfully as possible, by rendering each individual word of the source text into an equivalent drawn from the lexicon of the target text. Consequently the translator tends to hold the source text to be sacrosanct, and would see a free translation as a betrayal of the author's intention and a departure from the referential value of the original text.

A free translation, like a mirror image of a literal translation, is conceived of as its message rather than the medium, and thus sides with the
reader rather than the author. In fact, one may say there is relatively little
respect for the author's words, as long as the underlying message remains
intact. As the noted Bible translator Eugene Nida said,

> 'White as snow' may be rendered as 'white as egret feather' if the people of
> the receptor language are not acquainted with snow but speak of anything
> very white by this phrase (Nida 1964: 158).

In its extreme form, then, free translation may become cultural transla-
tion. However, the Orientalist translations cited above belong to neither
of these. From Ricci and Legge through to Lau, a former Professor of
Chinese at the esteemed School of Oriental and African Studies of the
University of London, who translated the Penguin Classics edition of
Analects of Confucius (Lau 1979), the goal of these Orientalist translators of
Chinese cultural texts seems to render Chinese culture as (in Said's termi-
nology) 'an integral part of European material civilization and culture' by
means of a 'supporting vocabulary'.

In 1907, after nearly fifty years as a missionary, the Rev. Griffith John
insisted that Confucianism, Buddhism and Taoism 'must pass away if the
countries which they dominate are to advance in religion, morality, and
civilization' (John 1907: 79-80). It is more than a coincidence that John
should mention morality, for this issue resurfaced half a century later
when the sinologist Arthur F. Wright claimed that fundamental and basic
to Chinese culture is a moral malaise, which he identified as the fault of
the Chinese language. For him, it was 'relatively poor in resources for
expressing abstractions [such] ... as truth' (Wright 1953: 286).

Recently, Orientalist sinology has been globalized, to the extent that
sinologists from diverse parts of the world have come to share their
values, like the missionaries of old. They insist their values and perspectives are universal, and see their actions as expressions of concern for the
social and moral well-being of the Chinese people. Like Griffith John
before them, they see the solution for the Chinese as depending on their
ability to accept the values and cosmogony of the centre, and reject those
in China's culture. These judgements indicate the widespread acceptance
of Orientalism, whose perspective has become natural. But if this analysis is correct, to be a good Chinese would require the Chinese to be
foreign, and deny much of their cultural heritage.

If Orientalism aims to make the Orient appear as an integral part of European civilization, then part of that objective involves diverting the gaze of the next generation, the students, and helping them to regard China's culture as European. A widely used modern text or source book on Chinese civilization asserts,

> The sacrifices to ancestors ... were of vital importance to the welfare of the family or clan, for the ancestors had the power to aid or punish their descendents according to their pleasure ... the character *di* of the compound *Shang-di* was used increasingly to mean not a supreme deity but the supreme ruler of human society, while the word *t'ien*, or Heaven, was more often employed to denote the power that governed all creation (De Bary et al. 1960: I/7).

Of the first part, Mote (1972) rightly said 'it is difficult to imagine what evidence exists for such an assertion'; of the second, he commented with equal clarity that

> references to 'supreme deity' and to 'power that governed all *creation*' can only bring to the mind of a Western student of theistic concepts. Should not the words *creator, creation* and *creature*, which are so misleading when talking about the Chinese world view, be rather scrupulously avoided (Mote 1972: 9-10).

Of course they should, if the aim is to understand Chinese culture and cosmogony, and to avoid Orientalism.

As if to counter Mote, Andrew Nathan insists that in cross-cultural studies involving China,

> the values the investigator believes to be valid can validly be applied to societies other than his own – what might be called evaluative universalism. The second choice is to base the judgement on values the investigator finds among those indigenous in the subject society ... the choice as the standard of evaluation is founded on the claim that a society can validly be judged only by the values that are among its own. I label this position cultural relativism ... The call for cultural relativism ... masked what was the projection of personal values, critical of American society, onto the Chinese revolution under the claim they were Chinese values (Nathan 1990: 295).

Nathan's proposition is hard to reconcile with pluralism. The calls to evaluate Chinese culture in such a way come not only from patriotic sinologists in the USA. At about the same time and on the other side of the world, a sinologist-translator, claimed that the Chinese tend to have an

> underdeveloped sense of independent personal identity [which] may be connected with the absence from all Chinese religions, except the minority

ones of Islam and the two Christianities, of a strong relationship between an individual soul and an omnipotent and judging deity (Jenner 1992: 230).

This judgment is by a W.J.F. Jenner, onetime Professor of Chinese and Head of the China Centre at the Australian National University. To Jenner, the refusal of most Chinese to embrace the 'jealous God' of the Book of Exodus is one of the causes of the 'tyranny of history' that has bedevilled China and a 'root of China's crisis', a perspective not far removed from that of Griffith John. Like the missionary-sinologists, Jenner wants the Chinese not only to reject much of their cultural and historical heritage, but also to embrace the Abrahamic god, if they are to be fully developed human beings. Such a position is highly ethnocentric.

Conclusion

Orientalist sinology is not, primarily, meant to enlighten us about China and her culture, but is rather a project to remake Chinese culture into what the Orientalists think it should be. Therefore the answer to the question of what being Chinese means would depend as much on who is asking as who is answering. The identity of the Chinese created by these Orientalist sinologists is based on a distorted image they created, in order to make the Chinese resemble those in the centre.

References

Bary, W.T. de, W-T. Chan, and B. Watson. 1960. *Sources of Chinese Tradition* vol. I. New York: Columbia University Press.

Bodde, D. 1961. 'Myths of Ancient China' in Kramer, S.N. (ed.) *Mythologies of the Ancient World*. Chicago: Quadrangle: 369-408.

Chan, A. 1996. 'Confucianism and Development in East Asia' in *Journal of Contemporary Asia* 26/1.

Chan, A. 1997. 'The *Sinless* Chinese: a Christian Translation Dilemma?' in Simms, K. (ed.) *Translating Sensitive Texts: Linguistic Aspects*. Amsterdam/Atlanta: Rodopi: 239-43.

Cohen, P.A. 1963. *Chine and Christianity: the Missionary Movement and the Growth of Anti-foreignism*. Cambridge Mass.: Harvard University Press.

Jakobson, R. 1971. 'On Linguistic Aspects of Translation' in idem, *Selected Writings II: Word and Language*. The Hague: Mouton: 260-66.

Jenner, W.J.F. 1992. *The Tyranny of History: the Roots of China's Crisis*. London: Allen Lane.

John, G. 1907. *A Voice from China*. London: James Clarke.

Lau, D.C. (transl.). 1979. *Analects of Confucius (Lun Yu)*. London: Penguin.

Legge, J. 1971. *Confucius: Confucian Analects, the Great Learning and the Doctrine of the Mean*. New York: Dover.

Legge, J., 1988. 'Preface' in *The Sacred Books of China: the Texts of Confucius*, new edition, part I. Delhi: Motilal Barnarsidass.

Legge, J. 1988a. 'Preface' in *The She King (She jing)*. Delhi: Motilal Banarsidass.

Major, J. 1978. 'Myth, Cosmology and the Origins of Chinese Science' in *Journal of Chinese Philosophy* 5/1: 1-20.

Mote, F.W. 1972. 'The Cosmological Gulf Between China and the West' in Buxbaum, D.C. and F. W. Mote (eds) *Transition and Permanence: Chinese History and Culture. A Festschrift in Honor of Dr. Hsiao Kung-chuan*. Hong Kong: Cathay: 3-21.

Nathan, A. 1990. 'The Place of Values in Cross-Cultural Studies: the Example of Democracy in China' in Cohen, P.A. and M. Goldman (eds) *Ideas Across Cultures: Essays on Chinese Thought in Honor of Benjamin I. Schwartz*. Boston: Harvard University Press.

Needham, J. 1951. 'Human Laws and Laws of Nature in China and the West' in *Journal of the History of Ideas* 12: 3-30 and 194-230.

Nida, E.A. 1964. *Towards a Science of Translating, with Special Reference to Principles and Procedures Involved in Bible Translating*. Leiden: Brill.

Pan, L. (ed.). 1999. *The Encyclopaedia of Overseas Chinese*. Richmond: Curzon.

Redding, S.C. 1995. 'Operationalizing the Post-Confucian Hypothesis: the Overseas Chinese Case' in Mun, K.C. Mun (ed.) *Chinese Style Enterprise Management*. Hong Kong: Chinese University of Hong Kong Press.

Rule, P.. 1986. *K'ung-tzu or Confucius? The Jesuit Interpretations of Confucianism*. Sydney: Allen & Unwin.

Said, E. 1995. *Orientalism*. London: Penguin. Second edition.

Wolferstan, B. 1909. *The Catholic Church in China from 1860 to 1907*. London: Sands; St Louis: Herder.

Wright, A.F. 1953. 'The Chinese Language and Foreign Ideas' in idem (ed.) *Studies in Chinese Thought*. Chicago: Chicago University Press.

GENDER

CHAPTER 11

HOW TO DO THINGS WITH GENDER: TRANSGENDERISM IN VIRGINIA WOOLF'S *ORLANDO*

Stef Craps

Orlando has often been regarded as little more than a playful interlude in Virginia Woolf's oeuvre, and has suffered considerable critical neglect as a result. The responsibility for the dismissive mode adopted by many critics partly lies with Woolf herself, who disparagingly described the novel as 'a joke', 'farce', 'a writer's holiday', 'an escapade' (quoted in Minow-Pinkney 1987: 117). When *Orlando* is not simply omitted from critical discussion altogether, it tends to be read as a fictionalized biography of Woolf's friend and lover Vita Sackville-West. Matching the novel's characters and events with their counterparts in the real world becomes the sole objective of critical inquiry (Cervetti 1996: 171-72). What this type of response hides from view, however, are the very serious, non-biographical concerns motivating the text's apparently frivolous play. These issues have only come to be appreciated in the last few years, which have seen a marked increase in scholarly work on the novel (Burns 1994, Cervetti 1996, Hovey 1997, Knopp 1988, Lawrence 1992, Minow-Pinkney 1987, Parkes 1994, Schaffer 1994, Watkins 1998). Taking my cue from some of these writings, I argue that *Orlando*, far from being an insignificant *jeu d'esprit*, is in fact a radical text, whose subversion of deep-seated and taken-for-granted assumptions about gendered behaviour is suppressed by its reduction to an escapade or a mere tribute to Vita Sackville-West.

Preliminaries

The dominant conception of gender in Western societies presupposes a causal relation between sex, gender and desire. The presumption is that there is first a sex that is expressed through a gender and then through a sexuality. All human beings belong to one of two discrete gender categories (either 'masculine' or 'feminine') permanently determined on the basis of biological – i.e. naturally given – sex characteristics (either 'male' or 'female'). Congruence is expected not only within and between a per-

son's sex and gender – meaning that one is either neatly male/masculine
or neatly female/feminine – but also between the areas of sex and gender
on the one hand and a person's sexuality on the other, with the default
option being that this will be heterosexual.

Though this system may seem obvious or natural, and the outline I
have given of it a generalized description of 'the way things are', it has
been argued that it is in fact an artificial conjunction of cultural constructs which has naturalized itself in order to conceal and hence perpetuate the power relations of which it is a product. According to Judith
Butler, the causal lines between sex, gender and desire can be exposed as
retrospectively and performatively produced fabrications:

> It may be that the very categories of sex, of sexual identity, of gender are
> produced and maintained in the *effects* of this compulsory performance [of
> heterosexuality], effects which are disingenuously renamed as causes, origins,
> disingenuously lined up within a causal or expressive sequence that the het-
> erosexual norm produces to legitimate itself as the origin of all sex (Butler
> 1991: 29).

The presumed continuities between sex, gender and desire are an illusion
set up by a power/knowledge regime which serves the interests of heterosexuality and – by casting male/masculine and female/feminine as a
hierarchical opposition – masculine hegemony.

'Intelligible' identities – intelligible within the terms of the dominant
sexual regime – are those which institute and maintain relations of coherence and continuity among sex, gender and desire. As Butler points out,
such 'coherent' subjects are constituted by a dynamic of repudiation and
exclusion. The formation of viable subjects requires the simultaneous
production of a domain of unviable (un)subjects – 'abjects' – who form
the 'constitutive outside' to the domain of the subject:

> The abject designates here precisely those 'unlivable' and 'uninhabitable' zones
> of social life which are nevertheless densely populated by those who do not
> enjoy the status of the subject, but whose living under the sign of the 'unlivable'
> is required to circumscribe the domain of the subject (Butler 1993: 3).

For Butler, the domain of abjection – that which the subject must exclude in order to constitute itself – offers a vantage point from which the
heteropatriarchal symbolic can be challenged: 'These exluded sites come
to bound the "human" as its constitutive outside, and to haunt those
boundaries as the persistent possibility of their disruption and rearticulation' (Butler 1993: 8). She makes a case for this threat of disruption to be

considered as a critical resource in the struggle to rearticulate the terms of symbolic legitimacy and intelligibility. In her view, the persistence and proliferation of gender identities that fail to conform to norms of cultural intelligibility 'provide critical opportunities to expose the limits and regulatory aims of that domain of intelligibility and, hence, to open up within the very terms of that matrix of intelligibility rival and subversive matrices of gender disorder' (Butler 1990: 17). By denaturalizing reified notions of gender, the domain of abject, delegitimated bodies can contribute to dismantling the restricting frames of masculinist domination and compulsory heterosexuality. The loss of gender norms would result in the meaning of what counts as a valued and valuable body in the world being vastly expanded.

If, as Butler claims, the domain of abjected alterity is populated by 'those [identities] in which gender does not follow from sex and those in which the practices of desire do not "follow" from either sex or gender' (Butler 1990: 17), then Orlando, the sex-changing, cross-dressing and bisexual protagonist of Woolf's novel, has all the right credentials to be considered one of its inhabitants. As an 'incoherent' or 'discontinuous' gendered being who fails to conform to the norms of cultural intelligibility, s/he can be seen to subvert and displace those naturalized and reified notions of gender that support masculine hegemony and heterosexist power.

Gender

A first glimpse of *Orlando*'s revolutionary conception of gender is afforded by the novel's opening sentence, which begins: 'He – for there could be no doubt of his sex, though the fashion of the time did something to disguise it [. . .]' (Woolf 1992: 13).[1] Calling the reader's attention immediately to gender, the narrator seems to protest too much, creating the very doubt that his words would deny.[2] Indeed, the interruptive qualification comically dismantles the male subject announced by the narrative's first word. In its muddling of the expectations of reading, the sly introduction is representative of the novel as a whole, which forces us

---

[1] All subsequent quotations from *Orlando* will be cited parenthetically by page number only.

[2] Throughout this article, I will designate the narrator as a male, though – as will become apparent later – there can be as much doubt of his sex as of Orlando's. Early on in the narrative, however, the narrator identifies himself as a male person (14), and for a long time this assertion goes unchallenged.

to reconsider virtually everything we thought we knew about gender and sexuality. The novel's protagonist, who lives through centuries, undergoes a sex change halfway through the narrative, and loves both men and women, is a transgressive figure who recognizes no borders or rules of time, gender or sexuality and fails to conform to any pre-established pattern.

Orlando's biographer, whose vision is that of hegemony, vainly tries to get a firm hold on his elusive subject. He casts himself as an objective reporter engaged in the factual exploration of a fixed identity:

> the first duty of a biographer [. . .] is to plod, without looking to right or left, in the indelible footprints of truth; unenticed by flowers; regardless of shade; on and on methodically till we fall plump into the grave and write *finis* on the tombstone above our heads. [. . .] Our simple duty is to state the facts (63).

The biographer naively believes that he will only have to follow a heroic figure going 'from deed to deed, from glory to glory, from office to office' (14). Little time elapses, however, before he 'must fly as fast as he can' (44) in pursuit of his historically and sexually mobile target, and very often he completely loses track of Orlando: 'we seem now to catch sight of her and then again to lose it' (211). Eventually, Orlando's biographer professes his irritation at seeing his subject 'slipping out of [his] grasp altogether' (255). 'Truth' and 'facts' prove elusive after all. Orlando escapes the understanding of the biographer and thus overcomes the authority which he represents.

The text marks subjectivity as multiple and shifting, and clearly implies that the biographer's attempt to find the 'single thread' (75) of personal identity is quite useless. In the words of Christy Burns, 'the notion of an essential self [is] comically reduced to a belief that Woolf's less than competent narrator struggles to defend, while the parody of that narrator's attempt results in the realization of the modern, constructive figuration of subjectivity' (1994: 346). Exasperated at his failure to pin Orlando down, the biographer exclaims that, 'when we write of a woman, everything is out of place – culminations and perorations; the accent never falls where it does with a man' (297-98). The assertion that the elusiveness of identity is typically feminine chimes in with Luce Irigaray's view of woman as being outside representation and always 'elsewhere' (1996: 317). To the dismay of the biographer, who wants everything to be predictable and in its place, woman refuses to be contained and tied down by his masculinist narrative paradigm.

That determining the truth of womanhood is anything but a simple matter also becomes apparent in the scene describing Orlando's sex change from male to female. In this scene, Woolf parodies those literary, philosophical and psychoanalytic discourses that represent woman as a veiled mystery which the male imagination seeks to penetrate. During his stay in Turkey as ambassador to King Charles, Orlando falls into a seven-day trance. The narrator insists that he would love to 'spare the reader' the outcome of this crisis, but spurred on by the trumpeted demands of 'Truth, Candour, and Honesty, the austere Gods who keep watch and ward by the inkpot of the biographer' (129), he observes the way in which the figures of Purity, Chastity, and Modesty struggle to veil the 'truth' of Orlando's sex. These veiling figures are banished from the scene by trumpets that blast 'Truth! Truth! Truth!' (132). Orlando awakes wholly naked and unclothed on his/her bed: 'He stretched himself. He rose. He stood upright in complete nakedness before us, and while the trumpets pealed Truth! Truth! Truth! we have no choice left but confess – he was a woman' (132).

As Mary Ann Doane points out, the representation of woman as veiled maps onto sexual difference the dialectic of truth and appearance. In the discourse of metaphysics, 'the function of the veil is to make truth profound, to ensure there is a depth that lurks behind the surface of things' (quoted in Lawrence 1992: 267 n.22). The theatrical unveiling of the female body in *Orlando* exposes as a metaphysical illusion the notion that gender identity is an intractable depth or inner substance. No bare, naked, essential truths are revealed in this passage; obscurity still functions. That the truth of femininity is anything but plain is evidenced by the pronoun slippage in the sentences announcing Orlando's transformation: 'we have no choice left but confess – *he* was a woman' (132; emphasis added); 'Orlando remained precisely as *he* had been. The change of sex, though it altered *their* future, did nothing whatever to alter *their* identity' (133; emphasis added). Human subjectivity is not unified and coherent but shifting and fluid. Orlando is composed of a multiplicity of selves none of which can lay claim to being more authentic or essential than the rest. Indeed, the narrator makes it clear that labelling Orlando either 'he' or 'she' signals nothing more than compliance with the social compulsion to tie human beings down to one of two genders: 'in future we must, for convention's sake, say "her" for "his", and "she" for "he"' (133). What is revealed in the moment of unveiling, then, is the arbitrariness and instability of the binary system of gender differentiation.

The feminization process which Orlando undergoes after her sex change reinforces the case against an essentialist view of gender. Orlando's physical change does not of itself entail a change of gender identity: 'The change of sex [. . .] did nothing whatever to alter their identity' (133). In fact, Orlando remains uninterested in her sex until she decides to sail from Turkey to England and so must dress as a 'lady'. She has been living with the gypsies and wearing Turkish trousers, and gypsy women, 'except in one or two important particulars, differ very little from the gipsy men' (147). The narrator comments that 'It is a strange fact, but a true one, that up to this moment she had scarcely given her sex a thought' (147). Orlando finds herself abruptly faced with the task of coming to terms with her new sex. Her feminine clothing now pressurizes her to conform to social expectations of gendered behaviour, and slowly but surely she becomes feminized.

She finds that her women's clothes have strange effects on the men on board the ship that brings her back to England. First, the Captain treats her with chivalrous condescension, offering to have an awning spread for her on deck, helping her to a slice of meat at dinner, and inviting her to go ashore with him in the long-boat. Next, the sight of her leg nearly causes a sailor on the mast to drop to his death with excitement. Orlando soon realizes what a woman is supposed to do in these situations, and acts out the required responses. She learns to flirt with the Captain, and resolves to keep her legs covered from now on. She discovers that many attributes and behaviours which are often thought to belong to women by nature are in fact the result of hard work: 'women are not (judging by my own short experience of the sex) obedient, chaste, scented, and exquisitely apparelled by nature. They can only attain these graces, without which they may enjoy none of the delights of life, by the most tedious discipline' (150). Such discipline is just what Orlando needs to further improve her gender performance. She learns to let her tears flow freely, as 'it is becoming in a woman to weep' (158), and to be shocked when men do the same: 'That men cry as frequently and as unreasonably as women, Orlando knew from her own experience as a man, but she was beginning to be aware that women should be shocked when men display emotion in their presence, and so, shocked she was' (172-73). In her (heterosexual) relationship with Shelmerdine, Orlando arrives at last at a conviction of 'rare and unexpected delight': "'I am a woman," she thought, "a real woman, at last"' (241). What finally convinces Orlando of the success of her gender performance is a feeling of maternal protectiveness incited by the odd vision of Shelmerdine as a 'boy [...] sucking peppermints' during his passionate struggle against the waves (241).

Orlando's efforts to achieve 'normal' gender status involve her in what, in the literature on transsexualism, is generally referred to as 'passing'. It is often argued that, in the pursuit of passing, transsexuals capitulate to the traditional sex/gender system that forbids transgressive violations. In their attempt to fade into the 'normal' population as a member of either gender, transsexuals can be seen to sustain the 'natural' attitude with respect to gender, which is made up of the assumptions that there are only two genders, that one's gender is invariant and permanent, that genitals are essential signs of gender, that there are no exceptions, and that gender dichotomy and gender membership are 'natural'. At the same time, however, transsexuals reveal the ways in which such a natural attitude is socially and culturally achieved. As Marjorie Garber points out, 'The phenomenon of *transsexualism* is both a confirmation of the constructedness of gender and a secondary recourse to essentialism – or, to put it a slightly different way, transsexualism demonstrates that essentialism *is* cultural construction' (1993: 109).

Transsexuality, then, is a position from which dominant discourses can be criticized. In her influential essay, 'The *Empire* Strikes Back: A Posttranssexual Manifesto', Sandy Stone asserts that the transsexual body has the potential to disrupt taken-for-granted assumptions about what constitutes legitimate gendered subjectivity, and to open up a space for other gender configurations:

> In the transsexual as text we may find the potential to map the refigured body onto conventional gender discourse and thereby disrupt it, to take advantage of the dissonances created by such a juxtaposition to fragment and reconstitute the elements of gender in new and unexpected geometries (1991: 296).

Woolf's novel, by making it abundantly clear that Orlando has to work hard at passing in her new gender status, reveals the extent to which the 'normally' sexed person is in fact a contingent practical accomplishment. Because Orlando has to work at establishing her credentials as a woman in a relatively self-conscious way, whereas 'normal' women – or men, for that matter – are under the illusion that they are just doing what comes naturally, she brings to the surface many of the tacit understandings that guide the creation and maintenance of our binary gender system. In a word, she makes us realize that we are all passing. All of us have to work hard at being men or women, at achieving culturally recognized identities, and in that sense we are all transsexuals.

This performative theory of gender is advanced in the novel itself in a lengthy aside in which the narrator meditates on the significance of clothes in relation to gender identity. Noting the changes in Orlando's behaviour and manners, the narrator remarks,

> What was said a short time ago about there being no change in Orlando the man and Orlando the woman was ceasing to be altogether true. [. . .] The change of clothes had, some philosophers will say, much to do with it. Vain trifles as they seem, clothes have, they say, more important offices than merely to keep us warm. They change our view of the world and the world's view of us (179).

Orlando's femininity is created, brought into being, through performance: by putting on the clothes of a woman and acting like one, Orlando effectively *becomes* a woman. The narrator goes on in the same vein: 'there is much to support the view that it is clothes that wear us and not we them; we may make them take the mould of arm or breast, but they mould our hearts, our brains, our tongues to their liking' (180). Rather than being a mere expression of an essential gender identity, clothes actively create the identity they are purported to reflect. Or, to quote Butler, 'There is no gender identity behind the expressions of gender; that identity is performatively constituted by the very "expressions" that are said to be its results' (1990: 25).

Though his own account of Orlando's cross-dressing adventures and transformation after her sex change provides strong support for the performative model of gender, in the next paragraph the narrator rejects the idea that clothes wear us, and professes a preference for a different (set of) belief(s):

> That is the view of some philosophers and wise ones, but on the whole, we incline to another. The difference between the sexes is, happily, one of great profundity. Clothes are but a symbol of something hid deep beneath. It was a change in Orlando herself that dictated her choice of a woman's dress and of a woman's sex. And perhaps in this she was only expressing rather more openly than usual – openness indeed was the soul of her nature – something that happens to most people without being thus plainly expressed. For here again, we come to a dilemma. Different though the sexes are, they intermix. In every human being a vacillation from one sex to the other takes place, and often it is only the clothes that keep the male or female likeness, while underneath the sex is the very opposite of what it is above (181).

In this knotty passage, the narrator perceives gender identity both as essentially related to sex and as androgynous. The essentialist definition, which is the one he gives first, reverses the relationship of priority between gender and sex proposed by the theory of gender performativity. In this view, gender reflects sex rather than the other way around. This biological sex is something 'of great profundity', 'hid deep beneath' a surface gender that expresses it.

The narrator goes on, however, to suggest that Orlando's nature comprises both male and female elements, which fluctuate according to psychological shifts and may be acted out or expressed. Indeed, the 'change in Orlando herself' cannot refer to her change of sex, because it 'dictated her choice of a woman's dress and of *a woman's sex*' (emphasis added). To interpret this change as a physical one would result in the statement's becoming nonsensical, as its first and last phrases would be co-referential. Moreover, later on the change is associated with a 'vacillation from one sex to the other' which is said to happen 'to most people' and hence may be assumed to be of a psychological rather than a physical nature. On the other hand, this psychological fluctuation cannot be what was meant by the 'something hid deep beneath' referred to earlier, as it allows the sexes to 'intermix', which would seem to imply that the difference between them is *not* one 'of great profundity'. Hence my suggestion that we regard the narrator's 'view' as a conflation of two distinct and conflicting constructions of gender identity rather than as one coherent theory.

The suggestion that in each individual the sexes 'intermix' invokes an ancient tradition of androgyny, going back to Plato, which idealizes the psychological or spiritual union of gendered opposites. In this tradition, androgyny often comes to mean a reconciliation of neatly complementary characteristics that are stereotypically masculine and feminine; an idealized synthesis of heteropatriarchal gender constructs that leaves existing power relations basically unchanged. However, androgyny can also be seen as a mode of resistance to established sexual norms and as a positive and liberating concept. Woolf has been associated with both positions. In *A Literature of Their Own*, Elaine Showalter famously accuses Woolf of being a 'bad mother' for betraying feminism by her 'flight' into androgyny and away from the field of political contestation (1977: 264). Makiko Minow-Pinkney, in contrast, reads Orlando's androgyny as a purposeful and subversive blurring of the socially constructed boundaries between genders: 'Androgyny in *Orlando* is not a resolution of

oppositions, but the throwing into a metonymic confusion of genders'
(1987: 122). According to Minow-Pinkney, androgyny in Woolf does not
reinscribe conventional ideas about sex and gender but functions as a
disruptive, chaotic force that exposes the artificiality of gender dichotomies and sexual dimorphism.

Androgyny is indeed presented in *Orlando* as a dynamic and fluctuat-
ing quality of identity that liberates the self from any supposed determinism of the body. During the process of her transformation into a
woman, Orlando at one point finds herself 'censuring both sexes equally,
as if she belonged to neither' (152). 'And indeed', the narrator goes on,
'for the time being, she seemed to vacillate; she was man; she was
woman; she knew the secrets, shared the weaknesses of each. It was a
most bewildering and whirligig state of mind to be in' (152). Identity,
then, is far less implicated in physical norms than is commonly believed
to be the case. The narrator also ends his long aside on the status of
clothes with an acknowledgement of the elusive and indeterminate character of Orlando's gender identity: 'Whether, then, Orlando was most
man or woman, it is difficult to say and cannot now be decided' (182).
The many instances of cross-dressing which the narrator records can be
seen as a literal realization of the vacillation between sexes said constantly to take place in all people. In the end, even without disguise,
Shelmerdine recognizes a man in Orlando, and Orlando a woman in
Shelmerdine (240, 246).

Through the concept of androgyny, the text opens up a space of
heterogeneity within unitary being. Gender is shown to be fluid and
multiple, irreducible to binary oppositions, which are exposed as unduly
regulatory and exclusionary. Butler confirms that the subject, as it is
constituted in contemporary hegemonic discourses, 'produces its coherence at the cost of its own complexity, the crossings of identifications of
which it is itself composed' (1993: 115). With Woolf, she celebrates the
incoherence of identity, envisaging

> an economy of difference [. . .] in which the matrices, the crossroads at
> which various identifications are formed and displaced, force a reworking of
> that logic of non-contradiction by which one identification is always and only
> purchased at the expense of another (1993: 118).

Sexuality

Another major area of subversion in *Orlando*, besides the dissolution of
gender dichotomies, is the contestation of the regime of compulsory

heterosexuality. The novel recounts how heterosexuality gets established as one of the norms that qualify a body for life within the domain of cultural intelligibility, only to contest this naturalization and to open up a space for alternative configurations of sexuality. Indeed, *Orlando* has been read as a kind of lesbian-feminist manifesto by critics such as Sherron Knopp and Elizabeth Meese. The text not only disrupts gender boundaries but also shakes the foundations of the entire edifice of heteronormativity.

Orlando enters the nineteenth century as a bemused observer of the apparent necessity for heterosexual coupling. To Orlando, 'the great discovery of marriage', by which people 'were somehow stuck together, couple after couple', 'did not seem to be Nature': 'there was no indissoluble alliance among the brutes that she could see' (231). The novel historicizes the institution of marriage by treating it as a curiosity of nineteenth-century society – a curiosity, moreover, which it goes on to condemn as indecent. Orlando opines that 'It was strange – it was distasteful; indeed, there was something in this indissolubility of bodies which was repugnant to her sense of decency and sanitation' (231-32). Yet, Orlando herself is not immune to this heterosexual contagion, and ends up submitting to 'the new discovery [...] that each man and each woman has another allotted to it for life, whom it supports, by whom it is supported, till death them do part' (234). Her longing for a husband is cast as unhealthy, as the cause of neurasthenic bouts of mania and lethargy. By thus presenting heterosexuality – rather than homosexuality – as deviant and pathological sexual behaviour, *Orlando* undermines the dominant sexuality's claim to naturalness and normativity.

Furthermore, it is strongly suggested in the novel that Orlando's capitulation to compulsory heterosexuality is not complete: 'She was married, true; but [. . .] if one liked other people, was it marriage? [. . .] She had her doubts' (252). Orlando finds that by marrying Shelmerdine, she has conformed just enough to slip by unnoticed in the age: 'she was extremely doubtful whether, if the spirit [of the age] had examined the contents of her mind carefully, it would not have found something highly contraband for which she would have had to pay the full fine. She had only escaped by the skin of her teeth' (253). Orlando's respectable marriage allows her to write overtly sapphic hymns to the charms of 'Egyptian girls' without censure (252). When the voice of the age interrogates her about her writing ('Are girls necessary?'), the narrator implies that

Orlando's heterosexual commitment to Shelmerdine allows her to elude
moral surveillance of her lesbian poetry:

> Are girls necessary? You have a husband at the Cape, you say? Ah, well,
> that'll do.
> And so the spirit passed on (253).

Allusions to homosexuality are not always so veiled, though. Earlier on
in the narrative, cross-dressing is used to introduce homosexual possibilities. The narrator explicitly states that Orlando, changing 'frequently
from one set of clothes to another' and living both sexes, 'reaped a two-
fold harvest [. . .]; the pleasures of life were increased and its experiences
multiplied' (211). Cross-dressing enables Orlando to enjoy 'the love of
both sexes equally' (211). By the time we get this declaration, lesbianism
has already been made somewhat palatable in the text by the (then) fantastic device of Orlando's sex change. Even after Orlando has become a
woman, it remains women that she loves, 'through the culpable laggardry
of the human frame to adapt itself to convention' (154). Despite her
change of sex, Orlando's former love for Sasha has not changed. The
Russian princess haunts the memory of Orlando the woman as powerfully and pervasively as she dominated the passions of Orlando the man;
indeed, 'if the consciousness of being of the same sex had any effect at
all, it was to quicken and deepen those feelings which she had had as a
man' (154). Through the device of Orlando's sex change, the novel '"ex-
culpates" the then shocking issue of lesbianism', achieving a 'cunning
naturalization' of it (Minow-Pinkney 1987: 134).

The narrator's insistence on the reality and profundity of a woman's
love for a woman gives the lie to men's belief that love between women
is impossible. This opinion finds expression in a passage which deserves
quoting in full, not only for the way in which it exposes the patriarchal
repression of lesbian eroticism, but also for the destabilization of the
narrator's gender which it enacts:

> it cannot be denied that when women get together – but hist – they are
> always careful to see that the doors are shut and that not a word of it gets
> into print. All they desire is – but hist again – is that not a man's step on the
> stair? All they desire, we were about to say when the gentleman took the very
> words out of our mouths. Women have no desires, says this gentleman,
> coming into Nell's parlour; only affectations. [. . .] 'It is well known', says Mr
> S.W., 'that when they lack the stimulus of the other sex, women can find
> nothing to say to each other [. . .].' And since [. . .] it is well known (Mr T.R.
> has proved it) 'that women are incapable of any feeling of affection for their

own sex and hold each other in the greatest aversion', what can we suppose
that women do when they seek out each other's society?

As that is not a question that can engage the attention of a sensible man,
let us, who enjoy the immunity of all biographers and historians from
any sex whatever, pass it over, and merely state that Orlando professed
great enjoyment in the society of her own sex, and leave it to the gentlemen to prove, as they are very fond of doing, that this is impossible
(209-10).

Women, according to the male authors cited by the narrator, can only
exist in relation to men. They have nothing to say to other members of
their own sex, whose company they dislike. The question as to 'what
women do when they seek out each other's society' is left hanging as the
narrator diverts attention to himself. Then he lets it be known that, contrary to what Mr S.W. and Mr T.R. think possible, 'Orlando professed
great enjoyment in the society of her own sex'. What exactly we are supposed to understand here by 'enjoyment' is not further specified, but it
would seem to pick up on the hanging question of the previous paragraph and thus may be read as a subtle hint at lesbian eroticism. Perhaps,
then, lesbian love-making is what women most desire.

The upholders of heteropatriarchal power, however, prevent
women's desire from getting into the order of representation. No sooner
do Orlando and her women friends try to speak of what they desire than
their words are snatched away, repressed and denied by a man bursting
in on the scene to declare with the full force of his masculine authority
that there is no such thing as female desire. As a result, the sentence
beginning, 'All they desire is [. . .]', is suspended in mid-air and left unfin-
ished.

Besides validating homosexual desire and denouncing its silencing,
this passage also calls into question the stability of the narrator's sex.
Like Orlando, the narrator, who up until then has always seemed male, is
revealed here to be 'a figure of perpetual oscillation' (Parkes 1994: 453).
Indeed, it is extremely difficult to pin the narrator down to one particular
sex in this passage. Having access to the women's quarters, he first appears to be a female observer, but then shifts to another realm where the
voice is implicitly detached from the women ('they' as opposed to 'we'),
yet not necessarily associated with the man whose step is heard on the
stair. The narrator assumes an ironic distance from Mr S.W. and his
appeal to the supposedly 'objective' authority of common knowledge and
the quasi-scientific 'proof' of Mr T.R. A few lines later he claims sexual

neutrality for himself, but this may be a male pose designed to give the air of impartial authority – the very strategy adopted by Mr S.W., in fact. It is indeed rather ironic to find the narrator dissociating himself from 'gentlemen' who are 'very fond' of proving things when, throughout the novel, the narrator's own anxieties betray an immense concern for 'facts' and 'truth'. The indeterminacy of the narrator's gender – which modulates from male to female to neutral in the space of just a few sentences – contributes to the text's overall project of dissolving reified gender categories.

Orlando's pushing at the boundaries of what it is possible to think in the areas of gender and sexuality may be understood as an attempt to prevent the closure of the gender system. By making gender trouble, the text hopes to effect a rearticulation of the terms of symbolic legitimacy and intelligibility which would result in gender configurations being proliferated outside the restricting frames of masculinist domination and compulsory heterosexuality. Without meaning to downplay *Orlando*'s humorous quality or to diminish the importance of Vita Sackville-West in Woolf's life and writing, we can reaffirm in conclusion that by reducing this novel to biography or gratuitous play, we risk rendering these subversive motives invisible and preventing them from influencing and altering other texts and discourses.

References

Burns, Christy L. 1994. 'Re-Dressing Feminist Identities: Tensions Between Essential and Constructed Selves in Virginia Woolf's *Orlando*' in *Twentieth Century Literature* 40(3): 342-64.

Butler, Judith. 1990. *Gender Trouble: Feminism and the Subversion of Identity*. New York: Routledge.

Butler, Judith. 1991. 'Imitation and Gender Insubordination' in Fuss, Diana (ed.) *Inside/Out: Lesbian Theories, Gay Theories*. London: Routledge: 13-31.

Butler, Judith. 1993. *Bodies that Matter: On the Discursive Limits of 'Sex'*. New York: Routledge.

Cervetti, Nancy. 1996. 'In the Breeches, Petticoats, and Pleasures of *Orlando*' in *Journal of Modern Literature* 20(2): 165-75.

Garber, Marjorie. 1993. *Vested Interests: Cross-Dressing and Cultural Anxiety*. London: Penguin.

Hovey, Jaime. 1997. '"Kissing a Negress in the Dark": Englishness as a Masquerade in Woolf's *Orlando*' in *PMLA* 112(3): 393-404.

Irigaray, Luce. 1996. "'The Powers of Discourse and the Subordination of the Feminine": this Sex which is not One' in Eagleton, Mary (ed.) *Feminist Literary Theory: A Reader*. 2nd ed. Oxford: Blackwell: 316-20.

Knopp, Sherron E. 1988. "'If I Saw You Would You Kiss Me?": Sapphism and the Subversiveness of Virginia Woolf's *Orlando*' in *PMLA* 103(1): 24-34.

Lawrence, Karen R. 1992. 'Orlando's Voyage Out' in *Modern Fiction Studies* 38(1): 253-77.

Meese, Elizabeth. 1997. 'When Virginia Looked at Vita, What did she See; or, Lesbian: Feminist: Woman – What's the Differ(e/a)nce?' in Warhol, Robyn R. and Diane Price Herndl (eds) *Feminisms: An Anthology of Literary Theory and Criticism*. Revised ed. Basingstoke: Macmillan: 467-81.

Minow-Pinkney, Makiko. 1987. *Virginia Woolf and the Problem of the Subject: Feminine Writing in the Major Novels*. Brighton: Harvester.

Parkes, Adam. 1994. 'Lesbianism, History, and Censorship: *The Well of Loneliness* and the Suppressed Randiness of Virginia Woolf's *Orlando*' in *Twentieth Century Literature* 40(4): 434-60.

Schaffer, Talia. 1994. 'Posing *Orlando*' in Kibbey, Ann, Kayann Short and Abouali Farmanfarmaian (eds) *Sexual Artifice: Persons, Images, Politics* (Genders 19). New York: New York UP: 26-63.

Showalter, Elaine. 1977. *A Literature of Their Own: British Women Novelists from Brontë to Lessing*. Princeton: Princeton UP.

Stone, Sandy. 1991. 'The *Empire* Strikes Back: a Posttranssexual Manifesto' in Epstein, Julia and Kristina Straub (eds) *Body Guards: the Cultural Politics of Gender Ambiguity*. New York: Routledge: 280-304.

Watkins, Susan. 1998. 'Sex Change and Media Change: from Woolf's to Potter's *Orlando*' in *Mosaic* 31(3): 41-59.

Woolf, Virginia. 1992. *Orlando: a Biography* (Oxford World's Classics). Bowlby, Rachel (ed.). Oxford: Oxford UP.

CHAPTER 12

(PORNO)GRAPHIC DEPICTIONS:
IMAGE AND SEXUAL IDENTITY

Mary Anne Franks

There are very few kinds of sexual imagery that incite almost unanimous social condemnation in today's society. Images of sado-masochism, group sex, and even rape and bestiality – while formerly controversial – have for the most part gone mainstream, or at least have become widely socially available and tolerated. However, it is still the case that the sexual representation of children is widely denounced. Few mainstream attempts have been made to justify the consumption or making of child pornography, and even those who are found to be associated with it tend to condemn themselves, to apologize profusely for their actions, and vow to seek help for what they admit is a terrible sickness. By contrast, consuming 'adult' pornography – even that of a violent nature – is not subject to widespread social censure, and it is not the case that the majority of adults feel compelled to hide the habit. Consuming adult pornography has even been openly admitted by people accused of viewing child pornography as a kind of defence and proof of 'normal' sexual proclivities. When 'Who' guitarist Pete Townshend was being investigated for downloading child pornography, he announced that while he despised child pornography, 'I've always been into [presumably adult] porn. I've used it all my life' (Aitkenhead 2004). When another music celebrity, Robert del Naja (vocalist for 'Massive Attack') was arrested on similar charges, he said, 'I've always been open about [adult] porn' (Petridis 2004), and referred to the fact that he had even contributed to the soundtrack for a porn film. As UK journalist Decca Aitkenhead writes,

> Fears over online child pornography have grown so great they have had an unexpected moral side effect, downgrading the adult variety to the humdrum. Even hardcore, illegal porn attracts little attention. The police are no longer interested, nor is the Government, and not one person has been sent to prison in Britain for adult cyberporn offences. Paedophilia has done for the top shelf what crack cocaine did for cannabis, re-branding what was once considered vice into an innocuous popular pastime (Aitkenhead 2004).

On the one hand, then, it would seem that Western society has become increasingly tolerant of (and also eager for) images of any number of heretofore taboo sexual practices among adults, while holding fast to (or even becoming more conservative in) conventional beliefs regarding the sexual representation of children. A very sharp determination is made here between what qualifies as a sexually acceptable portrayal of adults – that is to say, almost everything – and what qualifies as a sexually acceptable portrayal of children – that is to say, almost nothing. There could not be a more striking contrast between the lack of analysis and critical reflection offered or suggested in the former, and the decisive clarity of judgement in the latter. It would be only a slight overstatement to maintain that the taboo against child pornography is the only widely socially supported taboo left in the realm of sexual imagery. Child pornography is certainly the only form of pornography subject to legal regulation in Western countries. My interest here is not to provide a rationale for removing the taboo against the sexual representation of children, but rather to address what seems to be its converse – the utter lack of judgement or even critical dialogue regarding the sexual representations of adults. Contemporary Western society's reliance on the arbitrary and deceptively simple adult/child distinction fails to address any number of crucial issues concerning the relationship between sexual imagery and sexual identity – even those that should directly follow from the purported harm that child pornography inflicts on children and adults. My claim is that one cannot be genuinely consistent in arguing against child pornography while defending adult pornography, and I will demonstrate this by analysing the claims regarding image, identity, and autonomy in both cases.

   John Perry Barlow was purportedly the first person to use William Gibson's term 'cyberspace' to describe the global electronic universe of the Internet. In 1996, he published an on-line manifesto entitled, 'A Cyberspace Declaration of Independence' (Barlow 2003). In this manifesto, addressed to the 'Governments of the Industrialized World', Barlow describes cyberspace as 'a world that is both everywhere and nowhere,' but is 'not where bodies live.' In this utopian celebration of cyberspace, Barlow makes some interesting claims about identity: 'legal concepts of property, expression, identity, movement, and context do not apply to us. They are all based on matter, and there is no matter here. Our identities have no bodies, so, unlike you, we cannot obtain order by physical coercion.'

This almost religious belief in 'identity without body' – also without borders – could be seen as the defining belief of the increasingly global society of the twenty-first century. From software commercials set to the lyrics of 'I am, I am Superman, and I can do anything', to postmodern theories of the 'body without organs', identity is perceived as thoroughly malleable, limitless, infinitely changeable, but also infinitely powerful. As Barlow indicates, this fluidity and abstraction of identity is supposedly empowering. The conception of the new, fearless bodiless identity rests upon a rather old – at least as old as Humanism – and rather conservative belief in autonomy. It is not by accident that Barlow cites thinkers such as Thomas Jefferson in his manifesto; it should be recalled that the noble sentiment that 'all men are created equal and have certain unalienable rights' was asserted in the face of slavery and the disenfranchisement and subordination of women. But herein lies the paradox of bodiless identity: the fate of the real and limited bodies of citizens – the beaten slave, the girl sold into marriage – gives the lie to the abstraction of identity and the presumption of autonomy. Bodies *do* matter, and their rhetorical banishment from the realm of cyberspace results in many haunting returns. Consider how the very terrain on which such abstracting rhetoric is mapped is populated by bodies: cyberspace is filled with the fantasies of bodies, of imagined flesh, of compulsive and violent obsessions with sex, and many contorted revisions of autonomy are needed to keep alive the illusion of utopia. Barlow's dream of identity without bodies translates, even more now than in 1996, into a crude and unimaginative reality of bodies without identity. Cyberspace's volatile balance between being both somehow 'more real' than reality but also a fantasized 'other place' erupts precisely along the fault line of bodily autonomy, so greatly determined by the relationship between image and identity. This accounts to a great extent both for the existence of a phenomenon such as child pornography and for the desperate attempts to eradicate it.

The standard liberal defence for so-called 'adult' or 'mainstream' pornography has for a long time rested on rather facile conceptions of 'consent' possible (only) among adults, which in its turn rests on a simplistic notion of autonomy. 'Consenting *adults* can make any decisions about sexuality they want'; 'As *adults* we can simply change the channel if we don't like something'; 'We are after all *adults* who can make our own decisions about what we want to see or hear', etc. It is argued that not only is no participant harmed in the making of pornography, but also that no one's self-image or identity is harmed by pornography.

With child pornography, however, the rules are very different. Children are effectively posited as individuals who *cannot* consent. All it takes to provoke a wild shift in response from tolerance and even enthusiasm to criticism and moral condemnation is to insert the word 'child' just before the word 'pornography.' Suddenly one speaks not of consent and autonomy, but of coercion, deception, manipulation. According to conventional wisdom, not only are the actual children depicted in pornography harmed in the making of the product, but their self-image and identity suffers permanent damage. Also, it is argued that other children are harmed by child pornography, because presenting *any* child in a sexualized way makes *all* children more vulnerable to abuse. In the context of sexual imagery, children are conceived as a 'class' or identifiable subgroup of individuals, all of whom are at risk of sexual objectification if one is at risk. Furthermore, it is argued that child pornography also harms consumers, as it provides potential pedophiles with an opportunity to indulge their fantasies and encourages them to seek out more and more images – in other words, that child pornography also has an effect on adults' self-image and identity.

Children, then, do not have the capacity to consent to sex with or for adults, and their identity is both ongoing and collective, and thus there is the attendant fear that they may be seduced or manipulated into believing they have consented or should consent to such acts. Those children who appear in pornographic images are said to be victims, and those who make or consume the images are criminals in the eyes of the law and society. This stands in stark contrast to the billion-dollar industry of mainstream pornography by and for adults, legally and socially tolerated. It is fair to say, then, that at least one way of conceiving these strangely fine distinctions in pornography is along the lines of identity, between the consenting, fully autonomous, adult identity and the still-forming, nascent, impressionable child identity.

We might then call child pornography a development of harmful identity through imagery. In this assessment, one assumes that, first, a child's physical and mental identity is seriously damaged by being the object of a pornographic image. This is held to be true even if the child should claim that he or she was a willing participant. For as far as the law is concerned, this is impossible. Images of child pornography also produce a harmful identity in the producers, distributors, and consumers, as their participation in these images allows them to indulge, encourage, and justify a self-identity as predators. And finally, child pornography threatens the identity of all children, as these images present them to predators in a specifically victimized and sexualized manner, which can and does lead to child molestation. It would follow too that children who have been the victims of pornography, who have been taught to associate and accept the necessity of violation and exploitation in sexual relations, might grow up to be adults who continue to accept them.

But such adults would not be of concern in the general pornography debate. We are now in the world of *adult* fantasy, *adult* sexuality, *adult* consent. Once a child becomes an adult, harmful identity is somehow transformed into autonomous identity. Suddenly the individuals involved in pornography possess a powerful, fully self-aware identity, from the women who pose for Internet porn sites to the men who masturbate to their images. To the suggestion that such women are exploited or that men masturbating at their computers are unable to treat women as human beings, the standard liberal response is that these people are making their own free, harmless choices; they are not, after all, *children* who do not realise the full implications of the practices of which they are a part. The pornography industry, which in the US alone generates from nine to thirteen billion dollars a year, is supposedly a great testament to Western autonomy and freedom, where adults are free to pursue and enjoy all things sexual without harming themselves or others. Everyone can 'explore' his or her sexual identity in any way he or she sees fit.

Why, then, are the limits of this exploration so disturbingly consistent? Mainstream pornography overwhelmingly exhibits the female body, not the male. Consumers of mainstream pornography (as well as, incidentally, all other forms of pornography) are according to many studies over 95 per cent male. *Hustler* magazine prefers women in chains, threatened with weapons, or put through meat grinders. The image of sexual identity that pornography obsessively displays is of cut-and-paste women, with the artificially enhanced breasts of an über-sex object and the shaved genitals reminiscent of pre-pubescent girls. Adult sexual identity, far from being the dreamed-of 'bodiless identity,' is in fact insistently imaged in one particular body. And yet the lie goes unnoticed.

To explain this, one must consider the sheer omnipresence of pornographic images in Western society. It is one thing to assert that some individuals have made a conscious choice to produce certain images and certain individuals to buy them, but justifying the fact that all women (and men) are subsequently forced to view them (at magazine stands, newspaper stores, the phone booths in London) is quite another. In her book *The Imaginary Domain,* Drucilla Cornell writes,

> To strip someone forcibly of her self-image, particularly when that image is as basic as that of bodily integrity, is a violation. . . . It is the confrontation with the images in their inevitability, because they are allowed to pervade our public space so thoroughly, that itself constitutes the violation. . . . the images are those that have been encoded as the truth of our 'sex' in a heterosexual masculine symbolic. . . . it is the encoding of these images, through their domination of public space, that makes them seem as if they were the truth of sex and not just one particular imaginary (Cornell 1995: 148).

Cornell suggests that while pornography should not be censored, its public distribution should be restricted so that women might be left free to construct a different sexual imaginary for themselves. By affirming this, Cornell makes a clear link between sexual image and sexual identity. She therefore rejects the idea that any identity, even adult sexual identity, is 'without body' and fully autonomous. By the same token, however, Cornell maintains that one cannot and should not censor the production of pornography. Women, as adult citizens, must have the right to construct their sexual imaginaries in any way they choose, including by and through pornography.

The far too obvious observation to be made here is that every adult was also once a child. Modern Western societies are always-already embedded in the pornographic context; no woman alive today lived in a world before or separate from the one imposing a limited and limiting image of her sexuality. Women's sexual imaginaries are necessarily constructed by and through these images, which, as Cornell herself concedes, can and does prevent them from truly imagining a different sexual identity. To believe that when children become adults, previously manipulated and exploited identities are somehow transformed into subversive and autonomous ones, is to be blind to the fact that identity, especially sexual identity, is a process that begins as soon as we are capable of looking at images, and as soon as we are capable of being looked at as images. Like Barlow, Cornell asserts a fictional capacity of autonomy to hide the possible wounds in the bodies we image.

As Louis Althusser observed, the rhetoric of autonomy is often no more than a disguise for the brutal truth of subjection:

> the individual is interpellated as a (free) subject in order that he shall submit freely to the commandments of the Subject, i.e. in order that he shall (freely)

accept his subjection, i.e. in order that he shall make the gestures and actions of his subjection 'all by himself' (Althusser 1994: 136).

The construction of an *adult fantasy world* where all people are free and equal – where bodies truly do not matter – disguises the historical and statistical reality of sexuality, all too often characterized by violence, manipulation, and subordination. We wring our hands over child pornography and abuse, and agree that rape and domestic violence are crimes; and yet we consume and encourage sexual imagery that present childlike attributes as sexually tantalizing, and rape and beatings as sexually stimulating. We ignore the fact that the pornographic image, like all photographic images, is mute: it provides no indication of whether the act portrayed is consensual, it makes no distinction between the body of a fifteen-year old girl and that of a twenty-five year old, between a rape and a sex romp. We formally decry child pornography, rape, and domestic violence, but tolerate, endorse, and distribute imagery that present all of these in a sexual manner. We allow the sexualization, publication, and glorification of every possible inequality among individuals and excuse ourselves from the reality of abuse and violation with an anaesthetizing rhetoric of consenting adults and autonomous identity. We forget history – our own and that of others.

In the notes to *Dialectic of Enlightenment,* Theodor Adorno recounts the reservations of a physiologist regarding the use chloroform in surgery, which had recently become popular in his time. The physiologist (Pierre Flourens) writes that because a chloroformed patient has no memory of the operation, he is misled into believing that the chloroform prevented him from feeling any pain. What he doesn't know, writes Flourens, is that pain is actually experienced *more strongly* when a patient is anaesthetized – chloroform affects only the ability of the nervous system to retain sense impressions. It succeeds, in effect, in making the patient *lose his memory of pain.* Adorno considers that if mankind had taken Flourens's reservations seriously, 'the suspicion would then arise that our relationship with men and creation in general was like our relationship with ourself [*sic*] after an operation – oblivion for suffering. All objectification is a forgetting (Adorno & Horkheimer 1995: 230).

The anaesthetizing myth of identity fails to examine human relations and interactions in light of violation and pain. As Roland Barthes (1998) theorized, myth is that which decontextualizes and reifies, so that abuses and atrocities appear inevitable, ahistorical, and finally natural. The myth of sexual identity without bodies disciplines women into sexualizing their

subordination by offering no alternative sexual identity or even a space
free of pornographic imagery. It encourages the 75 per cent of sex industry workers who admit they were sexually abused as children to return to
the site of that violence every day and record and distribute it. It allows
men who refuse to view a woman simultaneously as a sexual and equal
human being to indulge in a split, predatory conception of the world
which marks off some humans as fit only for sexual use. It creates a
world in which anxiety, fear, and hatred determines the terrain on which
people come into their own sexual identities. The conception of an 'identity without body', free to embrace all images of all possible abuses and
violations, produces the body without identity: the physical, historical,
vulnerable body, broken into, butchered alive, and displayed, but with no
memory of pain.

References

Adorno, Theodor & Horkheimer, Max. 1995. *The Dialectic of Enlightenment*. Trans.
    John Cumming. Continuum: New York.
Aitkenhead, Decca. 2004. 'Net Porn'. On line at: http://observer.guardian.
    co.uk/review/story/0,6903,925264,00.html (accessed February 2004).
Althusser, Louis. 1994. 'Ideology and Ideological State Apparatuses' in Zizek,
    Slavoj (ed.) *Mapping Ideology*. London & New York: Verso.
Barlow, John Perry. 2003. 'A Cyberspace Declaration of Independence'. On line
    at: http://www.eff.org/~barlow/Declaration-Final.html (accessed Decem-
    ber 2003).
Barthes, Roland. 1998. 'Myth Today' in Sontag, Susan (ed.) *A Barthes Reader*.
    New York: Hill & Wang.
Cornell, Drucilla. 1995. *The Imaginary Domain: Abortion, Pornography, and Sexual
    Harassment*. London: Routledge.
Petridis, Alex. 2004. 'I've always been open about porn'. On line at: http://www.
    guardian.co.uk/friday_review/story/0,3605,933722,00.html (accessed Janu-
    ary 2004).

CHAPTER 13

WOMEN'S IMAGE AND NATIONAL IDENTITY IN THE INDIAN NATIONALIST MOVEMENT

Nuria López

During the nationalist and pro-independence movement that culminated in the independence of India from Great Britain in 1947, Indian women became a visible and active part of the anti-colonial struggle. They participated in public demonstrations against British rule and, at very early stages of the movement, they carried out several political activities hidden from the British authorities. Furthermore, Indian women were entrusted with the role of representing Indian tradition in order to prove that, in spite of Britain's superiority in the public domain, India was nevertheless superior in the private world of the home and the family. This private sphere, which had allegedly remained untouched by Westernization, became synonymous with a national Indian identity which could support Indians' demands for independence. As the central figures in the traditional family unit, Indian women had to conform to a series of *rules* which were to turn them into paragons of Indian traditional culture, that is, into symbols of Indian national identity. This essay will explore how Indian women adapted their appearance and behaviour in order to meet the new necessities of the nationalist cause, how they were affected by the nationalist symbolism attached to them during the independence movement, and to what extent their lives were changed by the role they undertook during the anti-colonial fight once this was over. In order to frame the main topic, we shall commence with some definitions of nation and the role of national identity in nationalist struggles. Nations, unlike states, do not have a political quality; their origin rather lies in cultural aspects that cannot be physically defined. Benedict Anderson, who has provided us with one of the most quoted definitions of nation, refers to its non-physical nature when he defines it as an *imagined community*,

> because the members of even the smallest nation will never know most of their fellow-members, meet them, or even hear of them, yet in the minds of each lives the image of their communion (Anderson 1983: 15).

If the nation is a product of the imagination of a group of people who perceive themselves as belonging to the same community, there must be some aspect that accounts for this imaginary link in their minds. Anderson points out that 'nations [...] always loom out of an immemorial past, and, still more important, glide into a limitless future' (1983: 19). Equally, Ernest Renan (1990: 19) stated that two things constitute the spiritual principle that is the nation: the possession of a common rich legacy of memories, and the desire to live together and perpetuate the value of the heritage received: a common heritage and a willingness to share a future.

With regard to the specific context of colonialism, the existence of a common cultural legacy from the past fulfils a role of paramount importance in the nationalist movements that lead colonies to independence. Since independence movements are based not only on political requests but also on the defence of the social customs, traditions and religious practices shared by a community, those fighting for their independence usually claim that their distinct culture is an important reason to justify their political autonomy. Furthermore, the rediscovery of the past in colonized societies contributes to the creation of a national identity free from the negative stereotypes imposed by the colonial process, which represses and manipulates the native character by claiming its inferiority and portraying it as a valueless identity.

On 15 August 1947, India became an independent country after more than two centuries under British control. In the face of the technological and economic superiority of the British, Indian nationalists resorted to the Indian family to create an oasis where Indian national identity could be preserved from Western influence. This division of the cultural world into the two different domains of the public (the economic, technological and political world) and the private (the world of the family, religion and indigenous tradition) allowed Indian nationalists to create, even within the colonial network, a space in which India was still the sovereign (Chatterjee 1990: 239).

It is at this moment when the relationship between Indian women and the Indian national identity becomes crucial in the context of the nationalist movement. Traditionally, the female terrain had been the domestic space (the home), and for this reason, the nationalist-orientated meaning assigned to the private sphere inevitably affected Indian women. They were entrusted with the role of proving the cultural superiority of India in the private world and became embodiments of the Indian national identity. Symbolism was to play an essential role in the independence movement, for political demands had to be supported by a mass movement, which could only be achieved by common symbols that could make Indians identify as a nation and fight together against British rule. To fulfil this purpose, Indian women were erected as nationalist symbols by becoming depositories of Indian culture. They were put in charge of showing that their behaviour and appearance were characteristic of the traditional Indian woman, or what amounts to the same thing, that they had not been influenced by the Westernization that British rule had produced in other domains.

In this respect, the role entrusted to Indian women of reaffirming the native culture meant a certain backward movement in relation to the very incipient emancipation of certain groups of women at the beginning of the nineteenth century, when a group of Western-educated Bengali intellectuals had defended the modernization of Indian women as a way of encouraging progress in India. They had provided their wives and daughters with an education in order to create Westernized Indian women who could become suitable companions for Indian men who had received a Western education. But the interests of nationalists regarding women were completely different, if not opposite, to those of the Bengali intellectuals in the nineteenth century.

The ideal nationalist Indian women had to prove to be more Indian, and less British, than ever. The superiority of Indian private life needed to be asserted in order to counteract the superiority of the British in the public domain and, therefore, Indian women, as living representations of the indigenous traditions, had to conform to a series of implicit rules that were used to measure the degree of their Westernization. Western manners went through a very careful selection, and the *memsahibs* (British women in India) were no longer the model that Indian women should imitate, since it was considered that Western women had adopted an attitude and a set of values that had led to the loss of spirituality and feminine virtues. It was the genuine Indian tradition that Indian women should follow, and there was one specific aspect that had to remain completely immune from any sign of Westernization: the spirituality of the Indian way of life.

Since the spirituality of Indian culture was mainly manifested at home, the traditionally feminine context, Indian women became the guardians of the spiritual values of their society. Indian mythology had traditionally portrayed Indian women as devoted, submissive, chaste, religious, benevolent and with a great capacity for self-sacrifice. During the nationalist movement, this mythological image was praised and self-sacrifice, devotion, submission, chastity, kindness, religiosity and benevolence became the essential characteristics of the ideal Indian woman. This new model of Indian woman, later known as the New Woman, was one of the most powerful manifestations of national identity. The spirituality of the New Women conferred on Indian women a status superior not only to Westernized Indian women but also to Western women themselves. According to nationalist discourses, the Westernized Indian women had not been able to preserve Indian traditions and had let themselves be dazzled by the material superiority of the West, whereas Western women had lost all feminine virtues and had happily abandoned their traditional role in their determination to enter the public, male world.

In order to display the preservation of feminine virtues and differentiate themselves from Westernized or Western women, the New Women had to take great care over their outward appearance and behaviour. Social relations should never make them neglect their duties in the home, and their religious practices could not be missed. More trivial aspects like dress were also important. The New Woman would never wear Western clothes, jewellery or make-up. Even the Bengali theatre at the end of the nineteenth century was put at the service of the nationalist cause by showing to the Indian public that the customs of the *memsahibs* were not signs of their superior civilization but, on the contrary, proofs of the decadent state of the private sphere of the Western world. Plays ridiculing Indian women who used make-up or Western jewellery and clothes became very popular and successful. Other habits or pastimes like reading novels, doing needlework or riding in open carriages were considered useless and were also criticized on the stage. This critique was intensified by a tendency to portray those women completely neglecting their homes (Chatterjee 1993: 122).

The nationalist attachment to traditional feminine behaviour has recently been seen as responsible for placing Indian women under a new patriarchy. This emphasis on the spiritual virtues of women conditioned female lives by imposing on them a remarkable religious devotion, and by intensifying their bond with the house and the family. Since the role of women as mothers had traditionally been the main objective of women in Indian society, motherhood was also considered a necessary occupation of the New Woman. In fact, as in many other anti-colonial nationalist movements, the figure of the woman as mother took an important place among the nationalist symbols. Women were seen as the mothers of the nation and soon became metaphors for the nation itself. This symbolism extolled the biological female capacity of giving birth and, therefore, it seems to have given some power to women. However, by reinforcing the identification of women with motherhood and emphasizing even more the traditional feminine roles, it made it more difficult for women to achieve at least some independence from the family and to enter public life.

The British had repeatedly pointed out that the backward situation of Indian women showed the uncivilized manners of the Indians, which at the same time was an indication that they were not prepared for self-rule. Faced with this critique from the British government, Indian nationalists needed to prove that they approved of the education of their women, and that ancient barbaric practices like the immolation of widows in the funeral pyres of their husbands (*sati*) were not longer in use. Thus, in spite of the traditional role entrusted to women, nationalists also proposed that the New Woman had to be an educated woman. Education can be considered as the only Western influence that was not rejected, though neither was it unconditionally accepted. Some arrangements had first to be made in order to make education suitable for the Indian women of the nationalist movement.

The fact that early schools were organized by Christian missionaries, and that education was administered in English, was seen as a threat for Indian women, for Christianity and the English language could constitute a harmful Western influence on them. In any case, it was believed that it was not necessary for Indian women to learn English because they were to stay at home and were not needed in the public sphere. These problems were solved when Indians themselves began to open schools for girls from the 1850s onwards and by the development of teaching material in the indigenous languages. The nationalist concept of education was closely related to the ideal of femininity. Whereas education for boys was meant to prepare them for the public world and even the political scene, schooling for girls was meant to make Indian women better housewives and mothers, that is, to make them more able to run the household and play the role of the perfect New Woman. Education was accepted as long as it did not jeopardize the traditional position of women in society and did not make them lose their feminine virtues, which it was thought had been the effect of education on Western women.

The participation of Indian women in the nationalist project was intensified when Gandhi became the leader of the nationalist movement after his return from South Africa in 1915. Bengali women had already collaborated actively in the fight against colonial rule in 1905, when the British ordered the partition of the province of Bengal. At that time women had used their traditional roles to mask a series of illegal activities such as hiding weapons or sheltering fugitives, and had joined men in the boycott of foreign goods in favour of the products made in Bengal (Forbes 1996: 123).

From the very beginning, Gandhi counted on both men and women for the non-violent struggle that he promoted. Arguing that India's poverty was caused to a large extent by the purchase of imported goods, he encouraged Indians to boycott foreign products. Gandhi's appeal to the Indians was extraordinary, and both Indian men and women from all parts of the country began to take part in the boycott, which became known as the *swadeshi* (from the country) movement. As part of the *swadeshi* movement, Gandhi made popular the activity of spinning, which allowed Indians to make their own cloth instead of buying the imported version from Britain. Spinning was a traditionally feminine activity, and the Mahatma encouraged women to spin every day, as he himself did. The spinning staff soon became a symbol of the anti-colonial fight, and served to idealize the traditional manual work of Indian women and make them a more visible part of the nationalist movement. However, it also reinforced the traditional image of women as passive full-time workers in the household.

This contradictory symbolism of the spinning staff is just an example of the ambiguities and double standards of nationalism in relation to the women's question. Under Gandhi's leadership, women not only joined the boycott and donated money and jewellery for the cause, but also participated in numerous demonstrations and meetings during the civil disobedience campaign in the 1930s. Both Indian men and the British were surprised at the determination and public presence of Indian women, as Jawaharlal Nehru, the first prime minister of independent India, pointed out:

> Most of us menfolk were in prison. And then a remarkable thing happened. Our women came to the front and took charge of the struggle. Women had always been there, of course, but now there was an avalanche of them, which took not only the British government but their own menfolk by surprise. Here were these women, women of the upper or middle classes, leading

sheltered lives in their homes, peasant women, working class women, rich women, poor women, pouring out in their tens of thousands in defiance of government order and police (cited in Liddle and Joshi 1986: 34).

However, in spite of the active participation of women in the civil disobedience campaign, the clear-cut division between the public and the private spheres did not disappear at all. In fact, Gandhi's ideas about the role of women in the nationalist movement contributed to the permanence of this public-private opposition. He certainly helped to make women an important and visible part of the pro-independence struggle, but he also opposed their participation in certain anti-colonial manifestations like the Salt March.[1] When Gandhi urged women to join the anti-colonial movement, he asked them to be like the ancient heroines, who had been faithful, brave, and had suffered with great dignity. He usually resorted to the well known Hindu legend of the demon Ravana and Sita to explain to his female followers what he expected from them. Sita, wife of the god Rama, was kidnapped by the demon Ravana. Rama spent many years looking for his wife before he could finally rescue her. Nevertheless, the god considered that his wife was indecent for having spent such a long time in the company of another man and decided to exile her. Sita, who had been an example of purity and faithfulness, accepted his husband's order with resignation and ended up wishing for her own death (Waterstone 1996: 53). The British, Gandhi said, were like the demon Ravana, and Indian women had to play the role of the long-suffering Sita (Forbes 1996: 150). Sita's suffering in silence and her unquestioning deference to her husband were the attributes that showed the great nobility of Indian women. Although the Mahatma maintained that women and men had equal intellectual capacities, he also encouraged women to conform to their traditional role in order to fight against the British colonization.

Although it is true that during the nationalist phase led by Gandhi, Indian women became a numerous and constant presence in public popular manifestations against British rule, it cannot be argued that women were given free access to public life. Once their duty to the nationalist cause was fulfilled, they were expected to return to their private domain and to continue playing their traditional role as wives and moth-

---

[1] Gandhi opposed the British monopoly over the salt in India. In March 1930, he started a 250 kilometre-long march towards the coast and hundreds of people joined in on the way. When they arrived at the coast they started to collect water, challenging the British law that only allowed buying salt in official shops.

ers. Besides, those women who joined men in public were discouraged
from becoming militants, which was the role designated to men. Parama
Roy refers to the distinct roles assigned to men and women in the Indian
nationalist struggle and explains that

> women are an atavistic and [the] authentic 'body' of national identities; they
> signify nationalism's link to a deep past, its conservative principle. Men on
> the other hand stand in for the modernity of nationalism, which is dynamic,
> aggressive, and revolutionary (Roy 1998: 137).

Hence, the symbolism attached to each sex determined the role of each
person in his or her fight against the colonial situation. Whereas men
were to be responsible for the dynamic fight, women were in charge of a
passive struggle that was identified with the preservation of traditional
spiritual values, and reinforced their bond to tradition. Indian women
were supposed to function as representative of some ideas rather than as
active defenders of anti-colonial beliefs. All the aspects that were extolled
as archetypal feminine virtues of Indian women (self-sacrifice, submission, etc.) emphasized the passive character of traditional women; the
household was portrayed as the feminine space par excellence, and
motherhood as the divine female gift. However, female active participation in the anti-colonial movement was not encouraged at all, and neither
was education intended to give women the opportunity to enter the
public world. Indian women did play an important role in the pro-independence movement, but it was a selective one, that praised and reinforced their traditional (and inferior) position in society.

India was declared an independent country in August 1947. In principle, the New Women were not needed anymore; they had already fulfilled their role in the anti-colonial struggle. If Indian women had undeni-
ably been given freedom from colonial domination, they had not been
given freedom from the patriarchal values of their society. India was free,
but Indian women were not. The idea of the New Women had guided
the conduct of Indian women for almost half a century, and it had inevitably become strongly rooted in Indian society. Should the 'New Woman
model' replaced by a new one, or should it continue to be the ideal
model for Indian woman even after 1947?

Shortly after independence, a report published by the University
Education Commission stated that a 'well-ordered home helps to make
well-ordered men' and that 'the greatest profession of women is and
probably will continue to be that of home-maker' (Desai and Krishnara:

1990: 140-41). The ideas regarding the role of women in society had not changed significantly after 1947. In 1973, *Femina*, a popular magazine for women, published a special issue to commemorate the coming of independence. The note that appeared on the cover read,

> To be a woman – a wife, a mother, an individual – in India means many things. It means that you are the store-house of tradition and culture and, in contrast a volcano of seething energy, of strength and power that can motivate a whole generation to change its values, its aspirations, its very concept of civilized life (cited in Forbes 1996: 227).

These words, written more than two decades after independence, echo the ideal of the New Woman, who was, above all, the 'store-house of tradition and culture'. Likewise, in 1971, the Ministry of Education and Social Welfare appointed a committee to examine the social status of women. The results of this examination, published in a report entitled *Toward Equality* (1974), showed that the status of Indian women after independence had declined. According to the report, Indian women were not aware of their legal rights, even though they were recognized in the 1950 Constitution, and many did not have the opportunity to achieve anything other than the traditional roles.

During the last two decades of the twentieth century the participation of Indian women in the public life of their country increased, and their access to higher education improved significantly, resulting in the formation of a new grouping of urban middle-class women who have been able to take up employment in the administrative, education and public health sectors. However, it is still generally believed that women must devote their life to housework and motherhood, and women working outside the house are very much regarded as guilty of rejecting tradition by entering the public domain traditionally reserved for men. Thus it can be argued that the role assigned to Indian women during the pro-independence struggle had negative implications for the Indian feminist movement that had started to develop at the end of the nineteenth century. The fulfilment of the traditional role, portrayed as the necessary sacrifice which Indian women had to make for the freedom of their country, did not meet the aspirations of those Indian women who wanted to achieve not only independence from the colonial power but also equality with their menfolk.

208 Nuria López

References

Anderson, Benedict. 1983. *Imagined Communities: Reflections on the Origin and Spread of Nationalism.* London: Verso.

Chatterjee, Partha. 1990. 'The Nationalist Resolution of the Women's Question' in Sangari, Kumkum and Sudesh Vaid (eds) *Recasting Women: Essays in Colonial History.* New Jersey: Rutgers University Press: 233-53.

Chatterjee, Partha. 1993. *The Nation and its Fragments.* Princeton: Princeton University Press.

Desai, Neera and M. Krishnara. 1990. *Women and Society in India.* New Delhi: Ajanta.

Forbes, Geraldine. 1996. *Women in Modern India.* Cambridge: Cambridge University Press.

Liddle, Joanna and Rama Joshi. 1986. *Daughters of Independence: Gender, Caste and Class in India.* London: Zed Books.

Renan, Ernest. 1990. 'What is a Nation?' in Bhabha, Homi K. (ed.) *Nation and Narration.* London: Routledge: 8-22.

Roy, Parama. 1998. *Indian Traffic: Identities in Question and Colonial and Postcolonial India.* Los Angeles: University of California Press.

Toward Equality. 1974. *Toward Equality: Report of the Committee on the Status of Women in India.* New Delhi: GOI Ministry of Education and Social Welfare.

Waterstone, Richard. 1996. *India.* Barcelona: Debate.

TEXT AND IDENTITY

CHAPTER 14

RESURRECTING *CARMEN*:
SEXUAL AND ETHNIC IDENTITY IN THE CINEMA

Ann Davies

In 1988 the Spanish playwright Antonio Gala wrote a play called *Carmen Carmen*, based on the Spanish gypsy *femme fatale* created by Prosper Mérimée (in his novella of 1845) and popularized in Bizet's opera (1875). Gala's Carmen is killed off four times in the course of the play, each time rising up shortly afterwards, only to be murdered again a while later. Gala's proposition – the repeated murder and resurrection of Carmen – is the subject for examination in this article. Carmen's story has become widely known in Western culture primarily as a result of the popularity of the opera, which forms an integral part of the standard repertoire of opera houses and companies. The reasons for its popularity seem fairly clear: they include a compelling storyline that includes a passionate sexual relationship, an attractive and vibrant central character, accessible music, the opportunity for colourful spectacle, and the chance to indulge in the exoticism of gypsy identities. Gala's play implies that there is another reason – the chance to see Carmen die at the end. The Carmen story is now familiar enough that many of us know its outcome in advance, and thus, as Gala indicates, its popularity derives partly from the satisfaction we derive from seeing Carmen die over and over again. *Carmen Carmen* hints at the possibility that our pleasure in the Carmen narrative lies not only in her death, but in its repetition – the fact that she has already died countless times on stage, on screen and on the page, and that in experiencing the narrative afresh we look forward to her dying yet again.

This article considers the repetition of Carmen's death by means of the cinematic remake.[1] The history of the Carmen story in the cinema quickly reveals a continual fascination with both the story and the char-

[1] The cinematic Carmen formed the focus of the Carmen Project at Newcastle University's Centre for Research into Film and Media, a project supported by funding from the Arts and Humanities Research Board. This article draws on research from that project.

acter and thus the constant climax of her death.[2] There are approximately
eighty – possibly more – Carmen films spanning the hundred or so years
of cinematic history, covering film genres such as art film, musicals,
filmed opera (naturally), cartoons, silent films and potential Hollywood
blockbusters. Many famous cinema names are connected with Carmen,
such as Charlie Chaplin, Cecil B. DeMille, Rita Hayworth, Jean-Luc
Godard, Plácido Domingo and the first film vamp Theda Bara. Such a
disparate collection of styles, stars and directors implies a fascination
with Carmen that goes beyond a specific time and place. Carmen's appeal
to the cinema is both broad and enduring, with a relevance that has
survived the far-reaching social changes that have occurred since the
time of Mérimée and Bizet.   Filmmakers have used Bizet as a text
(Francesco Rosi, in his 1984 version, for instance), and have plundered
him for incidental music, but they have nonetheless retold Carmen's
story in a greater variety of ways which, while varying the *mise-en-scène*,
retain the essential plot motifs of sexual passion and death. The cinema
Carmen has been a flamenco dancer (Carlos Saura's *Carmen* of 1983, and
Julio Diamante's *La Carmen* of 1975), a bank robber and kidnapper (Jean-
Luc Godard's *Prénom Carmen*, 1983), a singer who sides with the Spanish
resistance of 1808 (Tulio Demicheli's *Carmen la de Ronda*, 1959),[3] a peni-
tent (Florián Rey's *Carmen, la de Triana*, 1938),[4] even a dressmaker (Luis
César Amadori's *Carmen*, 1943). As Marshall Leicester (1994: 247) argues
in his essay on Carmen movies, a film has more scope for 'variance with
its original': the stage has not matched cinema's capacity to reinvent itself
and retell its stories in such innovative ways.

    Cinema carries an ambiguous status as an art form, being also an
industry that caters to a variety of popular tastes. Throughout its history
it has attempted to claim for itself a status as an art form comparable
with the higher artistic echelons such as opera, which partly explains why

---

[2] Not all Carmens die at the end of their films. Most notably, in *Carmen, la de
Triana*, don José rather than Carmen dies, with Carmen left to mourn over his coffin.
Some parodies and comedies preserve Carmen as well. In Chaplin's *Burlesque on
Carmen*, the final stabbing proves to be fake, while in Lotte Reiniger's animated *Carmen*
(1933), she rides off with Escamillo. These films are, however, the exception and not
the rule.
    [3] Released twice in the USA under the titles *The Devil Made a Woman* and *A Girl
Against Napoleon*.
    [4] A German version also appeared under the title *Andalusische Nächte*. It used
German dialogue and actors, but the same female protagonist as in the Spanish
Carmen, la de Triana, Imperio Argentina.

early filmmakers resorted to using operas such as *Carmen* as the basis for films, even though the early technology precluded a recorded soundtrack. Jennifer Batchelor comments, 'For an industry obsessed with having its product taken seriously as an art form, opera – the high art, *par excellence* – held obvious appeal. Opera was used to give cultural credence to the would-be seventh art' (Batchelor 1984: 28). The early opera film creates a hybrid cultural artefact that blurs cultural boundaries but nonetheless retains the tension between high and low culture in the encounter between an elite medium (opera) and a mass medium (cinema). As Nestor García Canclini, in his exploration of the hybridization of culture, remarks, 'The cultured, in the traditional sense, is not eliminated by the industrialization of symbolic goods' (García Canclini 1995: 4).

This tension between cultures also traces itself through the Carmen narrative. The story's central conflict derives from the clash of bourgeois and Bohemian cultures epitomized by the central male lead don José and his lover Carmen. Don José reminds us of the bourgeois audience of the Opéra-Comique that first saw Bizet's *Carmen* (and were consequently scandalized). The José character is a White male Northerner (from Navarre or the Basque country in the north of Spain), often a dutiful soldier and thus on the side of law and order, [5] and inherently bourgeois, so that even as he descends into a mire of criminality he dreams of settling down with Carmen in the supposed bliss of traditional domesticity. Carmen, on the other hand, is a highly sensual woman and a gypsy. A particular aspect of her Bohemian otherness is lawlessness: Carmen associates with criminals, which places her outside the law. Hence Carmen is other, not only in terms of gender but also in terms of race and class. Carmen's ethnicity and lawlessness are further emphasized in the contrast with the 'good' girl Micaela, who appeared first in Bizet's opera and in many films since. The Micaela character is clean, virtuous and *white* (from the same region as José), stressing the fact that Carmen's otherness and indeed her attraction lies very much in her lawless nature and her ethnicity. Thus don José's attraction towards Carmen parallels the attraction the bourgeois may feel towards the exotic, and the resulting relationship of the lovers is itself a hybrid in which their two different worlds encounter each other and inevitably generate tension. Jerrold

---

[5] In some versions of the film, José has in fact fled the law, having killed another man in defence of his honour. The defence of his honour, however, indicates that he still follows codes of manly virtue, and his commitment to his duty as a soldier implies his lawfulness.

Seigel stresses the simultaneous attraction and repulsion of the Bohemian lifestyle in nineteenth-century Paris, and observes the tendency of the Parisian bourgeois to attend Bohemian cabarets, which afforded them the opportunity to return to Bohemia again and again, in the knowledge that their secure bourgeois existence remained as a retreat (Seigel 1986: 240-241).[6] Seigel suggests that the Bohemian cabaret

> was a Bohemia for the bourgeoisie, a place where the increasingly organized and regulated life of the modern city could be left behind for an evening by those unable to escape it for longer. Here non-Bohemians might seek release from ordinary social boundaries, take part on the play of breaking conventions and violating tabus (Seigel 1986: 240).

In this sense, however, Bohemianism becomes a spectacle and the bourgeois a complicit audience, able to indulge in this offering of an alternative culture while nonetheless retaining their class status, in a move reminiscent of the hybridity of the opera film discussed above. This virtually Freudian *fort-da* movement thus occurs twice over with the cinematic Carmen, in which the encounter between opera and cinema parallels the encounter between bourgeois and Bohemian, and thus the resultant tension of these encounters raises the stakes for the resolution of the narrative.

Mérimée's original tale told Carmen's story from don José's, and thus from the bourgeois, point of view. The novella offers an unnamed narrator who encounters the bandit José, who subsequently recounts to the narrator his love affair with Carmen, and consequent fall from bourgeois grace as a soldier and upholder of the law, to his status as outlaw and murderer. Here we have Carmen's story at third hand, told twice over by both don José and a bourgeois narrator, so that she becomes the object of a double bourgeois gaze. The opera and cinema have tended to perpetuate Carmen as the object of such a gaze, as I will discuss in more detail below. Film theory has for some time now debated the function of the gaze, ever since Laura Mulvey's seminal article (1989) that assumed the audience as implicitly masculine, viewing women on screen as objects

---

[6] In Chapter 6 of his study, Seigel (1986) emphasizes the Bohemian as artist and eccentric rather than as gypsy, but acknowledges an anxiety in nineteenth-century Paris over the difference between the artist and the common criminal. He discusses the different reactions of some artists and commentators towards the marginal world of gypsies and criminals. Some wanted to create a distinction between the 'true' Bohemian artist and the common criminal; others embraced the concept of Bohemia in all its divergent meanings.

of a male gaze. According to Mulvey, viewers perceived the characters and events on screen as if they were heterosexual men, regardless of gender or of sexual preferences, so that other points of view disappeared beneath the compulsion to adopt this patriarchal male gaze. Many commentators have reacted against the over-simplistic binary opposition of patriarchal ideology as a filter through which one must view films (and Mulvey herself subsequently modified her position); new theories have appeared that allow the spectator a more active and more contextualized role in deriving meaning from a film, taking into account factors such as gender, race and class. This notion of audiences processing meaning in a contextualized setting has been described by Christine Gledhill as *negotiation*, which she defines thus:

> the term 'negotiation' implies the holding together of opposite sides in an ongoing process of give-and-take [...]Meaning is neither imposed, nor passively imbibed, but arises out of a struggle or negotiation between competing frames of reference, motivation and experience (Gledhill 1988: 67-68).

Although negotiation facilitates a greater flexibility in understanding how audiences process meaning through film, it does not necessarily dispense with Mulvey's male gaze. Binary oppositions such as male/female continue to be relevant. As Gledhill reminds us, negotiation holds together opposite poles, which allows for shifts in the spectatorial gaze, but also for axes of opposition that hark back to the male gaze. But male/female is not, of course, the only axis of opposition that can be used, and it might be better to think of this gaze as a *dominant* gaze that draws a crude axis of us/them or self/other, a position of hegemony that includes the notion of maleness but also ideas such as whiteness. The concept of negotiation means that this gaze is not inevitable but, being hegemonic, it carries a particular weight that requires effort to resist. Steve Neale makes this point when he argues that, though identification and desire (and thus alignment with a particular gaze) can be 'multiple, fluid, at points even contradictory'(Neale 1993: 10), they are by no means free floating:

> there is constant work to channel and regulate identification in relation to sexual division, in relation to the orders of gender, sexuality, and social identity and authority marking patriarchal society. Every film tends both to assume and actively to work to renew those orders, that division (Neale 1993: 11).

The gender axis discussed by Neale can be mapped on to the bourgeois/Bohemian axis without too much difficulty, particularly since it is

not by chance that in the Carmen narrative the male represents the bourgeois and the female the Bohemian. The dominant gaze includes the
male and patriarchal gaze, but it also includes the bourgeois gaze. In the
negotiation that ensues between bourgeois and Bohemian, then, the
former carries the greater power and weight and attempts to ensure that
the outcome of any negotiation is always in favour of the status quo.

In her study of Carmen, Evlyn Gould draws on Seigel to observe that
attitudes towards the Bohemian encompass a certain measure of ambiguity and ambivalence (Gould 1996: 20). These reactions allow a certain
mobility of identity. The capacity of Carmen to be other may be a constant of the story, but the notion of otherness is slippery and unstable: it
is simultaneously repulsive and attractive, and thus brings bourgeois
identity into question. Nonetheless the Carmen story does not encourage
total flexibility of identification. As we have already seen, Mérimée offered us Carmen as perceived by two bourgeois males, and most film
versions similarly encourage us to position ourselves alongside don José,
to the extent that we are encouraged to adopt his gaze. In Francesco
Rosi's *Carmen*, for instance, we first glimpse Carmen (Julia Migenes-Johnson) at the same time as José (Plácido Domingo) does, and at the same
angle – significantly, looking down on her from above. Bizet's opera also
offers Carmen precisely as a Bohemian performer in the Gypsy Song of
Act II, and some films emphasize this point by casting well-known sing-
ers to play the part of Carmen entertaining in the tavern, for the pleasure
of her audience both onscreen and off. In this way the cinema audience
watches the singer as much for her own self as for her incarnation as
Carmen, and thus becomes aligned with the diegetic audience in watching the Bohemian performance. These versions of Carmen function in a
way similar to the cabarets that Seigel discussed. A striking example of
this is the Spanish version *Carmen, la de Ronda*, in which Carmen is played
by the highly successful singer Sara Montiel. The film acts as a musical
showcase for Montiel, who (in the tradition of Spanish folkloric films) is
the only major character to sing. Thus Montiel performs as cabaret art-
iste for the pleasure specifically of don José (Maurice Ronet) who, along
with both the diegetic and the cinema audience, savours the pleasure of
her sexual allure, heightened by her sensuous singing style. Montiel as
star points to another aspect of Carmen as a spectacle of otherness that
is specific to the cinema-going experience: Carmen as a star vehicle.
Some Carmens are played by major stars such as Rita Hayworth (in *The
Loves of Carmen,* Charles Vidor, 1948), while Dorothy Dandridge's perfor-

mance in *Carmen Jones* (Otto Preminger, 1954) made her a major star too, the first black person to appear on the cover of *Life* magazine. In 1915, the first cinema vamp, Theda Bara, played the role (in Raoul Walsh's *Carmen*), and in the same year the popular opera star Geraldine Farrar acted the part in another *Carmen*, directed this time by Cecil B. DeMille, to general adulation in the United States. Carmen as a star vehicle becomes the spectacle, the display, of another form of otherness – the total otherness, unattainability, of the female film star – that on many occasions was deliberately emphasized by the ethnic otherness of the star in question (Dandridge, Hayworth and Bara, for instance: also Dolores del Río in Raoul Walsh's second attempt at a Carmen film, *The Loves of Carmen* of 1927).

A particularly powerful example of the power of the dominant gaze to treat its object as spectacle occurs in the pre-credit sequence of Saura's *Carmen*. The don José figure, here a choreographer called Antonio (Antonio Gades), observes a group of female dancers in a rehearsal studio as they go through some flamenco dance steps. Antonio is searching for the ideal woman to play Carmen in his proposed dance version of the story, and these opening shots of the film emphasize his gaze as he watches his female troupe, looking for the perfect other who will be his Carmen. In a sequence of shot and reverse-shot, he gazes at the women who perform for him in the hope of satisfying his requirements. There are many close-ups of his face and theirs so that, even though we hear the noise of the women's feet as they dance, we see very little of the steps. We see only the faces and the gaze. Moreover, while we see Antonio's gaze from an oblique angle, suggesting a neutral point of observation, we see the women directly from his point of view. From the very beginning, then, the camera stresses Antonio's gaze, and we are encouraged to identify with it: it is possible to resist such an identification, but its force remains powerful nonetheless. We should also note the consequence of Antonio's gaze: he rejects these woman who perform for him – who, like him, are part of a community which treats flamenco as a commodity of high culture, a refined art – and looks elsewhere for his inspiration, precisely to Carmen (Laura del Sol), who performs a despised form of flamenco in cabaret performances for foreign tourists.

This episode suggests, as many Carmen films do, the impulse to create an other, even within communities that are themselves 'other', thus implying that binary otherness is not inevitable but is nonetheless deliberately sought. In Saura's *Carmen*, Carmen is the outsider in an artistic community of flamenco performers wrapped up in their performance. They are established artists, keeping their art pure in the dance studio removed from the outside world: they deliberately marginalize themselves in order to preserve their artistic perfection. Carmen dances in a tourist night spot, peddling stereotypes of Spanishness: her art is impure, tainted. And of all the dancers, Carmen is the only one we see *arrive* from elsewhere. The other dancers are always already in the dance studio and we never see them in any other context. Carmen is therefore the outsider, who invades and disrupts the closed community of the troupe. Antonio's colleagues find little of merit in her, but Antonio has looked deliberately outside his troupe for something other than the artistic perfection it offers him.

Otto Preminger's *Carmen Jones* of 1954 also exemplifies a tendency deliberately to seek the other. The entire cast of the film is black, giving the impression of blackness as the norm: in fact it emphasizes the black community as other – white America becomes present through its very absence.[7] Within this community of racial otherness we witness the impulse to differentiate Carmen still further, as a sexual object of both the black and the white gaze. Dorothy Dandridge, who played this Carmen, had supposedly white facial features and appealed to notions of whiteness – an issue that has made Dandridge a somewhat problematic figure in black film studies. Dandridge was marketed as an object of male desire, described as a 'sizzling sex-bomb' for 'boys of all ages'[8] and indeed for all races, too. Within the film she is set up as an object of the black male gaze. A particular instance of this comes in the scene where the boxer Husky Miller arrives at Billy Pastor's and sings to the assembled crowd of his exploits in the ring ('Stand Up and Fight', to the tune of Bizet's Toreador's Song). The crowd gathers close around him to listen, but Carmen goes separately to a balcony to watch the scene and thus stands apart from everyone else, aloof and aloft. In this way she draws Husky Miller's attention. He gazes at her and immediately desires her, as the camera cuts back and forth between the two. The exchange of dialogue immediately after the song underscores the importance of Husky's gaze: he tells Carmen, 'I noticed you right off, up on the balcony. Did you notice me?' But his gaze is not the only one operative.

---

[7] Despite the premise of blackness as the norm, the film carries some racist elements. See McClary 1992: 131-135; Baldwin 1955.

[8] As described in the press book for *Carmen Jones* (available at the British Film Institute, London).

White men are watching her too, offscreen and behind the camera – director Otto Preminger and his crew. Thus both a black and a white male gaze holds Carmen in its sights and reinscribes her as other by marking her as a sexual object.

This dominant/other structure may therefore be actively sought, indicating that, even where we negotiate screen identities in a shifting environment, opposites remain desirable. As Seigel suggests, the Bohemian other served to displace social tensions way from the bourgeois centre:

> Bohemia offered the rest of society a special service of which few on either side were usually conscious. It gave powerful symbolic aid to bourgeois who needed to emphasize tradition and stability; for them, Bohemia was a way to project onto others the features of social disruption and moral uncertainty that rapid historical change called forth, to inoculate themselves against the negative effects of the dissolution of tradition that society as a whole was bringing about. [...] Bohemia was a revelation of tendencies nurtured by society as a whole, as revolution and innovation caused inherited structures and assumptions to give way (Seigel 1986: 146).

The dominant gaze acts as the means of displacement of these social tensions. But the dominant/other binary is also unstable. Carmen undermines the security of hegemonic identities by showing them to be wanting, inadequate. The don José gaze may be the dominant one, but it also reflects powerlessness, for Josés tend to be insecure and insanely jealous (a sign that Carmen is beyond their control). This insecurity often has a parallel in the deterioration of the male body, usually signalled by José's unshaven and ragged appearance as a result of the outlaw life in the mountains, undertaken because the sexual desire for Carmen drove him to break the law and to kill. A more extreme illustration of this loss of control is the shower scene in Godard's *Prénom Carmen*, where Joseph (Jacques Bonaffé) tries and fails to rape Carmen (Maruschka Detmers): he ends up collapsed on top of her, muttering his self-disgust. This springs from both a desire for control and an inability to realise that desire, symbolized by his sexual impotence. Such impotence is also implied – in a more comic vein – with the impossibly long scabbard of Charlie Chaplin's Darn Hosiery (in his *Burlesque on Carmen*, 1916) that hides his ridiculously short sword. But perhaps the most extreme example of all is the total disappearance of the male body and thus by implication the dominant gaze: in the Max Sennett comedy, *The Campus Carmen*

(1928) a woman (Carole Lombard) takes over the role of José, both personifying and parodying the male body.

Carmen's otherness, moreover, is also very attractive: it offers the temptation to defy and usurp the dominant gaze. Although many films (and the opera, too) introduce us to José first and then present Carmen as the object of his gaze, she wrests the male gaze away from its possessor and challenges it. Indeed, in some films – such as those directed by Otto Preminger, Raoul Walsh (in the 1927 version), and Charles Vidor and Ernst Lubitsch (1919) – Carmen spots José first and singles him out from the rest of the masculine crowd as the object of her gaze. Francesco Rosi's Carmen actually uses a mirror to spotlight the bull-fighter Escamillo as the erotic object of a gaze which she controls. In the scene at Billy Pastor's in *Carmen Jones* it is not only Husky Miller who looks at Carmen: she looks at him too as a possible object of desire, challenging the dominant gaze. But this alternative is not so simple either, since the desire to break free of any form of control – particularly male (or white) control – cannot go unpunished. Carmen usually dies as a result of her determination to live free from such control. Sometimes she must die even when she proves loyal to one man (as in Demicheli's *Carmen, la de Ronda*): her sexual otherness provides sufficient excuse for her death. Moreover, the desire to elude hegemonic constraints can be twisted back to suit the powers that be. Female audiences of Charles Vidor's *The Loves of Carmen*, for instance, were encouraged to identify with Rita Hayworth's Carmen through posters, adverts and a heavy promotional campaign; not with the idea that women should break free from male control but that they should buy the illusion of freedom – and desirability – through related fashion and merchandizing.

So *both* poles of this dominant/other axis prove both strong and weak, and a struggle arises for control, which neither side actually wins. It is in this limited space between the dominant reading and the alternative attractions and powers posed by the other that negotiation over identity can take place. Audiences interpret what they see on screen in a nuanced context in which their own identities retain the capacity to shift in an ongoing process. But nonetheless a need persists to displace social tension away from the centre and contain it. So we return to the notion of Freud's *fort-da,* which allows for the deliberate negotiation of control and its loss, with the eventual recovery of control – through Carmen's death – enabling the reaffirmation of the power behind the dominant gaze. The Carmen narrative threatens to undermine supposedly fixed identities, and thus we seek security in the knowledge that Carmen must die. Many people will already know the outcome of the story before they see a particular film version, and can enjoy the film safe in the knowledge that the other will eventually be killed. But the other is also pleasurable, attractive in its very danger – so we return again and again to watch Carmen, just as Seigel's Parisian bourgeoisie returned to the Bohemian cabarets time and again. As Seigel comments, in the cabaret,

> Bohemia was a realm of liberated fantasy, a space where – as in the uncon-
> scious Freud would begin to explore at the end of the century – wishes and
> anxieties associated with sexual passion, death, and violence eddied in and
> out of each other. Simply to enter the [cabaret] was to experience the perme-
> ability of these boundaries (Seigel 1986: 239-240).

The Carmen narrative facilitates the exploration of these fantasies, wishes and anxieties, safe in the knowledge that with her death the status quo – the bourgeois law – will be restored. The pleasure of *fort-da* is the pleasure we find in Carmen's constant death and resurrection, which allows us to step beyond boundaries, to indulge ourselves in the loss of control, in the knowledge that we retain the capacity to retreat back behind those same boundaries and regain the control we pretend to have lost.

The changes that have been rung with cinematic Carmens strongly imply the need to return to the scene of the crime and rehash the evidence; to try to fix the identities of both Carmen and of ourselves – a never-ending task since neither the dominant gaze nor the gaze of the other can be permanently fixed. But for as long as a Carmen film lasts, it offers the allure of a dissolution of identities even as it simultaneously tries to nail them back in place. This is why Carmen has proved so valuable to us. In a sense we know her story already, but we still come back to re-examine it, reinterpret in the light of our own new selves. As we renegotiate ourselves in response to new social tensions, we must renegotiate the other, too. Hence Carmen's perpetual death and resurrection, and hence her popularity in the cinema. With cinema's amazing capacity for remakes and new interpretations, in different languages and genres, the potential for exploration of otherness is that much greater. Cinema's ambiguous status as an art form, with its overtones of commerciality, of populism and pure schmaltz, makes it a hybrid vehicle wherein different identities can encounter each other in an endless play of lost and found – and thus an ideal format for Carmen's constant resurrection.

References

Baldwin, James. 1955. 'Life Straight in De Eye' in *Commentary* 19/1: 74-77.

Batchelor, Jennifer. 1984. 'From *Aida* to *Zauberflöte*' in *Screen* 25/3: 26-38.

Gala, Antonio. 1988. *Carmen Carmen*. Madrid: Espasa Calpe.

García Canclini, Néstor. 1995. *Hybrid Cultures: Strategies for Entering and Leaving Modernity* (tr. Christopher L. Chiappari and Silvia L. López). Minneapolis: University of Minnesota Press.

Gledhill, Christine. 1988. 'Pleasurable Negotiations', in Pribram, E. Deidre (ed.) *Female Spectators: Looking at Film and Television*. London: Verso: 64-89.

Gould, Evlyn. 1996. *The Fate of Carmen*. Baltimore: Johns Hopkins University Press.

Leicester, H. Marshall, Jr. 1994. 'Discourse and the Film Text: Four Readings of *Carmen*' in *Cambridge Opera Journal* 6/3: 245-282.

McClary, Susan. 1992. *Georges Bizet: Carmen*. Cambridge: Cambridge University Press.

Mulvey, Laura. 1989. 'Visual Pleasure and Narrative Cinema', in *Visual and Other Pleasures*. London: Macmillan: 29-37.

Neale, Steve. 1993. 'Masculinity as Spectacle: Reflections on Men and Mainstream Cinema' in Cohan, Steve and Ina Rae Hark (eds) *Screening the Male: Exploring Masculinities in Hollywood Cinema*. London: Routledge: 9-20.

Seigel, Jerrold. 1986. *Bohemian Paris: Culture, Politics, and the Boundaries of Bourgeois Life, 1830*. Baltimore: Johns Hopkins University Press.

CHAPTER 15

EMBODYING THE NATION:
VIVIANE ROMANCE IN *CARMEN* (1945) AND
RITA HAYWORTH IN *THE LOVES OF CARMEN* (1948)[1]

Phil Powrie

Since 1895 there have been some eighty film adaptations of the Carmen story, based either on Mérimée's novella (1845) or on Bizet's opera (1875), or a combination of both, making this the most adapted story in cinema history. It is not so difficult to see why this might be the case, since the story of Carmen, as Ann Davies says elsewhere in this volume, has 'a compelling storyline that includes a passionate sexual relationship, an attractive and vibrant central character, accessible music, the opportunity for colourful spectacle, and the chance to indulge in the exoticism of Gypsy identities'. Oddly enough, however, there are fewer stars playing Carmen in these eighty films than there are regular actresses or relative unknowns (who then may well have become stars as a result of playing Carmen, as with Dorothy Dandridge for example after *Carmen Jones* (USA, Preminger, 1954), or Julia Migenes-Johnson after *Carmen* (France/Italy, Rosi, 1984)). There have been some stars, however. Amongst the early ones, we find the opera singer Geraldine Farrar (1915), the vamps Theda Bara (1915) and Pola Negri (1918), Dolores del Rio (1927) and Imperio Argentina (1938). More recently, there has been pop singer Beyoncé Knowles in a hip-hop version (2001). In between the earlier versions and this most recent one, there were only three major stars: Sara Montiel (Spain, 1959), and the two who will be focused on in this chapter: Viviane Romance in *Carmen* (France, Christian-Jaque, 1942, released 1945), and Rita Hayworth in *The Loves of Carmen* (USA, Charles Vidor, 1948). There are a variety of reasons why it is appropriate to look at these two films. They were compared and contrasted in 1948 when *Carmen* was redistributed in the USA at the time of the release of *The Loves of Carmen*, the French Carmen being pitted against the American

[1] I would like to thank the Arts and Humanities Research Board for funding the research project which led to this chapter.

version by critics and indeed lawyers, as the distributors of Carmen complained that the American version plagiarized the French version. It is
true that the films have many similarities (although it is not clear that
plagiarism was involved). Both were super-productions in financial
terms; both fared badly at the hands of the critics, but both did well with
audiences, because they were star vehicles for major female stars of the
period.

There are several interrelated reasons why it is more appropriate to
analyse the function of stars, rather than just actors or actresses, in the
production of identity. First, and most importantly, stars are exemplary;
as Chris Perriam puts it, stars are 'epitomes, icons of states of affairs and
states of emotions' (Perriam 2003: 8). Second, they are not abstractly
exemplary, but exemplary within specific national contexts; they are 'intimate dramatizations of local myths and realities' (Babington 2001: 10).
Third, stars do not simply represent the national iconically, but also have
a key ideological function. Recalling Lévi-Strauss's definition of the function of myths, Ginette Vincendeau explains how stars 'reconcile contradictions that exist in the social roles expected of men and women at key
historical moments' (Vincendeau 2000: 35). Fourth, gender plays a vital
role in this process of resolution. Vincendeau points out how male stars
embody the nation very differently from female stars: 'Male stars elicit an
identification with public figures and actual historical events [...]. By
contrast, female stars, though they appear in historical drama, symbolize
the nation in ways which refer not to historical figures but to allegory on
the one hand and the body on the other' (2000: 36). Female stars, then,
'embody the nation' (Vincendeau 2000: 35), their function being to turn
image into identity by specific processes of allegory and embodiment at
any time, but even more so at key moments in a nation's history.

One of the more important moments of change in the twentieth
century was the Second World War. Women, in particular, played a vital
role. This happened during the war itself in France, where women were
famously active in the French Resistance, and in the USA, where they
entered the workplace in significant numbers, thus leading to the para-
noia of *film noir*, usually interpreted as a reaction to the social importance
of women in the workplace. They were important after the war, in
France because they were given the vote and therefore wielded power
which they had not hitherto held, and in the USA, as the consumers who
drove forward the emerging consumer society. The two films we have
chosen to examine, the French one made in 1942 but not released until

1945, and then re-released in the USA when the American film opened in 1948, capture this transitional period when the two nations were confronting social and political upheaval, and the condition of women was as a result changing rapidly. Comparing and contrasting two stars from different countries will allow us to explore the ways in which they help negotiate social and political change in and through the star image. Both films embody transition, located in the figure of the star, who creates an image of possible identities, even if transition is contingent on nation-specific contexts. Both films intimate, as might be expected of a narrative which ends by killing off its strong woman, that transition can only go so far, and must not include the independence represented by Carmen. Carmen embodies the nation, but this is so potentially dangerous that both films work to contain the mobilizing force of the image by killing off its embodiment.

Figure 15.1. Poster for *The Loves of Carmen* (USA, 1948, Charles Vidor).

In the first part of this chapter, we will argue that the films are very similar in a number of ways. The first of these is in the stress laid in both films on 'authenticity' and realism. Both *Carmen* and *The Loves of Carmen* are based on Mérimée's novella, rather than Bizet's opera, this being less important than the fact that this was an element emphasized by commentators or by distributors in the marketing of the films. Stressing that the films are adaptations of the novella functions in two ways. First, it suggests authenticity of origin, given that the novella came first. Second, opera as a musical genre can be construed as less 'realist' than prose fiction, so that gesturing to the novella rather than the opera is making a statement about the 'realism' of the text; indeed, the marketing campaign for *The Loves of Carmen* stressed that the film was 'not the opera' (see Figure 1). The emphasis on the authenticity and realism of the source text works together with another comment made about both films, namely that they work towards an authenticity of location. Commentators at the time pointed out, for example, that a Spanish painter was sent to Italy where the French film was made to ensure that an 'authentic' Spain was recreated. This attempt to authenticate seems to have worked: 'All of Spain breathes through these walls, these heat-laden squares, these shadow-streaked interiors', said a French reviewer of the French film (Sollies 1944). An American reviewer, while admitting that the film was less polished than the average Hollywood fare, turned this deficiency to the film's advantage, saying that 'the rough, newsreel-like quality of the photography often helps to create an effect of realism' (Helming 1947). Similarly for the later American film, much was made of the fact that Hayworth herself was part-Spanish, that her paternal grandmother had worked in a cigarette factory in Seville, and that two of her Spanish relatives were involved in authenticating the flamenco-style dancing (her father Eduardo Cansino as choreographer and her uncle Jose as a flamenco performer).

Such comments foreground authenticity as part of identification. We are being told that the films may be fantasies of a *femme fatale*, but they are less fantastical than previous versions: as one of the many posters in the marketing campaign for *The Loves of Carmen* claimed, 'The world is full of Carmens. They may not know it except in their most secret daydreams' (Figure 1). Authenticity of origin combines with realism of location as a frame for an image with which spectators can identify more readily. It is a similar process to the holiday snap, in which the distant view of the hills proves the presence of the photographed body ('This is me in the Pyrenées'), and locates it as an identity through the agency of desire ('You know it's me because I chose to have myself photographed in this location'). The analogy with the holiday snap is not as inappropriate as it might seem, since one of the features of both of these films is the emphasis on exotic locations, placing stars very much associated with the urban, as we shall see below, in the wide open outback as a metaphor for the freedom which will eventually be denied Carmen. This strategy serves to ground the films in a fantasied real, and facilitates identification with the female stars.

There is a second major similarity in the two films. Paratextual material such as reviews insisted in the case of both films that the identification should be with the female stars, and not the equally well-known male stars. This they did by diminishing the male stars in relation to the female ones.

Jean Marais was, unlike Viviane Romance, a recent star. He had achieved notoriety partly due to his lifestyle, as the openly gay partner of Jean Cocteau, and partly by his stunning Chanel-designed costume in Cocteau's stage version of *Oedipus* in 1937, where he appeared dressed only in loosely wound strips of bandage. By the time *Carmen* was released in 1945, he had become a film star – 'the first pop star', according to Soleil (2000: 105) - due to *L'Éternel retour* (1943), a reworking of the Tristan and Isolde legend scripted by Cocteau, and directed by Jean Delannoy. In *Carmen*, Marais not only has to contend with the generally weak persona that all don Josés have, but he also carries with him the other-worldliness of *L'Éternel retour*, a disconnectedness with the situation and, crucially, with Carmen herself. Significantly, perhaps, Marais makes no mention of Romance in the few hundred words he devotes to the making of *Carmen*, complaining of the director's 'bizarre orders for don José: "Be more Parisian"' (Marais 1975: 144). Contemporary reviews of *Carmen* all feminize or infantilize Marais: he is 'a brigand from operetta' (Sollies 1944); 'he can't resist being coquettish with his costumes' (Audisio 1945); his voice is 'juvenile and childish' (Jeanne), for which read that he is no match for Romance's earthy and very Parisian Carmen.

Glenn Ford was similarly infantilized, although in his case it might be argued that his roles prior to don José had tended in this direction anyway, and that in addition the film's dialogue constantly underscores it. In *Gilda* (1946), also directed by Charles Vidor, and also starring Rita Hayworth in the title role, Johnny/Ford's boss Mundsen/George Macready says disparagingly of Johnny: 'he's a boy'; and in *The Loves of Carmen*,

Carmen/Hayworth constantly calls don José 'little' or 'Joséito', an infantilization emphasized by Ford's chubby, fresh-faced features and don José's timidity in the face of Carmen's advances. Unsurprisingly, *The Hollywood Reporter* (1948) commented that Ford was like 'a schoolboy on his first visit to a peepshow', and Ford himself said of his role, 'It was disastrous, and I'm fortunate to have survived it' (Turner 1985).

Carmen may be a 'real woman' with whom we can identify, but don José is not a 'real man'. Whether this is in keeping with the male stars' previous roles and/or with the weakness of don José in the novella matters much less than the fact that the films emphasize identification with Carmen at the expense of don José. A third major similarity, then, is that Carmen must be strong, so that her death at the hand of the weak man can be justified. This is because what is at issue is the changing status of women during and immediately after World War Two in both countries.

It is no coincidence that *The Loves of Carmen* is essentially a replay of *Gilda*. *Gilda* was a *film noir*, and it is a commonplace of film theory and history that the paranoid atmosphere of *films noirs* translates the fear of returning GIs for women who had become newly independent by entering the workplace in large numbers. As if to underline this fact, *The Loves of Carmen* was the first picture part-produced by Hayworth's own production company, Beckworth, rather than just by Columbia, which had produced *Gilda*. The very extensive marketing of the American film included Dr Fredric Wertham's article 'Are Modern Women as Predatory as Carmen?', which was also broadcast on radio, underlining the threat posed by 'modern women'. That Hayworth was the quintessential modern woman was in no doubt; not only did she own her film company, but she carried a clear erotic charge, having been called 'The Love Goddess' in a famous issue of *Life* in 1947 (Sergeant 1947: 81); she therefore managed to combine sexual allure with business intelligence and independence. She was modern too in the role of Carmen, and not at all the dark Gypsy with as many faults as qualities, as described by Mérimée. His don José says of her that he 'didn't find her attractive' (1998: 21), and his narrator describes her thus: 'Her skin, though perfectly smooth, was nearly the colour of copper. Her eyes were slanting [...] her hair, perhaps rather coarse, and black with a blue sheen like a raven's wing, was long and shining [...] For every fault she had a quality which was perhaps the more striking from the contrast' (Mérimée 1998: 14). One of the more startling features of *The Loves of Carmen* is the fact that Hayworth plays Carmen like a pin-up, white teeth gleaming in disingenuous smiles, long legs flashing, her (originally dark) red-dyed hair never ruffled, and without the *caracol*, the kiss-curl, which is so stereotypically part of the image of Carmen, and which Romance did retain for her part.

Burch and Sellier have convincingly argued that French films in the immediate post-war period show the same development as American *noir*, with the emergence of weak men dominated by evil women (Burch and Sellier 2000: 52). They link this to the granting of the vote to women in 1944, suggesting that these films show 'a paranoid interpretation by men of their own predicament at the Liberation, fearful that they would not be able to recapture their pre-war position of dominance and seeing the emancipation of women as an attempt to destroy male identity'. Viviane Romance had shot to fame in Duvivier's *La Belle équipe* (1936), a key Popular Front film which recounts the story of a group of unemployed (male) friends who win the lottery and set up a riverside café. Gina is the ex-wife of one of them (Charles/Charles Vanel); she tries to worm herself back into the money by appealing to her ex-husband, but also by seducing Jean (Jean Gabin), whose passion for her brings him to kill Charles, so ending the utopian community. Romance became typecast as a vamp, her roles frequently being (as with Gina in *La Belle équipe*) that of the *femme fatale* who destroys men once she has ensnared them. By 1939, she was the top-ranking star in a poll for the weekly *Pour Vous* (Feydau 2001: 13).

In Gance's melodrama *Vénus aveugle* (released 1941 in Vichy, and 1943 in Paris), she plays an atypical role as a woman who has modelled for a brand of cigarettes, and who is going blind. She makes her boyfriend think she loves another so that he need not be saddled with a blind wife. She becomes a nightclub singer; the daughter she had by her boyfriend without him realizing it dies, and she becomes blind. The film is recognized by many as one of the worst of the Occupation, not helped by Gance's fawning dedication to Marshall Pétain in whom he suggested that France had become incarnated (Billard 1995: 378-79). Although the film was a flop, audiences faced with one their favourite stars playing a blind woman would have interpreted the film metaphorically: it was not Pétain but Romance who incarnated France, a France blinded and robbed of her future by the Occupation.

Having thus once embodied the nation in a sentimental allegory, it is also not difficult to see how Romance might have done so again for Carmen. Here, however, we find an interesting mismatch, similar to the mismatch between Hayworth as 'Love Goddess' and as Gypsy. Romance was seen as unsuitable for the role, given her Frenchness, indeed her 'Parisianness', which Christian-Jaque wanted her co-star to emulate, as we reported above. According to one reviewer, her persona in this film was straight out of an Offenbach operetta: she 'is not in the least bit like a Gypsy, giving the she-devil the flavour of *Vie parisienne*' (Audisio 1945);[2] meanwhile another considered that 'her Carmen is from Place Pigalle, or, if you like, a music-hall Carmen' (Jeanne 1945). This was so much her image that another reviewer complained about the rather literary turns of Romance's dialogue, which was in his view not only 'more Parisian than Sevillian', but prone to litotes, thereby imparting an incongruous preciousness where one might have expected 'a more direct language' (Leenhardt 1944). Her Parisianness, which makes her embody the nation in a move typical of France's Republican and centralized values, makes her a poor Carmen; in return, however, it makes her embody the contemporary woman in a far more obvious way than if she had been convincingly 'Sevillian'. And Carmen as a woman with a mind of her own would have resonated with the key political issue in 1944-45, women's suffrage. In January 1944, French women were finally given the vote, ostensibly to reward them for their part in the war, and more particularly their role in the Resistance, even if in practice this did not involve many women. Although the issue of women voting was much debated and indeed feared by many left-wing men because they were worried about a conservative backlash, when women voted for the first time in 1945 the usual distribution of the vote across the parties did not appear to have been affected. Nevertheless, it can be argued that the fact that women were voting for the first time had a psychological impact on many men.

We can see then how the two Carmens represent a change in the status of women during the 1940s in the two countries. Women were becoming stronger and more independent, and thus represented a threat. Unsurprisingly, both films attempt to neutralize that threat, in very similar ways. This they do, most obviously, by killing the *femme fatale* who represents a threat to order, discipline, and male pride. Given the popularity of the Carmen story, however, Carmen's death is expected. There are two ways in which these films work in rather more specific ways to neutralize the threat represented by Carmen before killing her off.

[2] *Vie parisienne* (1866), like *Carmen*, was scripted by Meilhac and Halévy.

Given that both stars embody modern women as much as they do the nation, a first strategy is to distance the stars both from the centrality of the national and from the 'ordinary' woman by emphasizing the exotic as different and marginal. Both star personas included a healthy dose of the exotic associated with the mysterious *femme fatale*. Rita Hayworth was born into a Latino family and started acting in films in 1926 under her family name of Cansino, with no less than three films where she played a character called Carmen. She changed her name and dyed her hair auburn in 1937 in order to escape the Latin connection, cultivating a glamorous image which brought her to stardom in the early 1940s in a series of musicals: *You'll Never Get Rich* (Lanfield, 1941) and *You Were Never Lovelier* (Seiter, 1942), both with Fred Astaire, and *Cover Girl* (Vidor, 1944), with Gene Kelly. However, the connection remains in a number of 1940s films. She has Latina roles in *Blood and Sand* (Mamoulian, 1941) as Dona Sol des Muire, a socialite who seduces a bullfighter away from his faithful Carmen (played by Linda Darnell), and in *You Were Never Lovelier* as Maria Acuna, the daughter of a rich Argentinian. When Hayworth does not play specifically Latina roles, there is often an exotic connection, especially in the last few films before *The Loves of Carmen*. In *Gilda* she is the wife of a South American casino owner; in *Down to Earth* (Hall, 1947) she plays the Greek goddess Terpsichore who creates mayhem in a Broadway musical; and in *The Lady from Shanghai* (Welles, 1947), where she is famously blonde-haired and American, she nevertheless has mysterious foreign connections.

In the case of Viviane Romance, of the seventeen films released in the period 1936-45, she plays a non-French native or a Frenchwoman living abroad in no less than seven, and nearly all of these prefigure her role as Carmen in one way or another. In *Naples au baiser de feu* (Genina, 1937) she plays an Italian who lures the Tino Rossi character away from his betrothed; in *Le Puritain* (Musso, 1937), she is Irish and introduces a disturbed young man to the underworld; in *La Maison de Maltais* (Chenal, 1938), she is from Marseille but living in Tunisia, and caught between two men, a smuggler and an explorer; in *Gibraltar* (Ozep, 1938), she is Spanish and seduces a soldier into betraying military secrets; in *Angélica* (Choux, 1939), she is a South American Madame; and in *Cartacalha, reine des gitans* (Mathot, 1941), she is a Gypsy dancer lured to Paris and torn between two men. In costume terms, *Gibraltar* and *Cartacalha* both prefigure *Carmen*, the first by the mantilla she wears, the second by the Gypsy costume.

The link with the exotic thus works paradoxically. It ensures that Romance and Hayworth would just about pass as versions of Carmen, despite the urban sophistication they had both cultivated as part of their star persona; but in injecting this image with Otherness, the exotic legitimizes the *femme fatale*'s death. The Otherness that guarantees both Carmen's independence and her 'authenticity' also guarantees that she must die, as not 'national' enough, too 'eccentric' in the etymological sense of off-centre.

The second way in which the films try to neutralize the threat represented by Carmen is by 'hystericizing' the film, by making the closure melodramatically excessive in relation to the supposed 'realism' and 'authenticity' striven for elsewhere. We are referring here to the well known argument concerning melodrama. Recalling that the function of melodrama is to work out the problems of patriarchal normalization, Geoffrey Nowell-Smith points out that the acceptance of the law by the rebellious son can only be achieved at the expense of repression, and that repression always resurfaces in melodrama as hysterical excess (in the Freudian sense) in relation to its attempt to conform to the patterns of realism:

> The laying out of the problems 'realistically' always allows for the generating of an excess which cannot be accommodated [...] The undischarged emotion which cannot be accommodated within the action, subordinated as it is to the demands of family/lineage/inheritance, is traditionally expressed in the music and, in the case of film, in certain elements of the *mise en scène*. That is to say, music and *mise en scène* do not just heighten the emotionality of an element of the action: to some extent they substitute for it [...] It is not just that the characters are often prone to hysteria, but that the film itself somatises its own unaccommodated excess, which thus appears displaced [...] Often, the 'hysterical' moment of the text can be identified as the point at which the realist representative convention breaks down (Nowell-Smith 1977: 117).

Both films stray from the novella in their final sequence, which is the point where they are most at odds with the so-called 'realism' which helped spectators work towards identification.

This was the feature most commented on in regard to the French film, despite the fact that on the surface it stays quite close to the novella. What commentators objected to was the tonality of this sequence, which they saw as quite different from the rest: a French reviewer in 1942 is exasperated by 'the syrupy light which congeals the finale' (Sollies 1944), and an English reviewer poked fun, saying that the finale 'is so swathed in studio mist that the appearance of Hecate and the Three Witches, or, more likely, the perturbéd spirit of Prosper Mérimée would not strike an incongruous note' (*Monthly Film Bulletin* 1949: 30). Other comments made suggested that this finale was somehow too Gothic, too expressionist, or even too German. Chirat and Barrot, writing in the 1970s, repeat the charge: 'We leave Bizet to find Wagner. We abandon Spain for Germany. In a landscape inspired by Gustave Doré, where you can see the incongruous influence of neo-Caligarism, Carmen dies' (1976: 58).

As for *The Loves of Carmen*, whereas it had remained close to the novella throughout as well, its finale veers alarmingly towards the opera. The finale is located no longer in the deserted place of the novella, transformed by Expressionist *mise en scène* in the French film, but outside the bull-ring. Why this change? First, and most obviously, the proximity of the bull-ring reminds us metaphorically of conflictual male-female relations. But more interestingly, there are generic constraints. *The Loves of Carmen* is closer to the Western by its use of outside locations and relations between outlaws than it is to the *film noir*, despite the shadow cast by *Gilda*. The Western is about male individuality, and its most obvious trope is the contrast between the wilderness and freedom on the one hand, and the city and social constraints on the other. By returning the outlaw to the city, the film is therefore emphasizing the threat to male independence. A second generic constraint is the shift in the same sequence from the Western trope just described (constraints of civilization) to melodrama: the interlocking staircases we see in the final scene, excessively empty, stressed by the black cat which scampers across the set, are no less a metaphor than the bull-ring. Indeed, they are more so, since there is no staircase in the libretto of the opera. The staircases are a metaphor for Carmen's bid for freedom, her flight away from the male and from patriarchal social and moral constraints. It is almost as if, as in a cartoon or a fairy-tale, the staircases appear magically before her as she struggles to get away, a hysterical somatization of her desire for freedom. This is underlined both by the melodramatic music and by the dialogue, as she shouts at don José, 'don't hang on to me; I can't stand anyone hanging on to me'.

We have suggested that these two films occur when they do for a specific and similar reason: to act as a vehicle for the expression of male anxiety about women at a particular historical conjuncture. At the same time, they try to work towards a neutralization of that threat, not just by rearticulating the death of the woman who wishes to remain free, but by hystericizing it. In the final part of this chapter, we shall explore ways in which the films are in reality very different from each other. That difference occurs in what might well have been felt was the weakest part of the argument so far, that both films help to articulate male anxiety about the advent of strong women. The key issue here is simply the dates. French women may well have played an important role in the Resistance, but this hardly represents the massive advent of women onto the labour market which is usually seen as the motivating factor for American *films noirs*. The French film's ethos is in fact very much that of the 1930s, largely because Viviane Romance was a pre-war star whose career never recovered from the interruption of World War Two.

Hayworth's image in *The Loves of Carmen* is also a throwback, one might argue, since she is cashing in on her pin-up image of the war years. But there is a difference, and it lies in the phenomenal attention to the film's promotion, costing $1 million to the film's $4 million production costs. The promotional campaign was much trumpeted at the time. Unusually, it used a number of people not associated with the film industry: a colour engineer, Howard Ketcham, who found the appropriate shade of magenta red, described in the Pressbook as the colour 'that psychologically everyone instinctively identifies with action, vivacity and passion', and which corresponded to 'the national mood of excitement'; a psychiatrist who wrote the 'world is full of Carmens' article referred to above; a dancer, Arthur Murray, who introduced flamenco in his 150 dance schools; a well-known novelist, Sophie Kerr, who wrote a thirty-day serialization for some 600 newspapers, and so on. Second, the promotional campaign was taken into small towns as well as the major cities. Third, some thirty-five manufacturers were used for tie-ins, such as shoes, handbags, cigarettes, hosiery, soap, cosmetics, hats, scarves, dresses, jewelry, and even dolls (*Showman's Trade Review* 1948: 21); remarkably, the Carmen dolls had $1 million in orders in the first twenty days on the market (despite which by 1995 it was so rare that it was worth $500).

The point we can draw from this list is that whereas the French film looks back to the 1930s, the American film looks forward to the consumerist 1950s. In that respect, the change from the novella at the end of the film is something we should return to. We considered it above from the point of view of don José because it was important to stress the film's *noir* aspect. However, we did not mention the fact that the film makes much more of Carmen's lover Lucas than does the novella. Wil-

liam Helling (1996) suggests that this ending is disturbing when compared with the novella, where Carmen dies for freedom rather than for a
new lover. This, of course, is intentional: Carmen must die from sexual
desire rather than the desire for freedom, because it is sexual desire
which motivates the move to buy the red frocks which signify it. A man-
ufacturer does not sell a frock because it represents freedom from the
tutelage of men, but because it suggests an illusory freedom to choose
within the chains of consumerist identifications. This was made all the
clearer in 1949 when the film was used by Aly Khan to entertain the
guests at his wedding to Hayworth, thus impressing Hayworth's image
not just on Hayworth herself (not a wife but a movie star), as well as on
the thousands of women who might have identified themselves with her.

   In conclusion, Carmen is a site of conflict which allows national
identity to be played out over her dead body. But these identities are
highly specific and rooted in the socio-political. Christian-Jaque's film is
primarily a sign of the resisting subject, still caught in a relatively un-
gendered fight against fascism. Vidor's Carmen, however, is an empty
sign waiting for the consumer to inhabit the colours and costumes on
display, 'a lacquered and lifeless creature' as Bosley Crowther said in his
New York Times review (Crowther 1948: 16). It is not for nothing that
many reviewers commented on the fact that not a hair of Hayworth's
famous red tresses is ever out of place, despite long trips on horseback,
bivouacs under the stars, or strenuous pseudo-flamenco posturing. In
other words, the image of Carmen serves multiple purposes, all of which
are connected to identity. She articulates a political crisis of identity (the
nation questioned or questioning itself) as well as a socio-cultural crisis
of identity (men made anxious by independent women), while neutraliz-
ing the threat that the image conjures up by ending up both dead and
fashionable at the same time.

References

Audisio, Gabriel. 1945. 'Un bon film français: *Carmen*' in *Action* (23 Feb. 1945).
Babington, Bruce (ed.). 2001. *British Stars and Stardom: from Alma Taylor to Sean
   Connery*. Manchester: Manchester University Press.
Billard, Pierre. 1995. *L'Age classique du cinéma français: du cinéma parlant à la Nouvelle
   Vague*. Paris: Flammarion.

Burch, Noël and Geneviève Sellier. 2000. 'Evil Women in the Post-War French Cinema' in Sieglohr, Ulrike (ed.) *Heroines Without Heroes: Reconstructing Female and National Identities in European Cinema, 1945-51*. London/New York: Cassell: 47-64.

Chirat, Raymond and Olivier Barrot. 1976. 'Christian-Jaque' in *Travelling* 47: np.

Crowther, Bosley. 1948. 'The Screen in Review' in *New York Times* (3 Sept. 1948): 16.

Feydeau, Alain. 2001. *Viviane Romance*. Paris: Pygmalion/Gérard Watelet.

Helling, William. 1996. 'Rita Hayworth's *The Loves of Carmen* as Literary Criticism' in *Literature Film Quarterly* 24/4: 445-51.

Helming, Ann. 1947. 'Good Acting Featured in *Carmen* Film' in *Hollywood Citizen News* (2 Aug. 1947).

Hollywood Reporter. 1948. 'The Loves of Carmen' in *The Hollywood Reporter* (18 Aug. 1948).

Jeanne, René. 1945. 'Encore une vieille connaissance' in *La France au combat* (1 Mar. 1945).

Leenhardt, Roger. 1944. '*Carmen*' in *Les Lettres françaises* (30 Dec. 1944).

Marais, Jean. 1975. *Histoires de ma vie*. Paris: Albin Michel.

Mérimée, Prosper. 1998. *Carmen and Other Stories* (tr., intro., notes by Nicholas Jotcham). Oxford: Oxford University Press.

Monthly Film Bulletin. 1949. '*Carmen*' in *Monthly Film Bulletin* 16/182: 29-30.

Nowell-Smith, Geoffrey. 1977. 'Minnelli and Melodrama' in *Screen* 18: 115-18.

Perriam, Chris. 2003. *Stars and Masculinities in Spanish Cinema* (Oxford Studies in Modern European Culture). Oxford: Oxford University Press.

Sergeant, Winthrop. 1947. 'The Cult of the Love Goddess in America' in *Life* (10 Nov. 1947): 81.

Showman's Trade Review. 1948. '*Carmen* Campaign to Reach the Small Towns' in *Showman's Trade Review* 49/7: 21.

Soleil, Christian. 2000. *Jean Marais: la voix brisée*. St-Étienne: Actes Graphiques.

Sollies, Jean. 1944. '*Carmen*' in *Gavroche* (28 Dec. 1944).

Turner, Adrian. 1985. 'Ford Popular' in *The Guardian* (15 Aug. 1985).

Vincendeau, Ginette. 2000. *Stars and Stardom in French Cinema*. London and New York: Continuum.

CHAPTER 16

BECOMING BUTTERFLY:
APPARATUSES OF CAPTURE AND EVASION

Joy James

This essay traces through time, space, and medium, a narrative that acti-
vates colonialist and imperialist inflexions of gender, race, and class in
the construction of identities: the Madame Butterfly story. The figure of
Madame Butterfly presents a tenacious though extremely unstable link,
from the time of its emergence as a dynamic representation of European
Orientalism through to its contemporary contestation in productions
such as the one under consideration here, David Cronenberg's 1993 film
M. Butterfly. Whether intended or not, animations of the Madame Butterfly trope are fraught with the effects of the competing forces at work in
notions of identity. This chapter is part of a larger project that seeks to
understand the specific qualities of movement entailed when unauthorized constituencies and marginal subjectivities come to take up audible,
and intelligible but constantly shifting positions in the larger body politic.

The enormously popular autobiographical travel-narrative, *Japan:
Madame Chrysanthemum*, written in 1887 by French naval officer Julien
Viaud under the *nom de plume*, Pierre Loti, is one of the earliest and – for
its time – most well known articulations of the Madame Butterfly story.
Viaud was in Japan in 1885. At that time Nagasaki was a treaty port
where French, American, and Russian navy personnel were often sta-
tioned for rest and relaxation leave. At the end of the nineteenth century
a practice evolved in Japan's treaty ports (as indeed it did throughout the
colonized world) whereby Western men entered into morganatic marriage arrangements with lower-class young women (Stoler 1995 and
1997).[1] These types of marriage arrangements were authorized by state
powers because it was thought that they discouraged 'unnatural' alliances,
protected the men from the potential for disease that they encountered
when frequenting the local prostitute populations and, at the same time,

---

[1] For an analysis of the way this practice works in the development of art in the
modern period, see Pollock 1992.

offered them all the comforts of home. Their 'wives' cooked for them, kept house, and acted as hostesses for their guests. Loti's *Madame Chrysanthemum* is a fictionalized account of an arrangement of this kind undertaken by Loti while he was in Japan.

In 1897, John Luther Long, an American lawyer who had never visited Japan, but whose sister was a missionary in Nagasaki, published in *Century Magazine* a story that echoed Loti's *Madame Chrysanthemum* (Quinn 1957: 625). Long titled his tale 'Madame Butterfly'. In this version of the story the French naval officer is replaced by an American, with whom the young Butterfly falls in love and has a child, whereas, in the Loti story there is no child and, indeed, the relationship is portrayed as a business arrangement that extends to the young woman: Chrysanthemum is not in the least romantically enamored with the European male protagonist. This narrative development in the Long story is notable in that it references what was rapidly becoming a problem for all colonizing countries: the growing population of mixed-blood children who troubled racial categories and thereby 'contaminated' boundaries of identity that held in place the supremacy of the bourgeois European male. Also interesting in the Long version is the insertion of a righteous moral tone, significant because it begins to map the incursions of the missionaries as they worked alongside and with the forces of imperial military domination. Italian-American playwright David Belasco subsequently worked closely with Long to produce a play based on, and with the same title as, Long's Butterfly story. The play opened in New York in 1899 and it was seeing Belasco's play that inspired Puccini to write his 1904 opera *Madama Butterfly*. The Butterfly trope continues to undergo metamorphosis. The popular success of the critically acclaimed film *M. Butterfly* demonstrates the continued power of this theme and its cultural stereotypes. Of course, *M. Butterfly* is just one of numerous cultural projects that engage this site of European colonization and its work in the constitution of subjects, domestic and foreign. The Cronenberg production offers a particularly potent mix of disruption and reinstatement of cultural stereotypes concerning proscriptions of identity.

Asian-American playwright David Henry Hwang wrote the film script for David Cronenberg's 1993 film, *M. Butterfly*. It is closely based on an award-winning play of the same title written by Hwang in 1986. Hwang tells us in his 'Afterword' written for the 1988 edition of the published script that he was inspired to write the play by a two-paragraph story that he read in *The New York Times* about a 'French diplomat who'd fallen in love and had a twenty-year relationship with a Chinese actress, who subsequently turned out to be not only a spy, but a man' (94). The diplomat, who supplied his lover with sensitive intelligence information, was tried for treason and imprisoned. Hwang goes on to reiterate that when 'attempting to account for the fact that he had never seen his "girlfriend" naked, [the diplomat, Bernard Bouriscot] was quoted as saying, "I thought she was very modest. I thought it was a Chinese custom"' (94). Hwang, aware that this was *not* a Chinese custom, said that when he read this story he had wondered what the diplomat thought he was getting in this Chinese actress...and the answer came to him clearly: 'He probably thought he had found Madame Butterfly' (95). Not surprisingly, then, Hwang's play and Cronenberg's film displace the Butterfly trope in significant ways.

Set to the music of Puccini's *Madama Butterfly*, the film *M. Butterfly* features actor John Lone in the title role playing a male opera singer masquerading as a female, Song Liling, who enters into a relationship with a luckless French diplomat, Rene Gallimard, played by Jeremy Irons, who twenty-years later as a result of his relationship with Song, is convicted of treason and put in prison. It is at the trial that Gallimard/Irons, in an electric moment of cinematic precision, is forced to confront the fact that she, Song Liling, is a he, when Lone dressed in suit and tie, his previously long and flowing black hair closely shorn, masculine and business-like, enters the French high court and fleetingly makes eye contact with his former lover. The intensity of the moment of contact in the courtroom is resumed in the back of the police van in which Song and Gallimard find themselves alone together while they are being transported to prison. In a scene as complex as any in recent cinema for its troubling implications, all the more notable for its subtlety, the lines of power and affliction are played out by the two characters: in a literal stripping-away of disguise and illusion, Song/Lone removes his clothes and in an appeal, by turns belligerent and poignant, asks Gallimard/Irons to acknowledge, through the experience of their love, his/her person. Gallimard/Irons is unable to meet Song/Lone in this ambiguously gendered terrain, and rather than affirming the 'identity' of his lover, affirms instead his love of the illusion: Song as the woman created by him.

After Gallimard is imprisoned he puts on a performance for his fellow inmates. On a small stage at the front of a large hall, the architecture of which is highly reminiscent of the opera house, Gallimard transforms

himself into 'Madame Butterfly'. His performance is orchestrated by a
recording, issuing from a portable tape-player that Gallimard has brought
along as part of his stage set, of the death-scene aria from Puccini's opera. As he applies costume and make-up, he recites, 'I have a vision – of
the Orient – that, deep within its almond eyes, there are still women –
women willing to sacrifice themselves for the love of a man. Even a man
whose love is completely without worth. Death with honour is better
than life with dishonour. At last, in a prison far from China, I have
found her. My name is Rene Gallimard – also known as Madame Butterfly' (Cronenberg 1993). This statement marks the completion of
Gallimard's transformation into 'Butterfly' and, after speaking these
words, he kills himself by slitting his throat with the sharp edge of the
small hand-mirror he used when applying his make-up.

    Gallimard's use of the mirror to commit suicide is, of course, highly
symbolic and begs for a Lacanian reading. However, while I have pursued a psychoanalytic analysis elsewhere, my argument here moves in a
different direction, and as such is more concerned with the ways in
which the Cronenberg/Hwang *M. Butterfly* can be considered a somewhat problematic re-presentation of some of the underlying tensions that
are masked in Pierre Loti's 1887 *Madame Chrysanthemum*. Such tensions, I
argue, are the material conditions of any and all constructions of identity.
I am particularly interested in how the complex assemblages of forces
that converge in the Cronenberg/Hwang production follow those found
in the nineteenth-century narratives mentioned above. For it is precisely
this fact of desires not pointing in a single direction (and we are indebted
here to Michel Foucault's work) that registers the complicated play of
competing forces in the construction of selves. The Butterfly narrative is
useful to present-day discussions regarding the relative advantage or
limitation of notions of the coherent 'subject' because it shows the ways
in which constantly changing configurations of identity are specifically
engendered by contingent historical and political conditions. It further
shows, importantly, that this mobility produces at any given moment,
open and unregulated as well as contained and defined spaces. These
spaces are the conditions of possibility for the emergence of new subjective experiences, and therefore of new definitions/configurations of
identity. Given this argument, I shall first discuss the material conditions
that lay behind and were indexed by the way that the Orient, 'woman'
and normative male sexuality were constituted in relation to one another
in Pierre Loti's writings.

Japan: Madame Chrysanthemum is a work that is intimately involved in the nineteenth-century project that sought to construct and secure the identity of the European bourgeois male. As Michel Foucault has famously argued in his later work, sexuality was of key importance in the construction of this identity (Foucault 1978). In *Madame Chrysanthemum*, as well as in Loti's earlier writings, the palpable presence of a homoerotic theme both compromised and complicated his involvement in this imperialist project. The point, as intimated earlier in the essay, is certainly not to try to secure static notions of identity or sexuality, indeed, as we well know at this point in the twenty-first century with its multiplicity of openly recognized manifestations to the contrary, these are unstable concepts. I shall call into play some of the readings activated in Loti's text and negotiated in his life, and see where they intersect with dominant ways of reading colonial sexuality. The immense popularity of Loti's *Madame Chrysanthemum* at the end of the nineteenth century was not only the result of a focus on a racialized, eroticized female subject, but also emerged from the evocation and play of other erotic charges and sexual identities. Loti's representation of Chrysanthemum is a complex one, and carries multivalent meanings: he evokes and engages popular racialized representations of the 'exotic woman' but his was also a subversive voice in relation to the construction of normative masculine identity. It is precisely this simultaneous installation of contrary ontological effects that arouse the interest: the possibility that while Loti's writing was doing the hegemonic work of empire it was *also* installing, albeit obliquely, unauthorized constituencies in the social body. While he was reiterating dominant tropes of the 'exotic woman', he was also constructing alternate imaginary spaces that opened onto very different sexual identities. While this reading does not fail to recognize the extremity of the misogynous and racist tendencies in Loti's work, it is also important to understand the way that these contradictory forces played themselves out, because such an understanding opens up possible spaces of conscious intervention in relation to current restrictive normative forces of containment.

Loti's privileged status is central to such a formulation because, at that moment in nineteenth-century hegemonic culture, it was not just any(body) that could transgress boundaries in this way. Rather, only those bodies that fall within the normative domain (even as it is being performatively redrawn, reconstituted, and rearticulated) were able to register a level of audibility/intelligiblity capable of engendering new social imaginaries. The following analysis suggests that for this process to take place it was essential that transgressive acts be located within a paradigm that at once embraces *and* resists that which is being transgressed. Loti's masquerade gives us just such a register to explore. In his work, foreign locales and bodies, sites of abjection for the European imaginary, are figured simultaneously as the playground of the privileged white male *and* as occasions for the disavowal of compulsory heterosexuality. That is, outside the parameters of Loti's power as a member of the elite, the acts explored here would have been unable to reach a level of audibility that were the very conditions of possibility that defined them as transgressive in the larger political domain. In other words, the strategic and transgressive use of iteration and citation in cultural production – in this case the evocation of a multiplicity of sexual imaginaries and cultures of experience – embraced a basic need for recognition felt by those whose lived existence fell outside definitions of normative identity. However, an important condition was that the voices of this acknowledgement were barely audible amidst the clamour of the hegemonic order, and would not, at that time, have been intelligible if they did not issue from a place situated firmly within dominant regimes of power. Pierre Loti was the embodiment of this positionality, and it is for this reason that the 'Loti effect' can be understood as a classic moment in the emergence of what became, in the twentieth century, gay history.

Pierre Loti was a celebrity in late nineteenth-century France. His elaborate masquerade balls, as well as his pronounced eccentricities, were infamous in Parisian society. Among the many examples of the formal recognition afforded him was his election in 1891 to the *Académie française*. Indeed, in being elected to this position he defeated the candidacy of Emile Zola. Membership in the *Académie* was, and still is,[2] revered by those wishing to enter the ranks of the forty 'immortals' that at any given time constitute one of the elites of the French literary world: the guardians of the French language. When Loti was inducted into the *Académie* he had reached the pinnacle of a structure of power that recalled the aristocracy of the *Ancien Régime*, clearly a force of cultural significance. Loti's books registered his influence: they were translated into many languages and were extremely successful, going through numerous

---

[2] See an Associated Press article carried in the 11 Dec. 2003 edition of the Canadian *Globe and Mail* newspaper, detailing the latest struggle in the *Académie's* history: the induction of former French president Valéry Giscard d'Estaing.

editions, both in France and around the world. In addition, monuments were erected in his honour in France, Turkey and Japan. Furthermore, in a testament to his popular influence, military records establish that when young male candidates for entry into the *École Navale* were asked to state what had inspired their naval vocation, the majority indicated that it was through reading Jules Verne and Pierre Loti. Loti can be seen as a figure writ large in the great nineteenth-century project that was dedicated to the assertion of European supremacy acted out through the body of the bourgeois male.

By the time he arrived in Japan, Loti was an old hand at turning his various ports-of-call into fictionalized travel narratives. Many of his stories are built around roughly the same plot: Western man travels to exotic land, meets 'Oriental' woman, who immediately recognizes the man as a superior being and falls in love with him; they have a relationship, and then the man moves on to the next port leaving the woman behind. More important for the purposes of this essay, however, is the fact that the passages where the prose is most alive and emotionally intense are those that are pervasive in the evocation of a distinctly homoerotic sensibility.

Loti's travel-narrative, a formulaic romance story built around his time in Japan, is for the most part a string of anecdotes and descriptive passages interspersed with stereotyped clichés about the country and its people. And, as suggested above, analysis reveals that rather than being structured around its title character – Madame Chrysanthemum – the narrative actually threads back and forth through the figure of the narrator's male-friend and companion, Yves, who as the object of the narrator's affections and loyalty, is the one who holds the storyline together. The vibrancy of the writing style when the author is talking about Yves, as well as this character's structural function within the narrative, indicate that the figure of Yves is of paramount importance.

In *Madame Chrysanthemum* Yves is a sailor and shipmate of Loti's who accompanies the narrator to Japan. The two friends are inseparable. It is Yves who suggests to Loti that he take a wife while he is in Japan and it is Yves who later picks out Loti's bride. However, very early in the story the narrator begins to express a possessive concern about the possible negative effects his young Japanese 'wife' may be having on his beloved friend Yves. This jealous worry and its resolution develop into the main narrative interest in the story. Chrysanthemum, rather than being a central character, is figured only as she is perceived, negatively, as a threat and a danger to the relationship between the two men: a foil to the main action of the story.

In the course of my investigations I went further into the body of Loti's work and also studied a collection of photographs of Loti, as well as accounts of his diaries and letters and a selection of his many drawings (like other men of his class, Loti was trained in fine art and was an accomplished draughtsman). It became clear that an emphasis on the expression of an ambiguous sexuality held a prominent place throughout Loti's life and work. He seems always to have been simultaneously constructing and transgressing the prescribed masculine identity of a nineteenth-century bourgeois male.

Three of Loti's drawings are provocative in this context: the example shown in Figure 1 was made in 1868-69 at the beginning of Loti's naval career. It is a composite sketch of Loti's fellow officers and shipmates. The men are each represented by head-and-shoulder drawings that are small in relation to the size of the paper, and fan out from the figure of the ship's captain located at the center of the page. Each discrete image is given its own space surrounded by large areas of white paper. By way of contrast, a later drawing (Figure 2), *circa* 1885-86, dealing with the same subject of Loti's shipmates, sets a very different tone. The men are not represented by pristine head-and-shoulder cameos. These men have bodies, and they are shown in different stages of undress. The scanty undershirts clothe virile, muscular forms that are no longer separated in pictorial space. The bodies touch, overlap and intermingle. A harlequin takes up his position as the centre of the composition and, as such, provides an evocative element alluding to Loti's love of the masquerade (a point to which we shall return). The figures are lyrically set against a fanciful cloud-swept sky, and a butterfly with a fluid gossamer train drifts out of the left frame of the drawing.

Figure 16.1. Pierre Loti, Composite drawing of shipmates, 1868-1869.
Source: Genet and Hervé 1988: 70.

Figure 16.2. Pierre Loti, Composite drawing of shipmates 1885-1886.
Source: Genet and Hervé 1988: 221.

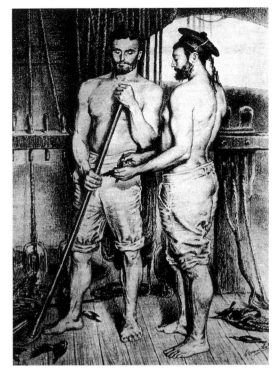

Figure 16.3. Pierre Loti, Extended study of two sailors, undated.
Source: Genet and Hervé 1988: 203.

Finally, the third drawing, illustrated here in Figure 3, is an example of a more sustained study executed around the same time as the one in Figure 2. In this image, two sailors are figured in a formal composition that ironically recalls eighteenth and nineteenth-century genre painting, with its moralizing narratives. The image features two ruggedly handsome young men, one of them sporting a sailor's cap, both of them naked to the waist, each wearing a pair of trousers rolled to the knees. In addition to an obviously erotic rendering – muscular limbs and chest, the draped soft lines of the cloth of the men's rolled trousers, and the close and familiar proximity of their bodies – the motif of the small, limp birds scattered over the deck and held in the hand alluded to particular eighteenth-century French genre paintings in which young women with dead birds signaled a loss of virginity; the motif of birds in flight had, in some cases, orgasmic associations. Loti was trained in the visual arts and would have been alert to the meanings he was calling up in these images: readings that also circulated in many forms of popular culture. Moreover, for Loti this practice was not restricted to visual art, and he employed similar strategies in his travel narratives where he also doubled and crossed specifically gendered tropes (Szyliowicz 1988).

The harlequin figure noted in the earlier drawing in Figure 2 stands as a reference to Loti's love of dress-up and disguise, a practice so obsessively pursued by him that it can be understood within today's definitions of 'cross-dressing'. (Indeed, the drawings in Figures 2 and 3 would not be out of place in twenty-first century gay visual culture, giving credence to the premise that the overall effect that Loti produced is one that can be understood as a foundational moment in a genealogy of present-day gay cultures.) Documents in the Loti archive reveal that his 'penchant for high heels, perfume, make-up, jewelry, and elegant dress extended far beyond the fancy-dress parties he loved; he often wore "accessories of feminine gear"' (Szyliowicz 1988:23). And he regularly wore excessive amounts of make-up (he 'frizzed and dyed his moustache', wore rouge and greasepaint and ran kohl around his eyes), and the lifts that he wore in his high-heeled boots made him walk almost on tiptoe. Documents in the archive also recount how Loti was the butt of endless jokes during active service in World War I because he continued to wear make-up and also wore an array of inappropriate costumes. Navy records document official reprimands delivered concerning his use of make-up (Blanch 1983: 188). Indeed, his excesses provoked numbers of amusing Loti caricatures in the publications of his time.

A caricature useful for our purposes here, and one of the many published in contemporary magazines, shows clearly that, by the early decades of the twentieth century, the ambivalent figure cut by Loti was not lost on the French public (Figure 4).[3] This image details a middle-aged Loti, dressed in the attire of a French naval officer, but wearing a Turkish fez rather than a French navy cap, poised atop the stylized form of a minaret, overlooking the great Turkish port city below, rimmed by an expanse of ocean dotted with naval vessels. In the drawing Loti is gazing into a hand-held mirror and applying makeup to his eyes as he balances – cross-legged, his high-heeled boots dangling in the foreground – on the pointed end of the minaret. The way that this image details the infamous high-heeled boots, the suggestion of make-up, the Turkish fez that re-

---

[3] From *Fantasia* (May 1913), reproduced in Genet and Hervé 1988: 436.

calls *Aziyadé* (another tremendously successful and well known fictional travel narrative that Loti wrote about his experiences in Turkey), suggests a familiar knowledge – on the part of at least some constituencies within the French public – of many of the closeted circumstances in his work and surrounding his person.

Figure 16.4. Caricature of Pierre Loti in the magazine *Fantasio* (May 1913).
Source: Genet and Hervé 1988: 436.

To begin with the caption of the caricature in Figure 4, 'Loti Pacha'. *Pacha – pasha* in English – was the term used for a Turkish officer of high rank. Loti, a high-ranking *French* naval officer who is, with the exception of the fez, identified as such by the uniform he is wearing, is designated as a 'Turk'. This caption alerts us to the first of many doubles in play here. Loti, as a representative of the French empire, is placed far above the ground in the imperial seat of omniscient power: an elevated position from which he is able to survey the entire expanse below. However, he does not occupy this position as intended. That is, he does not use the powers of surveillance provided by this position to police the events and activities over which he presides. Rather, he is lost in the image reflected back from the mirror held in front of him. He is immersed, deeply engaged in this surface. But for the viewers of this caricature, the reflection in the mirror is ambiguous at best. And we cannot leave this image without addressing the obvious sexual innuendo: another site of doubling. Loti's *Aziyadé* depicted the East as a place that permitted transgressive sexual practices: specifically, the penetration of men by other men; and on a more symbolic level, the penetration by the West of a feminized East (Gundermann 1994). This unflattering caricature of Loti certainly plays with such a perception. Loti straddled atop the obviously phallic representation of a mosque can be seen as being penetrated both in terms of (homo)sexual penetration and as a French subject being penetrated by the Turkish 'abject'.

It is notable, in relation to the construction of psychic imaginaries, that the intense masquerade Loti engaged in also found expression in the 'house of enchantment' that he created for himself in the family home at Rochefort. Although the elaboration of the nineteenth-century bourgeois interior has been recognized as significant by many theorists (Williams 1982), Loti created a particularly hermetic environment, one that prefigured the Paris Exposition of 1900 in its oppressive articulation of the material culture of many of France's colonial holdings. The interior he constructed seems to lurk in some twilight zone between ethnographic fascination and an obsessively articulated dream-world of the Other. There are many photographs and photogravures showing Loti reclining in these bizarre phantasmagorical spaces. He fashioned Turkish, Arabian, Japanese and Breton rooms, a Chinese pavilion, a Louis XVI salon, a Renaissance hall and a medieval room. Loti also possessed 'authentic' costumes to complement each of these settings, and these outfits had other more active, and sometimes dangerous, secret lives. Early in his naval career Loti began a practice that he was to sustain throughout his many years of service: when his ships reached port he went ashore fully disguised in local dress and wandered around fixed in the fantasy that he was perceived as a native. Feeling safely camouflaged Loti committed various infractions that violated the boundaries of local customs. If any of his fellow officers or shipmates came across him in his wanderings they knew that they were not to acknowledge him in any way (Blanch

1983:118). The experiences he gathered during these furtive outings were then woven into the stories of his travels. The photograph collection, housed in the Musée Pierre-Loti in Rochefort, France, contains dozens of pictures of Loti in the 'exotic' outfits he used for these excursions. The many extant photographs of Loti also feature him in costumes that were exotic portrayals of a mythic ideal past. A studio photograph of Loti dressed as Osiris, King of the Underworld, shows him ready to take part in a costume party given by one of his friends, Juliette Adams, on 20 February 1887, and illustrates the extremes to which he went in his entertainments. Nor was he alone in this; group photographs and archival paraphernalia from these social events (such as the elaborate and excessive menu cards) show that his friends and associates were also ready, willing, and financially able to participate in these extravagant fantasies.

The level of self-involvement, and the degree to which it is possible to understand these activities as attempts at the conscious construction of a collective imaginary, is gestured toward in Loti's 'Preface' to *Madame Chrysanthemum*. He presents this book as 'primarily' a tale about *himself* and the *effect* produced on him by Japan (emphasis in the original: Loti 1985). It is in keeping with other nineteenth-century cultural, social, economic, and institutional practices concerned with producing the self in relation to negative determinations of the Other, that Loti's representation of the European bourgeois male operates through the staged representation of a Japanese woman. Race and gender are not, of course, unusual co-ordinates in the larger discourses of identity being produced during this period.

Moreover, in relation to these productions, the autobiographical dimension of the widely used and popular genre of travel writing complicates and distorts the representation of non-European cultures and functions, therefore, as an insidiously seductive form of 'truth-telling' that proposes to offer an authoritative vision of a reality precisely rendered. The question of veracity is a relevant one in works that purport to be an accurate form of life-writing. When Loti writes, in *Madame Chrysanthemum*, about the architecture of his Japanese dwelling, and recites in great detail the intricacies of Japanese celebrations, he establishes himself as an authority on Japanese culture; then, when he slips into extreme, negative descriptions of the character of the young Japanese girl, Chrysanthemum, he carries that authority from the register of empirical claims into moralizing normative judgements.

Throughout his writing Loti engages dominant constructions of racialized female sexuality. In some works, such as the book *Aziyadé*, the woman is presented as sexually alluring and available, beautiful and mysterious, and devoted to the Western male protagonist. In other works, such as the Chrysanthemum story, this construction is so fragile that when the young Japanese 'wife' takes off her clothes for the daily bath, the narrator, in highly racist and misogynous descriptions, reduces Chrysanthemum to nothing more than her costume:

> A Japanese woman, deprived of her long dress and her huge sash with its pretentious bows, is nothing but a diminutive yellow being, with crooked legs and flat, unshapely bust; she has no longer a remnant of her artificial little charms which have completely disappeared in company with her costume (216).

In this interpretation of feminine identity as masquerade, Loti's text marks a strange resonance with his own intense involvement in disguise and masking as a way of playing with complex subjectivities: one that prefigures present-day theories of performativity in relation to the construction of identities. We might contrast his comments about Chrysanthemum with a description, taken from his journals, of Pierre Le Cor, the man upon whom the character of Yves was based, in a similar state of undress:

> When Pierre removes his clothes, one would think he were a Greek statue removing his coarse exterior, and one admires him. In the same bronzed alabaster, hard and polished, are outlined the mobile bulges of his muscles and the powerful lines of an ancient athlete (Szyliowicz 29).

In Loti's writing about the Orient, people and their customs and habits are consistently presented as static entities in ahistorical contexts. Sometimes they are vilified, and sometimes they are romanticized, but always they are diminished and stereotyped. Loti's preoccupation with sexuality was at the heart of his stories about non-European cultures. The construction of 'Madam Chrysanthemum' was not a construction of the Other at all – in this sense Loti admitted no alterity. Rather, the figure of Chrysanthemum was primarily a projection of the undecidability of his own identity, sexual and otherwise. Although this undecidability opened a space for the subversion of dominant prescriptions of sexuality, Loti's representations were also adamantly successful at performing the work of empire in nineteenth-century Europe.

If we now hold Loti's version of the Madame Butterfly theme alongside the Hwang/Cronenberg film, certain connections and dissonances
become clear. A century after *Madame Chrysanthemum* was first published,
the film *M. Butterfly* can be seen as foregrounding many of the silences
contained in Loti's work. By framing East/West relations in terms of
gender and sexuality this film complicates the conventional Butterfly
narrative, thereby substantially altering its power to define and contain
the figures it constructs. However, even though Hwang's play and
Cronenberg's and Hwang's film forge new readings that challenge earlier
versions of the story, and speak to the impossibility of the desire to fix
stable identities in Hwang's avowed embrace of the humanist vision of a
world united, the project falls far short of the radicality it proclaims.
Although the play is the more powerful of the two productions in its
complication of the stereotypes, Hwang's humanism works within a kind
of essentialism that fails adequately to address questions of difference.
This humanism is somewhat mitigated in the film with the injection of a
dose of Cronenberg nihilism but, the film nonetheless demonstrates (and
this is nowhere more obvious than in the closing scenes) that the specificity of any identity is always asserted at the price of occluding other
possibilities, and, moreover, that there is always a violence involved in
this suppression. In the end, the realization afforded by the film – as it
attempts to navigate and undo conventional aspects of the Madame
Butterfly story, and in so doing actually reinstates them – demands of its
viewers a rethinking of individual and collective subject formations
around notions of identity. Just as the 'Loti effect' diagrammed above
shows that the development of the figure of Madame Chrysanthemum is
replete with all manner of contingency, melded together in unspoken
ways to give shape to that which is clamouring to enter the hegemonic
domain, so too do current articulations of identity demand that we remain alert to the intricate webs of connection and disavowal that form
the very condition of possibility for those identities.

References

Blanch, Lesley. 1983. *Pierre Loti: Portrait of an Escapist*. London: Collins.
Cronenberg, David. 1993. *M. Butterfly*. Directed by David Cronenberg, Geffen
    Pictures.

Foucault, Michel. 1981. *The History of Sexuality: An Introduction* (tr. Robert Hurley). London: Penguin.

Genet, Christian and Daniel Hervé. 1988. *Pierre Loti l'enchanteur*. Gémozac: La Caillerie.

Gundermann, Christian. 1994. 'Orientalism, Homophobia, Masochism: Transfers between Pierre Loti's *Aziyadé* and Gilles Deleuze's "Coldness and Cruelty"' in *Diacritics* 24(2/3): 151-67.

Hwang, David Henry. 1988 (1986). *M. Butterfly*. New York: Plume.

Loti, Pierre. 1985. *Japan: Madam Chrysanthemum* (tr. Laura Ensor) (*Japan: Madame Chrysanthème,* Paris: Calmann-Lévy, 1887). London: KPI.

Pollock, Griselda. 1992. *Avant-Garde Gambits 1888-1893:Gender and the Colour of Art History*. London: Thames and Hudson.

Stoler, Ann Laura. 1995. *Race and the Education of Desire: Foucault's History of Sexuality and the Colonial Order of Things*. Durham: Duke University Press.

Stoler, Ann Laura. 1997. 'Making Empire Respectable: the Politics of Race and Sexual Morality in Twentieth-Century Colonial Cultures' in McClintock, Anne, Aamir Mulfti and Ella Shohat (eds) *Dangerous Liaisons: Gender, Nation and Postcolonial Perspectives*. Minneapolis: Minnesota University Press.

Szyliowicz, Irene L. 1988. *Pierre Loti and the Oriental Woman*. London: Macmillan.

Quinn, Arthur Hobson (ed.). 1957. *Representative American Plays: from 1762 to the Present*, 7th edition. New York: Appleton-Century Crofts.

Williams, Rosalind H. 1982. *Dream Worlds: Mass Consumption in Late Nineteenth-Century France*. Berkeley: University of California Press.

CHAPTER 17

TRANSLATION IN THE REHEARSAL ROOM:
SERIOUS PLAY AT THE CULTURAL INTERFACE

Gay McAuley

Even when working with classic (i.e. consecrated and well known) play texts, actors frequently modify the text during the course of the rehearsal process, either consciously through cuts and changes, or unconsciously through slips of the tongue and failures of memory. The text is thus reworked to fit the meanings being constructed by that group of actors through their performance. While this process occurs to a greater or lesser extent in any text-based rehearsal, it is greatly accentuated when the work involved is a translation from another language. Translation seems to destabilize the authority of the text, performance problems are likely to be seen first and foremost as translation problems and the tendency is to amend the text rather than search harder for a performance solution. This means that the rehearsal room is a wonderful place to observe the interface between cultures and the role of language in the construction and representation of identity. In Australia we routinely receive European classics through the filter of British or American English, which has a significant impact on the meanings actors are able to construct. In this chapter I draw on a performance project in which a group of Australian actors, starting from what they designated a 'neutral' translation of Molière's *Dom Juan*, modified the text in order to produce an Australian vernacular version, without adapting the fiction to locate it in an Australian setting. A comparative analysis is presented of five different versions of a fragment from this play: the original French, two published British translations, the 'neutral' and the Australian vernacular version. The minor textual differences are examined, and comment is offered on the significant impact these have in performance, on the ways in which this rehearsal process can construct characters and narrative moment, and on the value of rehearsal studies for cultural theorists interested in identity formation.

The theatre provides a valuable site for exploration of the ways in which individual and group identity is formed and manifested within society. It is not just that the theatre is one of the art forms where such identities are displayed and socially validated, but that it provides in its working practices a kind of laboratory where the processes of identity formation can be observed. In the theatre, and in particular in the character/narrative-based performance genres, artists work with a multiplicity of sign systems to create convincing characters and to explore the forces that motivate their actions. Accounts of rehearsal by practitioners and observers provide revealing examples of this process (see for example Callow 1985, Cole 1992, Sher 1985). Actors are in fact highly skilled and sensitive social semioticians, adept at recognizing and interpreting tiny details of intonation, gesture, dress and behaviour. Theatre practitioners usually exclude observers from the rehearsal process, but anyone who has been privileged to watch skilled actors at work will be able to affirm that the rehearsal room of a piece of character/narrative based theatre is an excellent place to observe the factors involved in the construction and manifestation of identity.

In the theatre, text has to become speech, which is to say that, not only are multiple paralinguistic features layered into each utterance, but that these must literally be embodied. Actors working with text pounce on tiny details of vocabulary, syntax, or even punctuation in order to tease out the implications for their characters and the physical incarnation of these characters. Many factors beyond the words themselves are, thus, brought into play in the creative process, and of course the given words, those the playwright has finally selected, offer multiple expressive possibilities to the actors, which is why any particular play text can give rise to such radically different productions.

Rehearsal room discourse is always revealing for the cultural theorist, but never more so than when the play being rehearsed is a translation. With a translated playtext, one is necessarily dealing with the interface between two (or more) cultures, and it seems that at the interface the mechanisms at work are more overt, or are more easily recognized as mechanisms rather than being masked by familiarity and glossed as 'natural' or 'true'. If a given play text can give rise to widely different productions, how much more is this the case when translation enters the equation. Rehearsal of a play in translation provides observers with the opportunity for intensive study of the function of language in relation to other signifying practices in the construction of character as well as many insights into prevailing attitudes to the cultures in question.

This chapter is structured around the presentation of a small fragment of text, part of a scene from Molière's *Dom Juan*, and a performance created by a group of Australian actors with this text.[1] In presenting the text that emerged from the actors' collective work process, I want to illustrate the way apparently minor details of grammar or syntax can have huge implications in performance, and how actors deal with the cultural minefield created by translation. The scene I am presenting is taken from Act II, where Don Juan has been attempting to seduce a peasant girl, Charlotte, and is interrupted by her boorish lover, Pierrot. The peasant scenes pose an immediate problem for translators, for Molière has written their dialogue in a robust and recognizable dialect, that of the Ile de France. English translators often choose some version of a Somerset burr, which functions inevitably to locate the action equally specifically, but somewhat confusingly, in the West of England. The group decided to explore the possibilities of using Australian vernacular for the peasant scenes while maintaining the location of the action in a kind of generalized seventeenth-century France. The task, as expressed by the director at different times in the rehearsal process, was to see if reference to one culture (Australia) can illuminate another (France), whether the power hierarchy and class issues could be clarified for Australian audiences through use of Australian speech, and whether the use of such speech could add to the humour of the scene, potentially somewhat compromised for modern audiences by the amount of physical violence.

Before discussing the scene in detail, however, attention should be drawn to a number of general points concerning the relationship between text and performance in contemporary theatre practice, especially where translation is involved. These points are all relevant to the ways in which theatre practice can be seen to illustrate the mechanisms at work in the construction and representation of identity.

Firstly, there are many varieties of English, and even many varieties of Australian English, but the relatively small population of Australia means that publishers and copyright agencies do not find it worth their while to

---

[1] The artists involved in the performance project were Beverly Blankenship (Director), Brandon Burke (Don Juan), Drew Forsythe (Sganarelle), Gillian Hyde (Charlotte), and Chris Truswell (Pierrot), and I acknowledge with gratitude their generosity in permitting academics to observe and document their rehearsal process.

bring out translations in Australian English. This does not constitute a
major problem in respect of literary genres such as prose and poetry, but
it is a serious drawback in the predominantly oral form of theatre, and
audiences in Australia routinely receive non-English theatre texts
through the filter of British or American English. It is perhaps only
because translated texts are accorded so little authority in the rehearsal
room and are routinely modified, that Australian audiences are able to
experience Chekhov's characters as located in Russia rather than in the
Home Counties (notwithstanding the obligatory samovar). It has proved
extremely revealing to ask actors to work systematically through the same
scene in a number of different translations (either emanating from different English speaking communities, or from the same linguistic community but over a period of time). Analysis of the results of these workshop
performances provides convincing evidence of the way that translators
inscribe what I have called 'performance indicators' into their texts, and
of the ideological load that such indicators can carry (see McAuley 1989:
59-80; 1994: 81-116; 1995: 111-125).

Secondly, in the contemporary theatre it is the director who, increasingly, carries the authorial responsibility for the whole production. This
means that the playtext, like every other aspect of the production, is
subject to the creative will of the director, and it can be cut, re-arranged,
amended, and can even have other texts interpolated into it. Depending
on the working method of the individual director, this re-writing may
occur before the rehearsal process (which may then proceed with a relatively stable written text) or it may occur substantially during the rehearsal process with changes being incorporated right up until opening
night. Of course, it is extremely likely that lapses of memory and slips of
the tongue have meant that the text in performance has always been
somewhat unstable, but in that case the agent of the change would have
been the actor rather than the director. Recording of the rehearsal process makes it possible to log the multiplicity of minor slips, the points at
which a given actor's memory recurringly fails, and to note the way that
some slips become enshrined as 'the text'. While I have not done such a
study over the whole run of a production, the work I have done on the
text in rehearsal suggests that, even in text-based theatre and even when
the text in question is well known and consecrated, it is shaped and
reworked in subtle ways to fit the meanings being constructed by that
group of actors for that production. This is to say that, although the text
plays a central role in the meaning making process, it is not a straitjacket

constraining the practitioners but it is, like the other elements that go to make up the production, raw material to be shaped.

This leads directly to my third general point which concerns the far more radical instability of translated texts in the performance-making process. If the verbal text is, in general, relatively unstable in contemporary theatre practice, this is greatly exacerbated in the case of translated texts, where the practitioners feel free to question the text and to amend it day by day as their performances develop. When working with a text in its original language, actors confronted by a performance problem will work to find a performance solution. When the text is a translation, their first assumption is that the problem is in the translation and they will consult the original (if anyone in the rehearsal room knows the source language) or another translation. They may adopt the other translator's solution, or they may amend the line themselves, but in either case their choice will be governed by the meanings they are creating in their production. The text is under construction just as much as the production that is taking shape through the same rehearsal process. While this kind of practice is probably, in Lawrence Venuti's term, one of the scandals of translation (Venuti 1998) and evidence of the low status accorded to translators in the theatre, as elsewhere, it does make for extremely interesting comparative cultural studies. Documenting the shifts and recording the discussion around changes suggested by the actors can reveal a great deal about the cultures engaged in the creative interplay.

In the Table printed at the end of this chapter, I have provided 5 different versions of the extract to be discussed here. In column 1 there is Molière's French original, written in 1665, banned after 15 performances, not performed again until 1841, rediscovered in 1947 and the subject of countless brilliant productions throughout the rest of the twentieth century. In column 2 there is John Wood's 1953 translation, published in the widely available and respected Penguin Classics; Christopher Hampton in column 3 brings the skills of a successful playwright to his 1974 translation, published by Faber, and in column 4 is the translation the Australian actors were given on the first day of rehearsal. This was prepared by Rex Cramphorn and modified by Beverly Blankenship, the director of the production in question. Column 5 gives the text, transcribed from a video recording of one of the performances, that Blankenship's actors produced as part of their conscious attempt to create an Australian vernacular version. The published translations are both British, a common situation confronting Australian theatre practitioners, and it will be noted that the translations have been produced at 20 year intervals, 1953, 1974 and 1991. This is another very important factor, as oral language dates much faster than the written, which drastically curtails the effective stage life of theatre translations, but does not lead to publishers bringing out new translations every five or six years.

The speeches are numbered and I have also numbered the elements within each speech, including stage directions. This facilitates direct comparison of the versions with each other and with Molière's text, and it also gives some indication of the actors' work process, for it seems to me that the translator's work process overlaps with that of the actor here. For an actor, each of my numbered phrases would probably be perceived as a 'thought', or an 'action' and each needs to be played, that is to say that a performance solution needs to be found for each. Justin Monjo, acting in a workshop production of Sophocles' *Antigone*, said, 'you play all the words you are given', and the rehearsal process made it clear that, even in text-based theatre, even when the text is a famous classic, the meaning is not *in* the words but is constructed by the actor (and the rest of the production team) *with* the words and is made manifest in the performance, using all the expressive resources the actor possesses. The segmentation into units in the tabular presentation makes it easy to see where one translation is significantly longer or shorter than the original, or where one translator has omitted a whole unit (indicated by xxx on the page) or inserted something not in the source text (e.g. Hampton 162 or Australian Actors 12). The latter instance is a result of having transcribed the text from a performance recording, as it was part of some improvised business: Chris Truswell, playing Pierrot, came on stage, walked right past Don Juan, saying 'Mornin' 'or on some occasions 'G'day', then did an elaborate double take as he realized the girl being actively seduced was his own fiancée.

Detailed analysis of even this brief fragment would exceed the scope of this chapter, so I shall restrict my remarks to a few key areas. The first of these concerns the nature and function of the peasant speech: is it comic in itself, does it function to indicate slow wittedness or simply the class gulf that separates Don Juan from both Charlotte and Pierrot, and how regionally specific is it? The answers to these questions differ from translation to translation. Molière gives the peasant characters a recognizable *patois* that, even today, French actors have no difficulty locating in the Ile de France. Don Juan may be a Spanish nobleman, and the location of the dramatic action may be Sicily, but the targets of Molière's satire are French, and the transparent ruse of the foreign setting is a tactic probably calculated to stir his critics to apoplexy. The peasants are clearly and undoubtedly French and, as Louis Jouvet advised students in his acting classes, you have to think of them speaking 'un langage ferme, solide, qui pourrait être aussi bien auvergnat' (Jouvet 1965: 139).The quality of groundedness that emerges from the French is certainly present in the Australian vernacular version, although of course it means that this translation cannot be transplanted far from its time and place of origin. This is also the problem with John Wood's choice of Somerset – or is it Sussex? – for his country bumpkins ("ee bain't go'n to be a-kissin' my intended'). Hampton takes the opposite tack and provides a neutral, rather bland translation that leaves it up to the actors to introduce accent or other markers of place. The problem with this strategy, however, is that the translation does not give the actor much to work with, in contrast to Molière's very colourful text. Furthermore, in a couple of places it appears that Hampton's Pierrot even strays into a middle-class register that might be somewhat confusing (32): 'Now, look here, just stop that' and (132) 'How dare you let him carry on with you like that'.

The care that Molière took with the details of the peasant speech suggests that it was in itself part of the comedy, and this is nowhere more evident than in the extraordinary range of expletives he gives to Pierrot. These are all corruptions of blasphemous phrases ('testigué' is 'tête de dieu', 'jernigué' is 'je renie dieu', 'palsanqué' is 'par le sang de dieu', etc.) and, although Pierrot swears nine times in this short extract, he achieves the remarkable feat of not repeating himself once. All the translators reduce the amount of cursing, Wood gives him six but, in keeping the religious connections – 'Lor' lumme', 'Lord help us' and 'Dang it' – loses much of the comic energy and colour. Hampton gives his Pierrot only two actual swear words – 'Christ' and 'Bluddyell', reduces others to simple exclamations like 'Oy' and 'Ey', and on other occasions (91, 119 and 152) omits the expletive entirely.The Australian actors were impressed by the comic inventiveness of Pierrot's cursing, but even they only managed six to Molière's nine expletives. Chris Truswell's Pierrot had already introduced the expansive verbal quality typical of country humour in his 'You're coming on as strong as a sheep farmer on shearing day' (15). The verbal elaboration here conveys something of the slower rhythm of life in the country (a city dweller would be half way down the street before Pierrot has reached his punchline), but the joke is nevertheless one for city dwellers. While the French Pierrot is getting entangled in the medical consequences of being overheated, the Australian actors chose a cheeky reference to a theme which townsfolk in Australia, and perhaps elsewhere, seem to find irresistibly comic, namely what it is that sheep farmers get up to with their sheep. For the cursing, he was able to maintain the religious connection with 'Jesus' (very commonly used in Australia), and the slightly comic 'Crikey', but for the series of expletives that punctuate the beating (Speech 11), religion gives way to bodily functions. There is a comic energy to his series of rhyming phrases, 'shit a brick', 'root a boot' and 'fuck a duck', and they make a good equivalent to the French Pierrot's seemingly unlimited range of invective while also preserving the notion of rhyme.

Contemporary audiences do not find much humour in the spectacle of aristocrats beating their servants or hapless peasants, so one of the problems with this scene for modern actors is how to handle the beating. The Australian actors questioned why Pierrot does not punch Don Juan, either when he first comes upon him kissing Charlotte, or when the assault begins. If he is restrained by his lowly position in the class hierarchy, then it becomes even more unseemly for Don Juan to persist in slapping him around. Translations that reduce his responses to 'Ow' and 'Oy' and 'Ouch' confirm his victim status and, in my view, put the comedy at risk. The robust verbal invective that Molière and the Australian actors give him functions to reassert his individuality, putting Don Juan in the wrong but without making too big a political point of it.

Speech 9 provides some interesting contrasts. 'Parce qu'ous êtes Monsieu' becomes 'Just because you're a gentleman', the 'just' carrying a suggestion of Australian egalitarianism, and the insertion of 'around here' in 93 makes a territorial claim ('you can't come around here and kiss our women'): Pierrot is on his own home turf and he is asserting his rights. Wood turns 94 into a rhetorical question rather than a direct challenge ('Why can't 'e go kiss 'is own women?'), which functions to makes it less aggressive. Hampton introduces some significant changes here: firstly, he shifts the issue from class to wealth ('Just because you've got money'), and then by changing 'caresser' to 'touch up', he brings in a more overt sexuality. There is a kind of vulgar materialism about this Pierrot which perhaps has its genesis in 1970s London, and it brings swift retribution. The first slap is a direct response to the insulting 'Go and touch up your own', and while this may provide some alleviation to the problem of aristocrats beating rustics who cannot fight back, it actually changes the dynamics of the scene. In Hampton's version, Pierrot attacks Don Juan so aggressively that the slap seems almost warranted, but then, somewhat inexplicably, Don Juan goes on hitting him even though he has ceased offering any provocation, thus creating a definite problem for the actors.

Molière initiates the slap by two monosyllables, an interrogative and an exclamation (101 and 111) which suggests that Pierrot stands up to the first warning issued by Don Juan. In the Australian version this gets elaborated in words: 'How dare you?', 'I dare all right, mate'. The decision to call him 'mate' – he has called him 'sir' in 13 – occasioned a discussion in the rehearsal room about the use of the term. It was generally agreed that 'mate' (stressing the imaginary inverted commas around the word) is insulting, and although it motivates Don Juan's first slap, it does not put Pierrot so far in the wrong as Hampton's translation does. It is also a strong affirmation of the individualism of this Pierrot, another indication of the different way in which class is manifested in Australia.

Mention has just been made of Molière's monosyllables: there are a good number of them in this short scene, and they seem to pose a considerable difficulty to the translator. 'Ah' (42) was omitted by all the translators; 81 was left intact by Wood and Hampton but transformed into a growl by Cramphorn and omitted by the actors; 101 and 111 have just been discussed, omitted by Hampton and elaborated into a verbal phrase by Cramphorn and the actors; and 'Oh' (115) was also omitted by Cramphorn and thus also by the Australian actors. French theatre practitioners stress that Molière wrote as an actor, with a living awareness of what happens to speech in performance. Jacques Lassalle, after directing the Comédie Française production of this play in 1993, commented that, while Molière's monosyllables are extraordinarily expressive, it is up to the actor to find and create the meaning. In dealing with these monosyllabic exclamations, he says,

> c'est tout le corps qui y passe. Un acteur moliéresque n'incarne véritablement Molière que lorsqu'il a su gérer un 'Ah!' [the actor's whole body is involved. An actor can only be said to truly embody Molière when he has discovered how to manage an 'Ah!'] (Lassalle 1995: 120).

The temptation for the translator is, as we have seen, to make the content explicit in some way but this tends to reduce the actor's scope; equally, where a translator is primarily concerned with the text on the page, some of these exclamations might appear redundant and the temptation then is to omit them. Following the very perceptive insight of Jacques Lassalle, however, it is evident that these monosyllabic interventions are extremely important, and the opportunity must be left for the actors to make their own meanings and to use whatever bodily resources they can in order to do so. Lassalle's reference to the body makes it clear that these are performance moments, and the way the actor 'manages' them will be full of implications for the character and the situation.

Another feature of translating for the stage is that the actor's trajectory in each speech has to be taken into account and this trajectory includes both the sequence of thoughts or emotional reactions of the character and the physical manifestation of this by the actor. In numbering the units or 'thoughts' within each speech, I have begun to indicate this breakdown, but I probably have not gone as far as the actors would do in rehearsal. For instance in 62 Molière seems to have given Charlotte three or even four micro-units: Et/laisse-le faire/aussi/Piarrot. While the linguistic content is clearly conveyed by Wood and Hampton, the rhythm of the speech they suggest is very different, and it seems that, while the 'et' and the 'aussi' do not have much linguistic meaning, they have a force and provide the occasion for performance possibilities that are lost in the straightforward 'Let him be/Pierrot' (2 units). Cramphorn's 'Oh/leave him alone/Pierrot' provides the actress with 3 micro-units, which Gillian Hyde elaborated into the crudely comic 'Piss off/Piarrot/and leave him alone'. The energy in this line came from her dismay at seeing her glittering opportunity threatened by the unwelcome reminder of her prior engagement, and it makes explicit her willing complicity in the seduction. She is certainly no victim, and she is also more aggressive towards Pierrot than any of the other versions: in 121 all versions, including the French, have her placating Pierrot ('Piarrot, ne te fâche point'), but the Australian Charlotte attacks him ('Yes, so simmer down, Piarrot'). The 'yes' here is another example of a micro-unit inserted by the actors: it was not written into the script but is the verbal trace left by the performative moment Gillian Hyde created there (picking up Pierrot's hat, dislodged during the fracas, and plonking it on his head).

There is much more that could be extracted from the comparative study of this brief fragment, but perhaps enough has been said to demonstrate the value of the rehearsal room for this kind of cross-cultural study. Theatre practitioners are necessarily working for their own place and time, even when the text at the centre of their work comes from another place and time. One of the most fascinating aspects of theatre as an art form is the way it negotiates the interface between 'there/then' and 'here/now', the transnational and the resolutely local, and actors are the agents of this negotiation. Although it would be unwise to attempt to draw weighty conclusions about Australia in the 1990s from the choices made by that particular group of actors in that performance project, the fact that they did set out consciously to make an Australian vernacular version makes their work rather revealing in this connection. Charlotte's assertiveness, Pierrot's sense of his rights, and the mockery of country manners from an implied city perspective probably say more about Australia in the 1990s than about France in the 1660s, but these elements both illuminate Molière's France, and create awareness of the continuities and discontinuities across time and place that make up the web of culture. In this analysis, I have also referred to other translations and the performance choices they imply, and this (albeit rather sketchy) comparative context functions to reveal the provisional nature of the characters and their story, and the way both are always under construction, continually shifting under the pressure of the multiplicity of factors at work in society.

The choice of such a small fragment of text and performance was determined by the prescribed length of this chapter, but the level of detail, fastidious as it may seem to some people, is methodologically very important, for it is with this level of detail that actors work in rehearsal. They map together thought, language, gesture and movement, constructing micro-units of behaviour, and their acute sensitivity to the shades of meaning in a word or phrase and their insights into all the other sign systems involved in the representation of character make them perceptive social commentators. I wanted also to show how the actors' creative process mirrors that of the translator, working through a text word by word, phrase by phrase. Rehearsal room talk concerning performance choices is invariably illuminating about the society in which the actors are working, and the distance in place and time between playwright and performers creates fascinating disjunctions (even when it is only a matter of a few years). When there is a translation involved the cultural interface being explored becomes even more complex and fascinating. While some of the issues I have raised, notably the radical interventions that routinely occur in rehearsal of a translated text, certainly pose ethical and intellectual questions that need to be pursued with both theatre practitioners and within translation studies, it is also clear that the work process involved in the creation of text/character/narrative-based theatre constitutes fruitful terrain for cultural theorists interested in identity formation.

Figure 17.1. Table of Molière, Dom Juan (Act II scene 3) Comparative Translations.

Molière, Dom Juan (Act II scene 3) Comparative Translations

Molière (1665) Eds Bordas	Wood (1953, Penguin)	Hampton (1974, Faber)	Cramphorn/Blankenship (1991)	Australian Actors (1991)
PIERROT 1. *(se mettant entre deux et poussant Don Juan)[1]* xxx Tout doucement, Monsieur,[3] tenez-vous, s'il vous plaît.[4] Vous vous échauffez trop[5] et vous pourriez gagner la purésie.[6]	PETER 1. *(interposing between them and pushing Don Juan)[1]* xxx Easy, maister,[3] steady on, if ye don't mind –[4] if ye be wax'n' that warm[5] ye'll be gett'n' 'eartburn.[6]	PIERROT 1. *(pushing Don Juan away)[1]* xxx Just a minute sir,[3] steady on, will you.[4] You'd better not get so worked up.[5] you'll have a stroke or something.[6]	PIERROT 1. *(between them, pushing)[1]* xxx Hold on a minute there, sir,[3] if you don't mind.[4] You're coming on a bit hot and strong –[5] you don't want to be overexciting yourself.[6]	PIERROT 1. xxx Mornin'.[2] Fair go there, sir[3] if you don't mind.[4] You're coming on as strong as a sheep farmer on shearing day.[5] You don't want to be overexciting yourself.[6]
DON JUAN 2. *(repoussant rudement Pierrot)[1]* Qui m'amène cet impertinent?[2]	DON JUAN 2. *(pushing him roughly)[1]* Where did this lout come from?[2]	DON JUAN 2. *(pushes Pierrot roughly)[1]* What's this buffoon think he's doing?[2]	DON JUAN 2. *(pushing Pierrot roughly)[1]* How dare this yokel interrupt me?[2]	DON JUAN 2. xxx Who is this twit?[2]
PIERROT 3. *(se remettant entre Don Juan et Charlotte)[1]* Je vous dis qu'ou vous tegniez,[2] et qu'ou ne caressiez point nos accordées.[3]	PETER 3. xxx I tell 'ee to keep off[2] 'ee bain't go'n' to be a-kissin' my intended.[3]	PIERROT 3. *(gets between Don Juan and Charlotte)[1]* Now, look here, just stop that,[2] keep your hands off my fiancée.[3]	PIERROT 3. xxx You'd better stop, that's all –[2] that girl you are kissing is engaged to me.[3]	PIERROT 3. xxx You'd better cut it out –[2] that female you're slobbering over is my fiancey.[3]
DON JUAN 4. *(continue de le repousser)[1]* Ah![2] Que de bruit![3]	DON JUAN 4. *(pushing him again)[1]* xxx What are you making a fuss about?[3]	DON JUAN 4. *(pushes him again)[1]* xxx Do you have to make such a noise?[3]	DON JUAN 4. *(continues pushing Pierrot)[1]* xxx What a fuss![3]	DON JUAN 4. xxx What a fuss![3]
PIERROT 5. Jerniquenne![1] Ce n'est pas comme ça qu'il faut pousser les gens[2]	PETER 5. Lumme![1] Don't 'ee be a-shov'n' folk like that.[2]	PIERROT 5. Ey,[1] stop pushing me around[2]	PIERROT 5. Hell![1] There is no need to push a person round.[2]	PIERROT 5. Jesus![1] There's no need to shove a bloke around.[2]
CHARLOTTE 6. *(prenant Pierrot par le bras)[1]* Et laisse-le faire aussi, Pierrot.[2]	CHARLOTTE 6. xxx Let him be, Peter.[2]	CHARLOTTE 6. *(takes Pierrot's arm)[1]* Let him be, Pierrot.[2]	CHARLOTTE 6. *(taking Pierrot by the arm)[1]* Oh, leave him alone, Pierrot.[2]	CHARLOTTE 6. xxx Piss off, Piarrot, and leave him alone.[2]

Molière	Wood	Hampton	Cramphorn/Blankenship	Australian Actors
PIERROT 7.	PETER 7.	PIERROT 7.	PIERROT 7.	PIERROT 7.
Quement![1]	How do 'ee mean,[1]	What do you mean,[1]	Why's that?[1]	What for?[1]
que je le laisse faire?[2]	let 'un be.[2]	let him be? Why should I?[2]	Why should I leave him alone?[2]	Why should I leave him alone?[2]
Je ne veux pas, moi.[3]	I bain't nowise for lett'n ' un be.[3]	xxx	xxx	xxx
DON JUAN 8.	DON JUAN 8.	DON JUAN 8.	DON JUAN 8.	DON JUAN 8.
Ah![1]	Ah![1]	Ah![1]	Grr![1]	xxx
PIERROT 9.	PETER 9.	PIERROT 9.	PIERROT 9.	PIERROT 9.
Testiguenne![1]	Confound 'ee![1]	xxx	I mean, what the hell![1]	I mean, crikey.[1]
parce qu' ous êtes Monsieu,[2]	Because 'ee be a gen'l'man[2]	Just because you've got money,[2]	Just because you're a gentleman[2]	Just because you're a gentleman[2]
ous viendrez caresser nos femmes à note barbe?[3]	do 'ee think 'ee can come kiss'n' our women under our very noses?[3]	you think you can go touching up our women in front of us.[3]	doesn't mean you can come and kiss our girls right under our noses.[3]	doesn't mean you can come around here and kiss our women right under our noses.[3]
Allez-v's-en caresser les vôtres.[4]	Why can't 'e go kiss 'is own women?[4]	Go and touch up your own.[4]	Go and kiss your own girls.[4]	Go and kiss your own women.[4]
DON JUAN 10.	DON JUAN 10.	DON JUAN 10.	DON JUAN 10.	DON JUAN 10.
Heu?[1]	Heh?[1]	What?[1]	How dare you?[1]	How dare you?[1]
		(He slaps Pierrot)		
PIERROT 11.	PETER 11.	PIERROT 11.	PIERROT 11.	PIERROT 11.
Heu![1]	Heh![1]	xxx	I dare all right.[1]	I dare all right, mate.[1]
(Don Juan lui donne un soufflet)[2]	*(Don Juan gives him a box on the ear)*[2]	xxx	*(Don Juan hits him)*[2]	xxx
Testigué! ne me frappez pas.[3]	Lord help us! Don't 'ee be a hitt'n' me.[3]	Oy, don't hit me.[3]	What are you doing?[3]	Shit a brick![3]
(Autre soufflet)[4]	*(Don Juan gives him another blow)*[4]	*(Another slap)*[4]	*(Another blow)*[4]	xxx
Oh! jerniguê![5]	Hey! What the...[5]	Ow, Christ.[5]	Stop that![5]	Root a boot![5]
(Autre soufflet)[6]	*(Another blow)*[6]	*(Another)*[6]	*(Another blow)*[6]	xxx
Ventrequé![7]	Lor' lumme![7]	Bluddyell.[7]	Ow?[7]	Fuck a duck![7]
(Autre soufflet)[8]	*(Another)*[8]	*(Another)*[8]	*(Another blow)*[8]	xxx
Palsanqué! Morquenne![9]	Hang it![9]	xxx	What the hell are you doing?[9]	What the bloody hell are you doing?[9]
ça n'est pas bian de battre les gens,[10]	that ain't no way to behave.[10]	It's not very nice, hitting people,[10]	You can't go round hitting people like that.[10]	You can't go round hitting people like that.[10]
et ce n'est pas là la récompense de v's avoir sauvé d'être nayé.[11]	That ain't no way to repay a feller that's saved 'ee from drown'n'.[11]	specially when they've just saved you from drowning.[11]	Especially when they've just saved you from drowning.[11]	Especially when they've just saved you from drowning[11]

Molière	Wood	Hampton	Cramphorn/Blankenship	Australian Actors
CHARLOTTE 12. Piarrot, ne te fâche point.[1]	CHARLOTTE 12. Now don't 'ee get mad, Peter.[1]	CHARLOTTE 12. Don't get angry, Pierrot.[1]	CHARLOTTE 12. Piarrot, there's no need to make such a fuss.[1]	CHARLOTTE 12. Yes, so simmer down, Piarrot.[1]
PIERROT 13. Je veux me fâcher;[1] et t'es une vilaine, toi,[2] d'endurer qu'on te cajole[3]	PETER 13. I will get mad if I want to[1] and it ain't noways right of 'ee[2] to be a-lett'n' un cajole 'ee so.[3]	PIERROT 13. I want to get angry.[1] How dare you let him[2] carry on with you like that?[3]	PIERROT 13. I want to make a fuss;[1] you ought to be ashamed of yourself,[2] letting him get round you like that.[3]	PIERROT 13. Simmer down? I'm spitting chips.[1] You ought to be ashamed of yourself,[2] letting him get round you like that.[3]
CHARLOTTE 14. Oh! Piarrot, ce n'est pas ce que tu penses.[1] Ce Monsieur veut m'épouser,[2] et tu ne dois pas te bouter en colère.[3]	CHARLOTTE 14. Oh, Peter, things bain't the way 'ee be thinking.[1] This gentleman be a-goin' to marry me[2] and there ain't no call for' ee to get mad.[3]	CHARLOTTE 14. It's not what you think, Pierrot.[1] This gentleman wants to marry me,[2] there's no point in getting all upset about it.[3]	CHARLOTTE 14. Oh, Piarrot, it's not like you think,[1] this gentleman wants to marry me,[2] so there's no need for you to get upset.[3]	CHARLOTTE 14. Turn it up, Piarrot, its not like that.[1] This gentleman wants to marry me,[2] so there's no need for you to kick up a stink.[3]
PIERROT 15. Quement?[1] Jerni![2] tu m'es promise.[3]	PIERROT 15. xxx Dang it![2] Bain't 'ee a-promised to me?[3]	PIERROT 15. What do you mean?[1] xxx You're engaged to me.[3]	PIERROT 15. No need?[1] xxx You're engaged to me.[3]	PIERROT 15. No need?[1] xxx You're my fiancay.[3]
CHARLOTTE 16. Ça n'y fait rien, Piarrot.[1] xxx Si tu m'aimes, ne dois-tu pas être bien aise[3] que je devienne Madame?[4]	CHARLOTTE 16. That don't make no matter, Peter.[1] xxx If 'ee do love me 'ee ought to be main glad[3] to see me a-goin' to be a lady.[4]	CHARLOTTE 16. That doesn't make any difference, Pierrot,[1] he doesn't mind.[2] If you love me, you ought to be pleased[3] I'm going up in the world.[4]	CHARLOTTE 16. Yes, but that's not the point, Piarrot -[1] xxx if you really cared about me, you'd be glad[3] to see me become a lady.[4]	CHARLOTTE 16. So what, Piarrot.[1] xxx If you really cared about me you'd be glad[3] to see me going up in the world.[4]
PIERROT 17. Jerniqué![1] non.[2] J'aime mieux te voir crevée[3] que de te voir à un autre.[4]	PETER 17. Lor' lumme![1] xxx I'd as soon see 'ee dead[3] as married to another feller.[4]	PIERROT 17. xxx Pleased?[2] I'd rather see you dead[3] than married to someone else.[4]	PIERROT 17. xxx No, I wouldn't.[2] I'd rather see you dead[3] than married to someone else.[4]	PIERROT 17. xxx No, I wouldn't.[2] I'd rather see you six foot under[3] than married to someone else.[4]

References

Callow, Simon. 1985. *Being an Actor.* London: Penguin Books.

Cole, Susan Letzler. 1992. *Directors in Rehearsal: a Hidden World.* New York and London: Routledge.

Cramphorn, Rex. 1991. Unpublished text in Cramphorn Archive, Department of Performance Studies, University of Sydney.

Hampton, Christopher. 1974. *Molière's Dom Juan.* London: Faber & Faber.

Jouvet, Louis. 1965. *Molière et la Comédie Classique.* Paris: Gallimard.

Lassalle, Jacques. 1995. 'Conversations sur *Dom Juan*' in *Théâtre d'Aujourd'hui* 4 : 120-123.

McAuley, Gay. 1989. 'Body, Space and Language: the Actor's Work on/with Text' in *Kodikas/Code: and International Journal of Semiotics* 12(1): 57-79.

McAuley, Gay. 1994. 'Performance Indicators in Playtext and Performance' in *Mediations: Sydney Essays in Honour of Ivan Barko.* Mount Nebo, Queensland: Boombana Publications: 81-115.

McAuley, Gay. 1995. 'Translation in the Performance Process' in Fitzpatrick, Tim (ed.) *About Performance* 1. Sydney: Centre for Performance Studies, University of Sydney: 111-125.

Molière. [1665] 1984. *Dom Juan.* Paris: Editions Bordas.

Sher, Antony. 1985. *The Year of the King: an Actor's Diary and Sketchbook.* London: Chatto & Windus.

Venuti, Lawrence. 1998. *The Scandals of Translation: Towards an Ethics of Difference.* London and New York: Routledge.

Wood, John. 1953. *Molière: Five Plays.* London: Penguin Press.

INDEX